# Alternative Educational Programmes, Schools and Social Justice

Alternative education caters and cares for students whose regular schools have failed and excluded them. Fifty years of international research reports that alternative settings are characterised by close and powerful staff–student relationships, a curriculum which is relevant, engaging and meaningful, and the strong sense of agency afforded young people by the opportunity to make decisions. Together, these three practices produce increased life chances for alternative education participants.

However, despite these apparent successes, alternative education seems to have had little impact on mainstream schools. This collection of papers addresses the important question – what might regular schools and teachers learn about socially just pedagogies from alternative education practices? In providing answers to this question, authors interrogate the taken-for-granted wisdom about alternative education while also taking account of ongoing policy shifts, differing locations and populations, and persistent and intersecting patterns of raced, classed and gendered inequalities. They draw on a range of theoretical and methodological approaches to interrogate the ways in which alternative schools and alternative education both challenge and legitimate the kinds of schooling most of us expect for our own and other people's children.

The chapters in this book were originally published as a special issue of *Critical Studies in Education*.

**Glenda McGregor** is a Senior Lecturer and Deputy Head of School (Academic) in the School of Education and Professional Studies at Griffith University, Australia. She teaches in the areas of globalisation and education, youth studies and history curriculum. Her research interests include sociology of youth, democratic and alternative forms of education, curriculum, and social justice and education.

**Martin Mills** is Professor and Director of the Teachers and Teaching Research Centre, Institute of Education, University College London, UK. His research interests include alternative education, new pedagogies, social justice issues in education and teachers' work. His most recent (co-authored) books are *The Politics of Differentiation in Schools* (2017, Routledge) and *Re-imagining Schooling for Education* (2017, Palgrave Macmillan).

**Pat Thomson** is Professor of Education at the University of Nottingham, UK. Her work centres on the ways in which educational practices can be made more equitable; her research currently focuses on arts and cultural education in schools, communities, galleries and museums. She is a former school leader of alternative and disadvantaged schools.

**Jodie Pennacchia** began her career working in learner support roles in mainstream and alternative schools. She has published work in the field of alternative education and is currently writing papers from her doctoral thesis, which explores the production of academy status in the context of an 'underperforming' school. She is a Researcher at the Learning and Work Institute, where her work evaluates the inclusivity of a range of education and training programmes.

# Alternative Educational Programmes, Schools and Social Justice

*Edited by*
Glenda McGregor, Martin Mills, Pat Thomson and Jodie Pennacchia

LONDON AND NEW YORK

First published 2018
by Routledge
2 Park Square, Milton Park, Abingdon, Oxon, OX14 4RN, UK

and by Routledge
711 Third Avenue, New York, NY 10017, USA

*Routledge is an imprint of the Taylor & Francis Group, an informa business*

© 2018 Taylor & Francis

All rights reserved. No part of this book may be reprinted or reproduced or utilised
in any form or by any electronic, mechanical, or other means, now known or
hereafter invented, including photocopying and recording, or in any information
storage or retrieval system, without permission in writing from the publishers.

*Trademark notice*: Product or corporate names may be trademarks or registered
trademarks, and are used only for identification and explanation without intent to
infringe.

*British Library Cataloguing in Publication Data*
A catalogue record for this book is available from the British Library

ISBN 13: 978-0-8153-8088-7

Typeset in TimesNewRomanPS
by diacriTech, Chennai

**Publisher's Note**
The publisher accepts responsibility for any inconsistencies that may have arisen
during the conversion of this book from journal articles to book chapters, namely
the possible inclusion of journal terminology.

**Disclaimer**
Every effort has been made to contact copyright holders for their permission to
reprint material in this book. The publishers would be grateful to hear from any
copyright holder who is not here acknowledged and will undertake to rectify any
errors or omissions in future editions of this book.

# Contents

| | |
|---|---|
| *Citation Information* | vii |
| *Notes on Contributors* | ix |

Introduction: Alternative programmes, alternative schools and
social justice     1
*Jodie Pennacchia, Pat Thomson, Martin Mills and Glenda McGregor*

1 Cracking with affect: relationality in young people's movements
in and out of mainstream schooling     6
*Jennifer Skattebol and Debra Hayes*

2 Young black males: resilience and the use of capital to transform
school 'failure'     21
*Cecile Wright, Uvanney Maylor and Sophie Becker*

3 Caught between a rock and a hard place: disruptive boys' views
on mainstream and special schools in New South Wales, Australia     35
*Linda J. Graham, Penny Van Bergen and Naomi Sweller*

4 'It's the best thing I've done in a long while': teenage mothers'
experiences of educational alternatives     55
*Kerry Vincent*

5 Meaningful education for returning-to-school students in a
comprehensive upper secondary school in Iceland     70
*Ingólfur Ásgeir Jóhannesson and Valgerður S. Bjarnadóttir*

6 Disciplinary regimes of 'care' and complementary alternative education     84
*Pat Thomson and Jodie Pennacchia*

7 Alternative education and social justice: considering issues of affective
and contributive justice     100
*Martin Mills, Glenda McGregor, Aspa Baroutsis, Kitty Te Riele and Debra Hayes*

## CONTENTS

8 The force of habit: channelling young bodies at alternative education spaces 116
*Peter Kraftl*

9 Teachers' work and innovation in alternative schools 131
*Nina Bascia and Rhiannon Maton*

*Index* 143

# Citation Information

The chapters in this book were originally published in the *Critical Studies in Education*, volume 57, issue 1 (February 2016). When citing this material, please use the original page numbering for each article, as follows:

**Introduction**
*Alternative programmes, alternative schools and social justice*
Jodie Pennacchia, Pat Thomson, Martin Mills and Glenda McGregor
*Critical Studies in Education*, volume 57, issue 1 (February 2016) pp. 1–5

**Chapter 1**
*Cracking with affect: relationality in young people's movements in and out of mainstream schooling*
Jennifer Skattebol and Debra Hayes
*Critical Studies in Education*, volume 57, issue 1 (February 2016) pp. 6–20

**Chapter 2**
*Young black males: resilience and the use of capital to transform school 'failure'*
Cecile Wright, Uvanney Maylor and Sophie Becker
*Critical Studies in Education*, volume 57, issue 1 (February 2016) pp. 21–34

**Chapter 3**
*Caught between a rock and a hard place: disruptive boys' views on mainstream and special schools in New South Wales, Australia*
Linda J. Graham, Penny Van Bergen and Naomi Sweller
*Critical Studies in Education*, volume 57, issue 1 (February 2016) pp. 35–54

**Chapter 4**
*'It's the best thing I've done in a long while': teenage mothers' experiences of educational alternatives*
Kerry Vincent
*Critical Studies in Education*, volume 57, issue 1 (February 2016) pp. 55–69

# CITATION INFORMATION

**Chapter 5**
*Meaningful education for returning-to-school students in a comprehensive upper secondary school in Iceland*
Ingólfur Ásgeir Jóhannesson and Valgerður S. Bjarnadóttir
*Critical Studies in Education*, volume 57, issue 1 (February 2016) pp. 70–83

**Chapter 6**
*Disciplinary regimes of 'care' and complementary alternative education*
Pat Thomson and Jodie Pennacchia
*Critical Studies in Education*, volume 57, issue 1 (February 2016) pp. 84–99

**Chapter 7**
*Alternative education and social justice: considering issues of affective and contributive justice*
Martin Mills, Glenda McGregor, Aspa Baroutsis, Kitty Te Riele and Debra Hayes
*Critical Studies in Education*, volume 57, issue 1 (February 2016) pp. 100–115

**Chapter 8**
*The force of habit: channelling young bodies at alternative education spaces*
Peter Kraftl
*Critical Studies in Education*, volume 57, issue 1 (February 2016) pp. 116–130

**Chapter 9**
*Teachers' work and innovation in alternative schools*
Nina Bascia and Rhiannon Maton
*Critical Studies in Education*, volume 57, issue 1 (February 2016) pp. 131–141

For any permission-related enquiries please visit:
http://www.tandfonline.com/page/help/permissions

# Notes on Contributors

**Aspa Baroutsis** is Research Associate at the Faculty of Education, The University of Queensland, Australia.

**Nina Bascia** is Professor and Director of the Collaborative Program in Educational Policy at the Ontario Institute for Studies in Education, University of Toronto, Canada.

**Sophie Becker** is a student social worker at Nottingham City Council, UK. She previously worked as a Research Assistant at Nottingham Trent University and the University of Nottingham, UK.

**Valgerður S. Bjarnadóttir** is a graduate student in the School of Education at the University of Iceland, Reykjavík.

**Linda J. Graham** is a Professor at the Faculty of Education, Early Childhood and Inclusive Education, Queensland University of Technology, Australia. She is also Faculty Research Group Leader of the Student Engagement, Learning and Behaviour Research Group.

**Debra Hayes** is an Associate Professor in the Faculty of Education and Social Work at the University of Sydney, Australia.

**Ingólfur Ásgeir Jóhannesson** is a Professor of Education at the University of Iceland, Reykjavík.

**Peter Kraftl** is Chair in Human Geography and College Director of Internationalisation at the University of Birmingham, UK.

**Rhiannon Maton** is an Assistant Professor in the SUNY (The State University of New York) Cortland School, USA, of Education's Foundations and Social Advocacy Department.

**Uvanney Maylor** is Director of the Institute for Research in Education at the University of Bedfordshire, UK.

**Glenda McGregor** is a Senior Lecturer and Deputy Head of School (Academic) in the School of Education and Professional Studies at Griffith University, Australia. She teaches in the areas of globalisation and education, youth studies and history curriculum. Her research interests include sociology of youth, democratic and alternative forms of education, curriculum, and social justice and education.

**Martin Mills** is Head of School in the School of Education at The University of Queensland, Australia. He is a Fellow of Academy of the Social Sciences in Australia (ASSA) and the immediate Past President of the Australian Association for Research in Education (AARE).

# NOTES ON CONTRIBUTORS

His research interests include the sociology of education, social justice in education, alternative schooling, gender and education, school reform and new pedagogies.

**Jodie Pennacchia** is a Researcher at the Learning and Work Institute and a doctoral candidate at the School of Sociology and Social Policy, the University of Nottingham, UK. Her research focuses on the ways education and training policies affect disadvantaged groups and the institutions that work with them.

**Kitty Te Riele** is an Honorary Professor at Victoria University, Australia. She held the position of Professorial Research Fellow at The Victoria Institute for Education, Diversity & Lifelong Learning.

**Jennifer Skattebol** conducts policy-relevant research with respect to children, young people and their families in contexts of disadvantage. She has expertise in the design of methodologies which are sensitive to the politics of marginalisation, and in incorporating educational and capacity-building elements in research design.

**Naomi Sweller** is a Senior Lecturer in the Department of Psychology, Macquarie University, Australia.

**Pat Thomson** is Professor of Education at the University of Nottingham, UK. Her work centres on the ways in which educational practices can be made more equitable; her research currently focuses on arts and cultural education in schools, communities, galleries and museums. She is a former school leader of alternative and disadvantaged schools.

**Penny Van Bergen** is a Senior Lecturer in Educational Psychology in the Department of Education, Macquarie University, Australia.

**Kerry Vincent** is Lecturer/Senior Lecturer at the School of Social Sciences, Nottingham Trent University, UK.

**Cecile Wright** is Professor of Sociology and Visiting Fellow at the Centre for Advanced Studies, Honorary Associate Professor at the School of Sociology and Social Work, and Professorial Fellow at the Institute of Mental Health, all at the University of Nottingham, UK.

# INTRODUCTION

## Alternative programmes, alternative schools and social justice

Jodie Pennacchia, Pat Thomson, Martin Mills and Glenda McGregor

Alternative educational programmes and alternative schools have been a feature of the educational landscape for some 50 years or more. These alternatives cater for children and young people who have generally experienced a variety of forms of exclusion during their schooling (Arnold, Yeomans, & Simpson, 2009; Sparkes & Glennerster, 2002). In some jurisdictions, a common aim of alternative education programmes is to return students to 'regular schools' (Slee, 2011). However, research suggests that young people who go back into regular schools from alternative programmes and short-term placements find it difficult, as nothing within the regular school has changed since they first left (Carswell, Hanlon, Watts, & O'Grady, 2014; Cox, 1999). Thus, alternative schools often aim to provide a permanent alternative route to further education, work or training. In so doing, they provide a convenient way for schools to continue unchanged, engaging in a range of exclusionary practices (Araújo, 2005; Mills, Riddell, & Hjörne, 2015). Whether young people return to regular school or continue with an alternative education programme, the regular school remains a critical social justice problem.

In this special issue, we report on recent international research that traces the ways in which the alternative schooling pathways play out across four national contexts. Among them, these papers take account of the variety of student populations, programme designs, spaces and policy issues that characterise alternative education, drawing attention to its flexible and dynamic nature (Aron, 2006; Kraftl, 2013). Our overarching concern is to present the range of social justice questions that arise from the alternative education of young people of compulsory schooling age. However, we want to do so in ways that explore these programmes in the context of educational provision at large, since what happens in alternative education is implicated in – and in turn implicates – practices in regular schools. This concern has led us to pose the following question: 'What might regular schools learn from alternative programmes and schools?' It is a question that invites a critical interrogation of what alternative education programmes can offer; how this can be viewed afresh in shifting policy contexts; and where the spaces for, and threats to, a more socially just education system might be found.

The papers collected together here propose a set of answers to this question. They address issues of school exclusion, the types and quality of education provided within alternative programmes and schools for those who reject and/or have been rejected by regular schools, the return of students into their original schooling contexts and the social justice implications of these issues. In doing so, the contributing authors have drawn on a range of theoretical resources and have taken account of the particular methodologies suited to understanding the experiences of young people attending alternative education programmes and schools.

In the opening paper, Jennifer Skattebol and Debra Hayes explore the education of Indigenous students in Australia in a context where race-based notions of deficit prevail, influencing how low levels of educational attainment are read by teachers and policy-makers. The authors advance a 'relational epistemology' (p. 8) as appropriate for understanding the alternative education and reintegration experiences of two Indigenous students, allowing moments of injustice and symbolic violence to come to the fore as the students gradually find it acceptable to be 'knowable' (p. 10). The authors' focus on affect brings emotions to the forefront of the stories being told and asks us to consider how 'educational experiences and affective states of individual students are underpinned by a myriad of collective legacies and social relations' (p. 9). In highlighting the importance of the collective and relational in the students' efforts to succeed, Skattebol and Hayes problematize the emphasis on the individualised subject within neo-liberal education practices, highlighting the way this might do a disservice to particular student groups.

Cecile Wright, Uvanney Maylor and Sophie Becker also consider the importance of collective resources in their exploration of the post-compulsory and post-exclusionary schooling experiences of young black males in the UK. They draw on Yosso's reworking of Bourdieu's concept of 'capital' to make sense of the ways these students resist labels of failure in order to transform negative schooling and educational experiences. Their findings illustrate a strong desire for educational success, high expectations from parents, and community infrastructure to be key to this process. This approach enables the authors to illustrate the structural inequalities of schooling whilst recognizing that young black men 'employ agentic strategies' (p. 29) to renegotiate their identity and to 'negotiate ways out of social disadvantage' (p. 25). Reflecting on the current policy context, they conclude that these students may need to be prepared not only for exam success but also for the 'resilience, self-esteem and resourcefulness' they will require to navigate uncertain futures in austerity Britain.

A focus on boys and young men continues in the third paper by Linda Graham, Penny Van Bergen and Naomi Sweller, who consider the educational experiences of a group of boys enrolled in special schools for disruptive behaviour in New South Wales, Australia. Whilst regular schools are demanding that more places be made available in behaviour schools, existing research has voiced concerns about the length of special school placements, a lack of specialist subject teaching, high levels of absenteeism and a focus on 'fixing' the young person. Although pupils tended to prefer the alternative programme, many still wanted to return to regular school, which they perceived as 'normal', 'better' and a space where they could interact with peers. The authors argue that if the social and academic needs of students are not being met in the special school context, the reform of regular schools becomes crucial. They contend that the very existence of alternative programmes is a barrier to such reform, 'forestalling the types of reforms that might otherwise lead to a more inclusive and effective system overall' (p. 50).

Kerry Vincent's paper considers the experiences of pregnant and mothering schoolgirls who have attended alternative education provisions in the UK. Using 'difference' as an analytical concept, Vincent explores the importance of the young women placed on continuing to access qualifications; developing greater confidence and being treated in non-stigmatising, non-authoritarian ways. The latter was particularly important in terms of the young women 'developing a more positive identity as a pregnant teenager' (p. 61). However, this paper also presents a number of potential problems for social justice: a lack of varied and challenging curricula and qualifications, young people's concerns about how

## ALTERNATIVE EDUCATIONAL PROGRAMMES

qualifications are viewed by employers, a lack of clarity over the progression routes qualifications offered, the funnelling of young women into gendered vocational options and/or routes into lower paid occupations. Vincent contends that these processes may continue gendered and classed patterns of inequality that exist in educational systems at large.

Ingólfur Ásgeir Jóhannesson and Valgerður S. Bjarnadóttir explore an innovative pedagogical approach designed to support students returning to academic upper secondary school in Iceland after previously 'dropping out'. The authors found that the innovative practices of this school – particularly an online learning platform and a new combined academic and vocational course – appealed to students because they supported their learning, planning and assessment. Students favoured the ongoing assessment processes because they reduced 'test anxiety' (p. 77), and noted the care, enthusiasm, commitment and listening practices of the teachers. Against a policy sway towards less flexibility and a focus on vocational learning for students returning to education, the authors highlight the right of all students to return to education and pursue the educational programs that interest them.

Pat Thomson and Jodie Pennacchia use a Foucauldian conceptual framework to consider the 'nature of the care on offer' (p. 95) in one therapeutic and one team building complementary alternative provision. Against a backdrop of the performative swing in alternative education in England, the authors highlight some of the ways these two provisions operated against the dominant model. The pedagogies of care observed offered young people a different set of choices about 'the ways in which they could exercise power' (p. 92). Rather than this being focused on developing compliance with the aim of reintegration, these programmes offered more dynamic ways for students to participate in the life of the school, moving away from a 'conform/resist' binary. Whilst not wanting to overemphasise the benefits of the alternative programmes, this research suggests these programmes were 'directed towards a more generous vision of education' (p. 96).

Drawing on the work of Ravaisson and Dewey, Peter Kraftl's paper offers a conceptual language through which to interrogate the habit forming/altering practices of alternative education, and how these relate to the practices that take place in regular schools. Kraftl uses the concepts of '(re)calibration' and 'contagion' (p. 116) to make sense of a number of vignettes drawn from research visits to observe homeschooling, care forms and forest schools. This paper explores the malleability of habit, its moral characteristics in locating what is 'good' and 'bad', but also its collective quality. Kraftl contends that considering the collective quality of habit forming might offer a potentially radical approach because it 'runs against the grains of contemporary neoliberal educational praxes' (p. 128). Yet he maintains how fraught the processes of habit formation are, and the ambiguity with which they are understood in alternative programmes, acknowledging the possibility for these practices to continue in the dominant neo-liberal vein.

The paper by Martin Mills, Glenda McGregor, Aspa Baroutsis, Kitty Te Riele and Debra Hayes considers the ways in which three alternative schools in Australia provide a socially just education for their students. They build on Fraser's work on social justice, adding the categories of affective justice and contributive justice, which 'pay attention to inequalities in relational care and individual potential for meaningful participation' (p. 111). Whilst support, respect and caring aspects of affective justice were strong in the alternative provisions, the authors suggest that this alone is not sufficient to address the needs of young people. Voicing concern over the level of academic challenge they found in some instances, they argue the importance of ensuring contributive justice is incorporated alongside affective justice. They argue contributive justice is present where young people have the opportunity to engage in more complex learning tasks, which extend their capacities, develop competence, enable a sense of pride and prepare them for evolving societal contexts.

Nina Bascia and Rhiannon Maton's paper considers the ways innovation stems both from teacher practices and structures of publicly funded alternative schools in Toronto, Canada. Through the concepts of tight and loose coupling, Bascia and Maton explore the ways alternative schools may be buffered from some of the standardisation practices which restrict the work of teachers in regular schools. In this buffered space, alternative school teachers have found ways to innovate, using student voice to inform curriculum, and developing cross-curricular courses through departmental collaborations. This helps the schools to cater for students who 'do not conform' to mainstream structures; however, at present, there continues to be limited opportunities for these practices to inform what is happening in the majority of schools.

Taken together, these papers present the many opportunities and resources offered by alternative education programmes and schools in a variety of international contexts. A common thread which emerges is the importance of 'collectivism'. Programmes are collectively developed and run, provide opportunities for young people to work as collectives, and thus stand apart from the dominant individualising approach to education promoted through neo-liberal ideologies and practices (Apple, 2005). Yet common themes, such as the rigidity and impermeability of regular schools, also emerge as a cause for concern, highlighting existing and future barriers to social justice for young people who experience educational exclusion. The papers suggest that ongoing work is needed to ensure more challenging curricula are available to students accessing alternative education provision. This is vital for challenging notions of individual deficit, which continue to prevail as a way of justifying young people's exclusion and low educational attainment. Rich curricular choices also facilitate Basil Bernstein's contention that education should assist students to 'think the un-thinkable and the not yet thought' (Bernstein, 2000, p. 30). A remaining concern is whether the very existence of alternative education permits the continued unjust practices of regular schooling contexts. The continued presence of this possibility necessitates further research, and calls for systematic inquiry which investigates how practices of collaboration between regular and alternative education sites can be developed and sustained.

## References

Apple, M. W. (2005). Education, markets, and an audit culture. *Critical Quarterly, 47*(1–2), 11–29. doi:10.1111/criq.2005.47.issue-1-2

Araújo, M. (2005). Disruptive or disrupted? A qualitative study on the construction of indiscipline. *International Journal of Inclusive Education, 9*(3), 241–268. doi:10.1080/09596410500059730

Arnold, C., Yeomans, J., & Simpson, S. (2009). *Excluded from school. Complex discourses and psychological perspectives*. Stoke on Trent: Trentham Books.

Aron, L. Y. (2006). *An overview of alternative education*. Washington, DC: The Urban Institute.

Bernstein, B. (2000). *Pedagogy, symbolic control and identity* (2nd ed.). Oxford: Rowman & Littlefield Publishers.

Carswell, S. B., Hanlon, T. E., Watts, A. M., & O'Grady, K. A. (2014). Prevention-related research targeting African-American alternative education program students. *Education and Urban Society, 46*(4), 434–449.

Cox, S. M. (1999). An assessment of an alternative education program for at-risk delinquent youth. *Journal of Research in Crime and Delinquency, 36*, 323–336. doi:10.1177/0022427899036003004

Kraftl, P. (2013). *Geographies of alternative education: Diverse learning spaces for children and young people*. Bristol: Policy Press.

Mills, M., Riddell, S., & Hjörne, E. (2015). After exclusion what? *International Journal of Inclusive Education, 19*(6), 561–567. doi:10.1080/13603116.2014.961674

Slee, R. (2011). *The irregular school. Exclusion, schooling and inclusive education*. London: Routledge.

Sparkes, J., & Glennerster, H. (2002). Preventing social exclusion: Education's contribution. In J. Hills, J. Le Grand, & D. Piachaud (Eds.), *Understanding social exclusion*. Oxford: Oxford University Press.

# Cracking with affect: relationality in young people's movements in and out of mainstream schooling

Jennifer Skattebol and Debra Hayes

This paper focusses on the schooling stories of two young women who moved from mainstream schooling into alternative learning program set up for Indigenous students and back into mainstream schooling to complete their Year 12 education. The manner in which these young women narrated their stories is understood through the prism of Indigenous notions of relatedness and affect theory and is as revealing as the actual reporting of the events and rationales in these young women's schooling trajectories. Young people's insights into the challenges of mainstream pedagogies and promises of relational pedagogies invite us to consider what could be different in structures and processes which aim to deliver educational equity. We argue there is a need for more research which offers rich accounts of the emotional and relational fields which underpin student subjectivities and engagement.

## Introduction

In the 2012 Australian census, the number of Indigenous students staying on to Year 12 exceeded 50 per cent for the first time (ABS, 2014; Dreise & Thomson, 2014). While clearly an improvement on past figures, many schools continue to serve Indigenous students poorly. They are not enabling Indigenous students to perform alongside their non-Indigenous peers on most measures of educational participation and achievement. Successive national governments have attempted to address the issue through educational policies, the most potent of which are those that aim to improve school attendance (Department of Prime Minister and Cabinet, 2014). A recent strategy, the Compact for Young Australians, received bipartisan political support to potentially penalise families whose children have poor attendance by having their parenting payments suspended (Te Riele, 2011). This constructs the problem as one within families and works to reinforce implicit race-based assumptions that low levels of educational attainment are a result of incompetent child rearing (Beresford, 2003). This kind of policy emphasis on measurable and incremental improvements in attendance and retention displaces efforts to understand why many Indigenous students disengage from schooling institutions and how policies and institutional practices might converge to alienate young people from learning in the institutional contexts available to them. Smyth and Hattam (2001) argue that research and policy that engage a 'sociological imagination' might redress the issue through offering deeper understandings of young people's lives and experiences: 'it is not sufficient to merely research the reasons young people give for deciding to leave school, but we also need to understand something about how they construct their subjectivity or lived experience, sociologically speaking' (p.402).

Our purpose in this paper is twofold: to use a sociological lens to better understand how young people who are excluded from school construct their subjectivities; and to consider how these experiences might be accessed and interpreted, sociologically speaking. Drawing upon a larger study of a community-based alternative learning program, which catered mainly to Indigenous students (see Hayes, 2012, 2013), we share the schooling stories told to us by two young women. These two were significant because they were the only students in the program to opt to return to mainstream schooling to complete year 12. Over time, the way these young women constructed their schooling subjectivities changed. These shifts illuminated some of the barriers to and facilitators of schooling engagement and completion. We put to work storying devices (such as photo elicitation techniques) to facilitate access to these young peoples' stories; and tracked the affect and relational dynamics that flowed around their stories. We argue that attention to the contexts and processes of storytelling is integral to understanding how these young people constructed and reconstructed their schooling subjectivities, and subsequently navigated the system.

The affective dimensions of the interviews were striking and they repeatedly drew our attention to the social relations between the research participants as a group, between them and other members of the school community, and between ourselves as researchers and the students as research participants. Aboriginal scholar Karen Martin's (2008) generous and detailed work on indigenous methodologies offers a roadmap for engaging relational epistemologies in order to understand such relations and their place in indigenous ontologies. While there are many dimensions and layers to her work, Martin reminds us that accessing what was important to these students was only visible with an understanding of the complex and multifaceted social relations that shaped their subjectivities.

The question of how social relations shape schooling subjectivities has been explored in several studies with Indigenous students who find school difficult to engage. Research focussed on an earlier version of the alternative program attended by students in our study offers a platform for considering this question. The coordinator of the program, Dorothy Bottrell (2007) drew upon her established relationships with her participants to understand their perspectives on schooling and truancy. She showed how these perspectives were shaped by their experiences within and outside school. Through interviews with 12 girls, aged 13–24 years, she came to understand their resistance to school as resilience to the exclusionary social relations in their school in the face of 'pressures, expectations of failure and inability to change' (p. 604).

Elsewhere, the significance of social fields beyond the school on student's participation in schooling has been highlighted. In a study of non-formal place-based learning, Tracy Friedel (2009) warns of a tendency to misunderstand Indigenous young people's refusal to participate in formal learning programs as rebelliousness or apathy. She argues that they are often enacting subjectivities and relationship responsibilities that are invisible or inadequately recognised in schools. Findings from her research illustrate how students were 'regularly and actively affiliate[d] with ancestrally important places and with relatives near and far. Moving within and across geographical boundaries, youth consider themselves counter to the way they were perceived by ... educators' (p. 536).

These studies underscore the importance of adopting a sociological imagination that places the notion of relationality at the centre of research design. We ask what this lens can contribute to discussions about alternative and mainstream schooling, and to research at these sites. In the next section we consider Martin's call for relational epistemologies and how affect theory can be put to use analytically in such an endeavour. We then assemble a narrative that addresses the affective content of the interviews as well as the salient events that underpinned young people's disengagement and reengagement with school. We conclude by arguing that schooling and research processes are profoundly relational and argue the need for more research explicitly framed by attention to relationality.

## Relational epistemologies

Indigenous scholars have identified a plethora of injuries and injustices that result from Western research practices and epistemologies (Nakata, 2007; Smith, 2012). The enduring legacy is distrust about research and towards researchers. Martin and Mirraboopa (2003) contend that epistemologies respectful of Indigenous ways of being insist on a 'truly relational' approach where 'all things are recognised and respected for their place in the overall system', including the reasons Indigenous people have to distrust research.

For Martin (2008), indigenist research is based on an ontological premise of related-ness and composed of three components – Ways of Knowing, Being and Doing. *Ways of Knowing* are about one's stories of relatedness – of who one is and where one comes from; *Ways of Being* require that one is respectful, responsible and accountable to one's stories of knowing; and *Ways of Doing* require that one's processes and practices of daily living serve and are served by relatedness. Martin (2008) developed this framework by paying close attention to how an Aboriginal community regulated outsiders and argues these processes are informed by and congruent with Aboriginal ontologies. She describes how she was engaged in a series of 'enfoldments and evolvements', which regulated and mediated her deepening engagement. From this she identified a number of relational subject positions for researchers: stranger/unknown outsider, whiteman/known outsider, and friend/known outsider. She argues these positions are regarded as temporary states and that through respectful interactions that fulfil conditions of 'honesty, co-operation and respect' (Martin, 2008, p. 10) outsiders are able to move and 'come amongst' or 'come alongside' to understand issues of importance to the community.

As researchers, understanding the worldviews of Indigenous young people requires attention to one's own place, one's own accountabilities and ensuring one's processes serve relatedness. Martin (2008, p. 1) lucidly argues, researchers should not act as though we are 'entering a frontier' where people have no understanding of research practice or histories. This view works to 'perpetuate fictions of ideological, physical or intellectual terra nullius'. Instead, we should tread with awareness of the legacies of our trade, knowing and accounting for ourselves. Research about schooling can be of particular concern because of its role as a key mechanism of colonisation and the dehumanisation of Aboriginal people.

These insights are both ontological and epistemological. They offer a way into the field as well as a way of understanding what happens there. Martin's insights supported us – as non-Indigenous researchers – to think about our own social positioning and how it might impact on what the Indigenous students in the alternative learning program might share about themselves, how they were responsible and accountable for themselves, and how relationality might underpin their processes and practices of daily life, including engagement in research. We entered the field slowly and negotiated extensively with community elders and stakeholders in order to accumulate enough community trust to 'come alongside' young people. These processes required reflexive tools that supported us to work through distrust and divergent worldviews towards encounters where we could check our understandings. Paying attention to affective signals allowed us to read our own place in the relational field as well as how the students were placed in their own fields of relationships.

## Affect as a 'relational' epistemological tool

Affect is 'principally elided with the concept of emotion where emotions are understood as profoundly social' (Maxwell & Aggleton, 2013, p. 5). As an epistemological tool that signals important social relations, affect is powerful because it can be both blinding and illuminating. Wetherell (2013) notes 'an intriguing feature of affect is its spectacular demonstration of the limits of human agency ... it arrives unbidden and we find ourselves in a state of grief, anxiety, rage or euphoria' (p. 221). Affect is a powerful lens for thinking about social relations and participation because affect 'accumulates across both relatedness and interruptions to relatedness' (Seigworth & Gregg, 2010, p. 2). It marks both belonging and non-belonging. While hugely variable in its intensities, affect is a marker of relatedness, desire and agency.

Affect theory and attention to emotional landscapes have gained some traction in educational research where, historically, emphasis has been on rationality, reason and cognition. Psycho-social or psychoanalytic concepts have been employed to better understand gendered, classed and racialised power in education and how affect patterns are socialised according to historical collective experiences (Boler, 1999; Britzman, 1998; Skattebol, 2010; Walkerdine, Lucey, & Melody, 2002). It informs socio-cultural–spatial analyses that map the emotional geographies of education to better account for student agency (Kenway & Youdell, 2011). This work encourages us to look closely at joy, shame, anger, fear, excitement and other emotions as central rather than peripheral to the stories being told. Furthermore, it demonstrates how educational experiences and affective states of individual students are underpinned by a myriad of collective legacies and social relations.

The legacy of widespread education system failures in relation to Aboriginal and Torres Strait Islander communities means that researchers need to be sensitive to collective and intergenerational experiences of schooling. Students do not simply have their own experience of school but are affectively enmeshed in the experiences of those closest to them. Affect is thus a powerful epistemological lens that sensitises researchers to historical and collective experiences, and signals how and when we might 'come alongside' our research participants.

## Affective storytelling

In the evaluation of the alternative learning program, we found students were wary of school and of outsiders. As a consequence, they were somewhat reluctant research participants. At the time of writing, interviews have been conducted with seven students, with three of the students doing multiple interviews over an 18-month period. Young people were invited in person, and via Facebook and individual phone calls by friends (both known outsiders and insiders) to participate in the research. It took months to actually come face to face with students and even longer to persuade them to talk to us formally. Our key supporter was Gareth – a friend/known outsider (Martin, 2008). He worked with young people in the community and in the education program. He supported us in many ways – offering perspectives on the community, introducing us to everyone including young people, being a trusted physical presence in interviews and selecting photographs from the learning program to jog young people's memories and stimulate conversation. These photographs proved critical to enable 'easy' and 'light' interactions with young people. They captured work in the classroom, process work on projects with community artists, outings to corporate venues, camps and events showcasing their work to their families and local community. The initial research encounters crackled with affect. We often felt like we were being circled by a cautious flock of birds – landing tentatively, quick to sense any danger and remaining only as long as there were no sudden moves, by us or by the flock.

We eventually settled down to work with small groups of ex-students. These encounters inevitably began in awkward clipped and minimalist ways, but usually transformed and built in affect as students reminisced and reworked narratives with each other, and relentlessly teased Gareth whenever he appeared in photographs. The images of their time in the program transported participants back into shared pleasurable experiences and turned around what might otherwise have been experienced as a stressful performance-based schooling activity. The insights signalled by these shifts in tenor of hot and cold emotions have informed our analysis; and we have attended to the flows of affect in both conducting and analysing interviews. Tuning in to these flows of intensity has been instrumental in recognising the importance of incidents which were often obfuscated by young people's storytelling styles and devices. Young people frequently used fooling around and competitive displays of bravado to disarm injustices within the institutional cultures of mainstream schooling. These devices often acted as signals that anecdotes contained reference to potent forms of symbolic violence.

Analysis of the sequencing of when and how events were told has revealed important insights. These young people did not appear to want their worlds to be immediately knowable. In early interviews, young people typically flagged most of the issues that we have come to see as important over time. Insights were offered in a scattergun fashion, and painful incidents tended to be hinted at but understated. Mazzei and Jackson (2012) describe discursive currents from history, policy, practice and people's varied lifeworlds as 'noise' which shapes what can and cannot be spoken in any given situation. The multiple encounters required by indigenist methods (Martin & Mirraboopa, 2003) build understandings of the complex discursive landscapes that shape the meanings of research participants. Obfuscated stories sharpened our awareness of surveillance, intrusions and the symbolic violence of being typecast as the 'problem' and how this plays out in subsequent social relationships.

We have viewed each interview as an increment in 'coming alongside', and this allowed us to listen without jumping in on tentative or oblique offerings. In subsequent interviews we could gently reopen a space for young people to discuss understated issues and check the impressions we were forming. Our sense is that this reopening operated as a point of recognition for the students, in terms of both the import of the issue and the care they required to be able to discuss it. Sustained contact enabled us to not only see change over time; but it also allowed us to build their trust that we were making a serious effort to understand their worlds and would represent this as best as we could.

The students brought considerable expertise to the research process itself. This expertise resonates with Martin's call to rethink the idea that research is a frontier and participants are naive to the power that permeates research and thus vulnerable in the process. Our participants expected that we already had access to information about them, and they were aware of the limitations of confidentiality and the personal nature of disclosure. They were well practiced in regulating outsiders to manage intrusions. They often deflected attention away from themselves in interviews by adopting the role of interrogator, and disrupted the traditional power dynamic between researcher and researched. At other times they simply refused questions – sometimes bluntly and sometimes feigning a lack of knowledge. They were highly skilled in maintaining their own and other people's personal privacy and were quite cynical and resistant about having information collected about them, their families and communities.

In recognition of ontological differences between Aboriginal and non-Aboriginal communities, we analysed transcripts with outside Aboriginal experts. The interpretations of a number of researchers with greater and lesser distance to the research participants and contexts have enriched our analysis. We offer our interpretations of our data as a 'form of provisional and mobile understandings' (Thomson, 2009, p. 11) rather than as unmediated truths about young people's lives.

## Told stories of schooling structures and processes

Toss and Willa were two students in the alternative education program (hereafter the annex) who returned to mainstream schooling. The annex was one campus of multi-campus high school that catered to an inner-city catchment area. It operated out of a youth centre in an area where there was considerable public housing and had been set up specifically to address the schooling disengagement of Indigenous students. It was a community initiative but operated under the school structure. In the late 1990s, under neoliberal education reforms that emphasised schooling 'choice', the local school in Toss and Willa's neighbourhood struggled for enrolments. It was amalgamated into a multi-campus facility that drew enrolments from six major suburbs. This scale enabled the school to attract and retain a bigger and higher achieving student population because it could offer an array of subject choices. The breadth of subject offerings in restructured multi-campus high schools mimics the kind of 'intensive cultivation' described by Kenway and Fahey (2014) in elite private schools that seek 'to ensure their students' gain entrance to similarly elite universities and thus to the economic and other benefits that accrue in the labour market or as owners of business and industry. Such schools make much of their high curriculum standards as well as their extensive offerings (p. 182). Unfortunately, these advantages were lost to the students who ended up in the annex for a range of complex reasons.

It was clear from young people's told stories that the schools they had attended had attempted to facilitate the inclusion of Indigenous students. They described subsidy programs, Aboriginal Liaison Officers, and Aboriginal and Torres Strait Islander curricula offerings. However, these inclusion efforts were often scuttled by poor understandings of students' histories, everyday lives and consequent vulnerabilities. Schooling structures, processes and relations frequently touched on trigger points that caused them to retreat from school.

The issue of subsidies was one such trigger point. Toss, Willa and all the students in the program were entitled to subsidies yet refused many of the 'richer learning' subjects on offer in their school. They maintained that affordability was not the reason for their refusal. Toss noted, '*No we don't miss out on anything because we don't pay for anything ... we're poverty blacks*'. On this remark, she looked at Willa and they collapsed into laughter. The laughter was deeply revealing. We followed up the phrase with them in a later interview when we had much more trust with them. When asked about what 'poverty black' meant, they exchanged quiet glances. Toss requested a repeat of the question and listened carefully. She began her response in a low slow formal register:

# ALTERNATIVE EDUCATIONAL PROGRAMMES

That term, that just means we just play the black card and get everything for free.

She broke into laughter and continued:

But we shouldn't... that's really bad.

They both stood up and grabbed at each other. Toss was almost incomprehensible when she added:

That is really bad getting it on tape.

The term again provoked a heightened flow of affect – from highly cautious to anxiously self-conscious and then to a shared rebellious joy. This heightened affect indicates the symbolic power of the term to discredit Toss and her family, and perhaps her desire to reject its power. She indicated that subsidy system designed to ameliorate material disadvantage dovetailed with deficit 'handout' discourses that frame using redistributive resources as 'playing a black card' (Pederson et al., 2006). These diminishing discourses endure across generations and circulate in various forms in the media, in popular discourse, in hate speech and have strong historicity. As schooling systems are embedded in this broader context, the subsidy system and application process within schools was clearly an unsafe equity mechanism for these young people.

Toss, Willa and their peers in the annex were attuned to a plethora of deficit discourses about Aboriginal people. They were acutely aware of discourses, noted earlier in the paper, that regard schooling difficulties as a result of incompetent child rearing (Beresford, 2003). Toss and Willa discussed their interactions with school systems, teachers and other students in a way that indicated they often felt hypervisible as 'poor' students and that others regarded them as from dysfunctional families. They often colluded to manage the images of their families in efforts to ward off the stigma that circulated around them. Regardless of how innocuous teachers may have perceived the process of applying for subsidies or extra supports, the girls believed such applications amplified negative views about their families. For them, the schooling structures that were designed to support equity were fields of social relations saturated with long-standing deficit views. Most often they exercised their agency to refuse things that required additional fees and thus refused any chance of being embroiled in handout discourses. The consequence of this meant they not only had limited subject choice but also missed out on potentially enriching experiences (such as excursions) in the subjects they were in.

Their home lives were financially under-resourced. In their own words, Toss and Willa 'didn't get out much'. Holidays were rare. Toss had been on one trip away from home and she described this trip as profoundly unsettling. Her family drove half way across two states to the '*mission country*' where her father was raised. Once there, Toss refused to get out of the car. She said she was shocked by the living conditions and desperate to come home. The home lives they described included significant care responsibilities for younger siblings and sometimes for adults. As a result, they were often absent, late and/or in difficult moods at school. The notion that school could be a place of respite when households were stressed appealed to them. Toss remarked '*school sometimes comes to an advantage, because you just want to get out the house.*' However, more often than not, they discussed mainstream school as an unsafe place because the processes of the school demanded them to behave in ways that dismantled the tactics they had developed to feel safe. Willa indicated that teachers did not respect their privacy or safeguard information:

# ALTERNATIVE EDUCATIONAL PROGRAMMES

> When the teachers know there's something wrong – you go to every class and teachers stare at you like something's wrong with you. Then they'd be funny with you ... because they know your business. They don't say nothing to you about it, but they just know and it pisses you off. The whole school finds out, they all know if one teacher knows. You don't want them to feel sorry for you. You don't want the teacher's sympathy; they're the last person who you want to feel sorry for you, because it just makes you more angry ... like we're dumb black kids.

Toss and Willa not only missed a significant amount of content because of school absences but also had few opportunities to draw on their out-of-school knowledge at school. Aboriginal studies was available but they described it as a relatively low-status subject that only attracted small numbers of primarily Indigenous students. There was little transfer of content across subjects. For example, Toss's mum came from Far North Queensland and she was well rehearsed in the persuasive language of the Mabo native title judgement – noting, '*I get taught that stuff every day, my mum just drills it into my head*.' This knowledge was of value in Aboriginal Studies but was not deployed as an example of genre writing that could help them in high-stakes English assessment tasks. In spite of her deep knowledge of a very persuasive text, Toss did not understand the term 'persuasive writing', so did not even attempt to answer any related questions in her National Assessment Program – Literacy and Numeracy test. She internalised her results as not being good at English.

They were allocated support teachers but Toss and Willa found much of the support was delivered in a way that heightened their sense of visibility as a 'poor' student. Toss experienced the Aboriginal support teacher as overly vigilant, a constant presence, and this undermined her sense of competence:

> Toss: It's like we actually need assistance 24/7. In some cases we are right to go to class, we can do it but she's always up our asses. She won't let us go to class by ourselves.
>
> Jen: So is that something that makes you feel less inclined to go to class?
>
> Willa: Makes you feel dumb.

They dealt with their self-consciousness about gaps in their content knowledge in ways that often brought them into direct conflict with teachers. It is easy to imagine that their interactions with teachers might have sometimes flowed like our discussion about 'poverty blacks' and ended in uncontained laughter. They felt teachers thought they did not take school seriously and were quick to label them as behaviour problems. Willa said:

> You'd walk into the classroom and the teachers would have a go at you about something and you didn't often know what it was, so you'd just walk out again on your own.

The consequence of breaching classroom rules and poor attendance eventually saw them sent to the annex. While the school and the families saw the annex as a positive schooling option, Toss and Willa saw this as unequal treatment and felt they had been '*run out of school*'. They noted that other, non-black, students who were similarly challenged by the mainstream system were permitted to stay in the system, while they were sent to the annex. Willa again:

> they repeated one...they were going to send one to another behaviour school, but they didn't end up, she just stayed there.

## ALTERNATIVE EDUCATIONAL PROGRAMMES

The annex was not a place of status in their eyes. Willa stated *'who would want to go to school in a youthie except for black kids'*.

### Systems of containment and amplification

Like the alternative education spaces described by Nairn and Higgins (2011), the annex carried stigma yet provided space to breathe. It was a hiatus in a trajectory of increasing educational failure. They indicated they could arrive and leave when they liked, get *'a feed'* and participate or not depending on their mood and energy levels. In this educational landscape their emotions were allowed, the pedagogy was relationship based. A young Aboriginal woman who had graduated from the school several years earlier would call them and yell down the phone *'get yourself down 'ere!'* (much as she had when she called them to join our research project). In the space of the annex, having an Aboriginal support teacher was articulated as supportive not as claustrophobic. This is important because it highlights how an intervention in one social field might be experienced very differently from the same intervention in another social field.

Within the annex, they began to *'get out more'*. Excursions grew out of classroom discussions. They were a long time in the making, small in scale and student driven and organised. They selected destinations that aligned to their own knowledge. They became cartographers – charting and controlling their own learning journeys.

In all their talk about learning, the event that generated most affect in the retelling is a camp. It was different from the excursions they had deliberately missed in the past, Toss said:

> This time we wanted to go because we were all together. We were the people that we knew and we hang around with, so yeah, we all wanted to go.

The presence of others who understood their struggles muted the burden of visibility they felt at school and made a critical difference to their desires to participate. They relished making budgets, requesting authorisations, timetabling, and permissions work that made their ideas come to life. Their chosen destination was an island that had once housed a psychiatric hospital. Their interest in this place was entirely relational – one student had visited before and wanted to visit again; and more than one student had a family member who had been housed there in the psychiatric ward. The place had salience in their families and community. Indeed, it resonated with their own experience of being sent offshore of the school to the annex. In Karen Martin and Booran Mirraboopa's (2003) terms, the pedagogy connected to their *Ways of Knowing*.

All of the students became highly animated when looking at photographs of the camp. Downcast eyes and single-sentence answers gave way to rushes of talk and peals of giggles. Toss and Willa told of fear and excitement when they first landed on the island, spirits rising. They raced around its boundaries in the dark, loud in their attempts at silence, abrim with silliness. They tried to connect to each other, metres apart, through Facebook.

> Toss: Yeah, we were like ... try and find signal on the island, that was just the most devastating thing about it. When you found a signal you had to stand in one spot.
>
> Willa: Yeah, like you were standing there like ... do not touch me, do not move. I'm trying to figure out what I'm doing.
>
> Toss: then you'll lose it.

# ALTERNATIVE EDUCATIONAL PROGRAMMES

They sought out the known in this unknown landscape. They played at being prisoners, convicts, conquerors.

> Willa: We ran that island bro...teachers couldn't find us for ages.
> Toss: They're all looking with their torches.
> Willa: We're like quick, quick, quick. Some of us on the floor, me and Toss ... we... It was our idea right, we made that.
> Toss: Because we were all like ... kidbrain

Their victorious claims '*We ran that island Bro*'...'*It was our idea right, we made that*' communicate the ownership and joy of controlling their own lives and learning. They explain their frenzy as a return to a carefree childlike state, which they felicitously name as '*kidbrain*'. 'Kidbrain' was clearly an embodied state of joy and devoid of responsibility. Given the demands of managing complex responsibilities in their home lives and complex social dynamics at school, one can only imagine that 'kidbrain' was hard to come by. There are two ways to read such a state: one is that they were emotionally out of control, making trouble. The other is that they were in a state of heightened engagement with the experience – buoyed by their own capability and agency in making it happen, thrilled at being on the threshold of new knowledge about a place where they had historical relational connections. Their night of cavorting on the island was clearly something of a legend. Teachers, principals and youth workers all shared the story with us. These educators indicated that while 'kidbrain' was difficult for them to manage as responsible adults, they were proud of their capacity to enable such joy. 'Kidbrain' was not considered disruptive or transgressive in the code of conduct of the annex.

Unlike mainstream school, students described the annex as that which provided a safe place for them when things were difficult at home. The annex was a place to go when they wanted to find their friends (or indeed have a sleep). Their relationality and sociability was amplified and permitted in this space.

## Individuation and relatedness

The idea of returning to mainstream school germinated for Toss and Willa some time around the organisation of the camp. They spurred each other on to consider aiming for credentials with power rather than the low-level certificates available through alternative providers, such as technical schools and registered training organisations. They saw returning to mainstream as a task of remaking themselves as individualised learners. They understood this to be the orientation and attitude of successful school students. So they worked hard at individualism and independence and at leaving behind their successes as co-learners with each other and with the teachers at the annex. It was clearly an effort. They frequently referred to their need to '*keep their heads down*' and avoid being called into 'relatedness' by other students. They distanced themselves from the other annex students, often referring to them in interviews as '*dumb*' and '*idiots*'. These references were in direct contradiction to their insightful stories – told at other times – about the hardships facing these same students, and their insistence that intelligence had no bearing on why learning was difficult for students in the annex.

The journey from the annex back to mainstream was unprecedented and there were few considered supports. For their part, Toss and Willa enacted singularity to signal they were no longer trouble makers. '*Keeping their heads down*' meant performing 'successful' student and was a mantra that supported them to downplay relatedness with each other.

Alternative learning spaces do not operate in isolation but are constituted through and in distinction from the bigger system of mainstream schooling. The flow between mainstream and alternative education spaces tends to be unidirectional. The way these spaces are physically located and the resources available in them communicate the level of value conferred on the students they serve by the broader system (Van Ingen & Halas, 2006). Nairn and Higgins (2011) state:

> Alternative education might provide a refuge or a liminal space for students to rework their identities as troublemakers but equally their location [and idea they are for] trouble makers might amplify this aspect of their identities (p. 185).

Little had changed for them on the main campus: the structures, processes and pedagogy that failed in the past were still present; there was no transition, no in-between space, they simply went back to school with a teacher at their sides to help them with work. The irony of their shared insistence that the journey back to mainstream was solitary is that Toss – a year older – returned to the main campus to complete her studies a year before Willa. She marked time waiting for Willa – often missing school. She said she was going to '*put her head down*' when Willa arrived. As soon as this happened, she kicked in big time. She was at Willa's house picking her up for school every day, studying, making goals together and focussed only on schoolwork so she was not distracted by Willa or anyone else.

While the structures and processes were the same, they did experience a change in their relationship with teachers. They felt teachers were now proud of them and offering continual positive reinforcement. Toss enthusiastically noted:

> I just get along with all the teachers. Yeah and they really help. They always tell me that I've improved this year because they send me commendation letters. I get them all just student letters in the mail. My mum gets so excited so I just always give them to my mum.

In spite of this encouragement, the environment remained one that was difficult and challenging. Six months later, Willa remained regular at school, fairly white knuckled and repeating that she was keeping her head down. Toss was rarely attending.

A year later Toss unexpectedly returned to country. Once left alone in a school full of potential graduates, Willa bumped up against her better-off counterparts around the canteen in the morning where there was a '*free feed*'. She did not identify with them and thought they were middle-class kids faking their troubles. Nevertheless, she got through the year and graduated.

However, alone in an interview for the first time, her joy at having achieved her goal was surprisingly muted. It is hard to know if this was because graduating was an anticlimax or whether she was missing Toss. She said that Toss was proud of her and expressed faith in Toss's judgement that returning to country was a positive future-oriented decision. We can hope that Toss's experience of exercising agency in an education setting and learning successfully will position her well in any future attempts to gain credentials or work. In this she would achieve her goals of moving away from welfare and public housing.

Toss and Willa resisted the push and pull of other students in the annex, who typically moved off into other training opportunities, entry-level placements or parenthood. They moved against the flow back into the territory of mainstream school to gain a foothold in the competitive field of educational attainment. They were somewhat better supported by teachers – their stand-out efforts to return no doubt shored-up beliefs that the system delivered equity of opportunity. However, they were still subject to the indignities of hypervisible targeted supports. Unfortunately, there is little evidence at the time of writing that the overarching structures and core beliefs in the mainstream institution were modified to reflect the important pedagogical knowledge about student learning gained in the annex.

What kept these students in school and what failed them exceeds mechanistic and punitive policy interventions to improve school attendance. The environments they occupied – the school, the annex, the family, the community, the mission and the street – were all porous and open to enduring beliefs and transformational hopes about schooling attainment. For Toss and Willa, the group momentum of people from their own community urging them to '*get to school*' supported their aspirations to complete school like their middle-class counterparts (Hayes & Skattebol, 2015). In spite of saying they had to go it alone at school, it was clear their efforts to succeed at school were not individualised but collective and relational. They helped each other keep their '*heads down*'. Furthermore, they both made a substantial contribution to a new narrative in their community that students can move into alternative learning spaces and back again into mainstream environments.

**Conclusion**

In a transnational study of re-engagement programs across Europe, Heidegger et al. (2005) reported that successful programs assisted students to view challenges as a series of achievable thresholds instead of insurmountable problems. The stories told by students in the annex help open out understanding of challenges faced by some Indigenous students as they move through the school system and why some disengage from schooling institutions. In the annex, Toss and Willa were able to cross the thresholds of some of these challenges and imagine themselves as students like 'the others' who complete school. Reconstructing their identity as learners, even after a difficult break and exclusion from normalised schooling trajectories, was made possible, at least in part, by the social relations they developed with the teachers, their peers and each other. For Toss and Willa, this process required opportunities to learn in ways that recognised and respected the social relations that mattered to them. Their stories show how the challenge of remaining engaged at school requires far more considered and relationship-based interventions than those enshrined in policy that penalise families when young people's school attendance drops.

The schooling stories from students in the annex were marked by continuous sociocentric identifications – the '*kids like us*' and the '*we*' of poverty blacks. This emphasis on relatedness suggests a different *Way of Knowing* the self to the individualised notions of students that underpin much education practice. Opportunities to access resources available in the school system were often in direct conflict with their obligations to be responsible to each other and to their families and communities – *Ways of Being*. The historical and collective trauma experienced by Indigenous people means these responsibilities often require silence and refusals to any processes that intrude on collective vulnerabilities. Schooling structures and processes that do not take account of these obligations, or that amplify stigma, failed these young people as equity initiatives. Indeed, schooling processes need to be sensitive to the plethora of messages that communicate negative race-based assumptions about Indigenous students and their families.

Our use of affect theory afforded us the opportunity to make meaning of the stories that Toss and Willa told about their movements between mainstream and alternative schooling in terms of the social relations embedded in and across these sites. It has contributed a 'relational lens that searches for identities and connections between people, histories and place' that can support healing and reconciling 'some of the dire impacts of physical dispossession and social fragmentation' (Martin & Mirraboopa, 2003). It has helped us understand the limits of reason, of the immediately knowable and communicable, the nature of embodied affective storytelling, of entanglements and relational states. These things are often tangible in the study of young people who are poorly served.

There is a need for more relational accounts of schooling that grapple with the inequalities that striate social relations between students that come to school with material and educational capital valued in the system and those that do not. The emotional landscapes of schools, and particularly those of students designated as 'unsuccessful', offer important insights into the social relations produced by neoliberal education reforms. Perhaps, just as importantly, accounts of these emotional landscapes offer insights into how policy and the practices that flow from it could be done 'otherwise' to benefit those who are disadvantaged under the current system. We argue that making sense of these stories is critical for interrogating how educational policy, structures and processes might become more attentive to social relations.

## Acknowledgements

We would like to acknowledge the support and insights of community elders, Dr Gareth Jenkins and Dr Margaret Raven, who helped us access the young people and understand their worlds.

## References

ABS. (2014). *Schools, Australia, 2014*. Catalogue number 4221.0. Canberra: Australian Bureau of Statistics. Retrieved from http://www.abs.gov.au/ausstats/abs@.nsf/mf/4221.0

Beresford, Q. (2003). The context of Aboriginal education. In Q. Beresford & G. Partington (Eds.), *Reform and resistance in Aboriginal education: The Australian experience* (pp. 10–25). Perth: University of Western Australia Press.

Boler, M. (1999). *Feeling power: Emotions and education*. New York, NY: Routledge.

Bottrell, D. (2007). Resistance, resilience and social identities: Reframing 'problem youth' and the problem of schooling. *Journal of Youth Studies*, *10*(5), 597–616. doi:10.1080/13676260701602662

Britzman, D. (1998). *Lost subjects, contested objects: Toward a psychoanalytic inquiry of learning*. Albany: State University of New York Press.

## ALTERNATIVE EDUCATIONAL PROGRAMMES

Department of Prime Minister and Cabinet [DPM&C]. (2014, April 22). Indigenous advancement strategy. *Children and Schooling*. Retrieved from http://www.indigenous.gov.au/children-and-schooling

Dreise, T., & Thomson, S. (2014). *Unfinished business: PISA shows indigenous youth are being left behind*. Retrieved from http://research.acer.edu.au/indigenous_education/37

Friedel, T. L. (2009). *Urban indigenous youths' perspectives on identity, place and place-based learning and the implications for education* (NR55347 Ph.D.). University of Alberta (Canada), Ann Arbor, MI. ProQuest Central database.

Hayes, D. (2012). Re-engaging marginalised young people in learning: The contribution of informal learning and community-based collaborations. *Journal of Education Policy, 27*(5), 641–653. doi:10.1080/02680939.2012.710018. Special Issue: What Would a Socially Just Education System Look Like?

Hayes, D. (2013). Customization in schooling markets: The relationship between curriculum and pedagogy in a 'pop-up' learning project, and the epistemic opportunities afforded by students' interests and backgrounds. *International Journal of School Disaffection, 10*(2), 3–22.

Hayes, D., & Skattebol, J. (2015). Education and belonging. In J. Wyn & H. Cahill (Eds.), *Handbook of children & youth studies* (pp. 517–528). Singapore: Springer.

Heidegger, G., Niemeyer, B., Petersen, W., Ruelens, L., Heikkinen, A., Herno, M., & Frazao, L. (2005). Re-integration: Transnational evaluation of social and professional re-integration programmes for young people. *Final Report*. Retrieved from http://www.biat.uni-flensburg.de/biat.www/index_projekte.htm

Kenway, J., & Fahey, J. (2014). Staying ahead of the game: The globalising practices of elite schools. *Globalisation, Societies and Education, 12*(2), 177–195. doi:10.1080/14767724.2014.890885

Kenway, J., & Youdell, D. (2011). The emotional geographies of education: Beginning a conversation. *Emotion, Space and Society, 4*(3), 131–136. doi:10.1016/j.emospa.2011.07.001

Martin, K., & Mirraboopa, B. (2003). Ways of knowing, being and doing: A theoretical framework and methods for indigenous and indigenist re-search. *Journal of Australian Studies, 27*(76), 203–214. doi:10.1080/14443050309387838

Martin, K. L. (2008). *Please knock before you enter: Aboriginal regulation of outsiders and the implications for researchers*. Brisbane: Post Pressed.

Maxwell, C., & Aggleton, P. (2013). Introduction: Privilege, agency and affect – understanding the production and effects of action. In C. Maxwell & P. Aggleton (Eds.), *Privilege, agency and affect: Understanding the production and effects of action* (pp. 1–14). Houndmills: Palgrave Macmillan.

Mazzei, L. A., & Jackson, Y. (2012). Complicating voice in a refusal to "Let participants speak for themselves". *Qualitative Inquiry, 18*(9), 745–751. doi:10.1177/1077800412453017

Nairn, K., & Higgins, J. (2011). The emotional geographies of neoliberal school reforms: Spaces of refuge and containment. *Emotion, Space and Society, 4*, 180–186. doi:10.1016/j.emospa.2010.10.001

Nakata, M. (2007). *Disciplining the savages: Savaging the disciplines*. Canberra: Aboriginal Studies Press.

Pedersen, A., Dudgeon, P., Watt, S., & Griffiths, B. (2006). Attitudes toward Indigenous Australians: The issue of "special treatment". *Australian Psychologist, 41*(2), 85–94. doi:10.1080/00050060600585502

Seigworth, G. J., & Gregg, M. (2010). An inventory of shimmers. In G. J. Seigworth & M. Gregg (Eds.), *The affect theory reader* (pp. 1–25). Durham: Duke University Press.

Skattebol, J. (2010). Affect: A tool to support pedagogical change. *Discourse: Studies in the Cultural Politics of Education, 31*(1), 75–91.

Smith, A. (2012). Indigeneity, settler colonialism, white supremacy. In D. Martinez HoSang, O. LaBennett, & L. Pulido (Eds.), *Racial formation in the twenty-first century* (pp. 66–90). Berkley: University of California Press.

Smyth, J., & Hattam, R. (2001). 'Voiced' research as a sociology for understanding 'dropping out' of school. *British Journal of Sociology of Education, 22*(3), 401–415. doi:10.1080/01425690120068006

Te Riele, K. (2011). Raising educational attainment: How young people's experiences speak back to the compact with young Australians. *Critical Studies in Education, 52*(1), 93–107. doi:10.1080/17508487.2011.536515

## ALTERNATIVE EDUCATIONAL PROGRAMMES

Thomson, R. (2009) *Intensity and insight: Qualitative longitudinal methods as a route to the psychosocial* (Timescapes Working Paper Series No. 3). ISSN: 1758 3349.

Van Ingen, C., & Halas, J. (2006). Claiming space: Aboriginal students within school landscapes. *Children's Geographies, 4*(3), 379–398. doi:10.1080/14733280601005856

Walkerdine, V., Lucey, H., & Melody, J. (2002). *Growing up girl: Psychosocial explorations of gender & class*. London: Palgrave.

Wetherell, M. (2013). Feeling rules, atmospheres and affective practice: Some reflections on the analysis of emotional episodes. In C. Maxwell & P. Aggleton (Eds.), *Privilege, agency and affect: Understanding the production and effects of action* (pp. 221–239). Houndmills: Palgrave MacMillian.

# Young black males: resilience and the use of capital to transform school 'failure'

Cecile Wright, Uvanney Maylor and Sophie Becker

This article addresses the idea of 'failure' of young black males with respect to schooling. Perceptions of black masculinity are often linked to 'underperformance' in the context of school academic achievement. This article addresses how young black men, by great personal effort, recover from school 'failure'. It explores how young black men, despite negative school experiences, see possibilities for their future and how they seek to transform school 'failure' into personal and educational 'success'. Low attainment combined with permanent/temporary exclusion from school does not necessarily deter young black men from pursuing their education. This low attainment is used by some to make a renewed attempt at educational progression in a different post-school learning environment. Yosso's concept of 'community cultural wealth' provides an understanding of how different forms of capital are accessed by young black men to form a 'turnaround narrative'. This article considers the complex ways in which young black males work to transform their negative school experience. Their narratives reveal a determination to succeed and the ways in which cultivation of this determination by the family, organisational/community agents promotes a sense of possibility. However, it remains to be seen how, in the UK, the cuts to vital local services and support will impact on this sense of possibility.

## Introduction

The portrait of black masculinity that emerges in this work perpetually constructs black men as 'failures' .... Yet, there has never been a time in the history of the United States when black folks, particularly black men, have not been enraged by the dominant culture's stereotypical, fantastical representations of black masculinity .... (Hooks, 1992, p. 89)

Hooks' comment exemplifies the dominant negative stereotypical narrative of black men in the United Kingdom (UK) and the United States (US) societies. It portrays the presence of black males as problematic to the extent that black males are considered to have 'failed'.

Indeed, it is widely recognised that part of the wider perception of black masculinity is the notion of 'failure'. This is evident particularly within the context of education and with regard to black boys in the UK and the US in relation to them being labelled as 'underperforming'. This has, in turn, been reflected in US and UK statistics relating to black male academic achievement (e.g. DfE (Department for Education), 2013; Farkas, 2003; REACH, 2007; Strand, 2010) and black male unemployment. For example, the Office for National Statistics (ONS) (2012) reported that in 2011, 55.9% of black males aged 16–24 in the UK were unemployed which is more than double the proportion of white males (23.9%) in the same age group (see also Institute for Public Policy Research (IPPR), 2010). Moreover, it is suggested that a discourse of 'failing black masculinity' (Reynolds, 2006; Sewell, 1997), especially in its overrepresentation of black males in the criminal justice system (House of Commons Home Affairs Committee, 2007) has been important in influencing how educational statistics on academic achievement are explained by the media and the government (Gillborn, 2008; Mocombe, Tomlin, & Wright, 2014).

This article examines the experiences of young black men excluded from school and how they negotiate their futures. This is particularly with respect to transforming school 'failure' into 'success'. The article commences with a review of the literature with regard to educational 'failure', exclusion and potential success. This is followed by an examination of intersectionality, forms of capital and their utilisation to achieve success. There then follows the findings of the authors' study into how young black men excluded from school engaged in a 'turnaround narrative' to transform their negative school experience.

## Literature review: education and the othering of black students

As mentioned previously both within the US and the UK the presence of young black people within the respective education systems has been framed within a discourse of 'problematic students' because of their perceived alien demands and identities (King, 2005; Ladson-Billings, 2006; Majors, 2001; Wright, Standen, & Patel, 2010). Within both contexts young black men are seen as the most problematic group (Goff, Jackson, Di Leone, Culotta, & DiTomasso, 2014; Gosai, 2009; Sewell, 1997). Yet schooling, underpinned by the 'permanence of structural racism' (Dumas, 2014, p. 20), 'is a site of suffering' (Dumas, 2014, p. 2) for black students as a whole (Leonardo, 2009).Within the UK, young people of African-Caribbean heritage, particularly young black men, feature disproportionately in terms of low educational achievement and high rates of exclusion from school (DfE, 2013; Graham & Robinson, 2004; Richardson, 2005). This is compared to Chinese and Indian heritage children who are consistently denoted as high achievers in terms of 5A*–C GCSE (general certificate in secondary education) passes (including English and mathematics), followed by white British, Bangladeshi and Pakistani heritage children (DfE 2013; Strand 2014). At an individual level, attaining 5A*–C at GCSE is the measure which is used by the UK government (through the Department for Education (DfE)) to judge student success. At the school level, individual and cross school comparisons of success are determined by a floor level target of 40% of pupils at a school attaining five GCSE grades between A* and C, including passes in English and maths (Adams, 2015; the DfE 2015). As well as these defined and measurable criteria of schooling success, Tett (2014) suggests that students' notions of success and failure are informed by their experiences of teaching and learning. She found that adults who had been positioned 'failures' at school had 'learners identities' that had been 'constituted by the dominant discourses of education where people are divided into high or low achievers, intelligent or ignorant, capable or incapable'.

While such labels are experienced by all students in English schools it could be argued that contentions of being 'capable' are undermined by national GCSE results which positions African-Caribbean males in comparison to students from other ethnic groups as not just underachievers, but as failures, likely to fail (even if supported) and therefore

## ALTERNATIVE EDUCATIONAL PROGRAMMES

not worth bothering about because of the persistent underachievement of the African-Caribbean group as a whole. If unchallenged these notions of 'failure' become internalised and negative learner identities can be difficult to escape (Youdell, 2003). A further problem is that rather than being regarded as individuals, stereotyped notions of black failure held by teachers can serve to limit a student's ambitions because they are constantly told their goals are impossible to achieve (Maylor, 2014).

The considerable variation in educational achievement for young black men is also linked to high exclusion rates (Blair, 2001; Christian, 2005; DfES, 2006). Exclusion from school, particularly black student exclusion, is an extremely urgent issue (Office of the Children's Commissioner, 2012), especially as Britain's official exclusion figures for black students far outstrip those of other countries in Europe and North America (Mocombe et al., 2014). However, even in the US, school exclusion and suspension figures indicate that significantly high numbers of black students, particularly males, are being suspended and/or excluded, often for relatively minor incidents and at a much higher rate than their white counterparts (see, e.g., Gardner, Ford, & Miranda, 2001; Gregory & Thompson, 2010; NAEP, 2008; Skiba, Trachok, Chung, Baker, & Hughes, 2012).

A related topic of discussion and debate are the negative consequences related to school suspension/exclusion, namely, school disengagement, school dropout, poor retention and ultimately school failure (Eitle and Elite, 2004).This racial–ethnic and gendered disparity in exclusionary practices has also become an integral part of the debate and discussion relating to closing the black/white achievement gap in both the UK (e.g. Gillborn, 2008; Strand, 2010, 2014) and the US (e.g. National Assessment Education Progress (NCES), 2009; US Department of Education 2014). In 2014, US government concern about the high school suspension rates and the relatively poor educational and employment outcomes of young black males when compared to white students underscored the launching of a national government initiative – 'My Brother's Keeper'. This was designed to close the educational and employment gap by fostering educational and employment opportunities for boys and young black men, as explained by the US President Barack Obama who said:

> As a black student, you are far less likely than a white student to be able to read proficiently by the time you are in 4th grade. By the time you reach high school, you're far more likely to have been suspended or expelled. .... Black kids are nearly four times as likely [as white kids] to be suspended. And if a student has been suspended even once by the time they're in 9th grade they are twice as likely to drop out. .... we know young black men are twice as likely as young white men to be 'disconnected' – not in school, not working. ... Fewer young black and Latino men participate in the labor force compared to young white men. And all of this translates into higher unemployment rates and poverty rates as adults. (Obama, 2014, online)

Obama's comment concerning the educational outcomes of 'Black kids' resonates strongly with the situation in the UK, but a number of writers go beyond this, for instance, the works of Channer (1995), Rhamie (2007), Byfield (2008) and Wright et al. (2010), by offering evidence of young black people's successful personal and educational outcomes of post-compulsory education. Moreover, this article posits, as Rhamie (2007) points out, that it is important to explore all aspects of black students' experiences within the education system, not only the pattern of differentiated attainment, 'but also the factors that fracture that pattern and enable academic success' (p. 4). Indeed with respect to the pervasive discourses of 'failing' young black people, particularly males, a number of researchers have been critical of what is considered to be the normalised 'absence and the pathologised presences of the non-western subjects in the academy' (Phoenix, 1998, p. 860). This is despite the fact that, according to Owen (2006), within the UK there is an overrepresentation of young black people in higher education compared to their presence in the population.

Low attainment at 16 is not the disaster which is often portrayed to be, as it can be regarded by certain groups of young black people as a platform for making a fresh start in a new learning environment on a journey to improve longer-term career prospects. An understanding of how low GCSE attainment can lead to renewed self-belief in a non-mainstream school environment is needed to gain a sense of educational progression of young black people. One route for this is further education, as further education colleges offer opportunities and courses for black young people who have been alienated by their experience of school (DfES, 2003). Indeed it is evident that African-Caribbean males are more likely to continue their studies in further education than white males (Strand, 2012). Data also suggest that the proportion of UK domiciled black students pursuing higher education degree courses has increased since the academic year 2003/04 (ECU, 2014). The desire for further and higher education study highlights the commitment of young black people to challenge conceptions of black 'failure'.

Similarly, findings from the US also suggest that black students at the post-secondary education stage 'obtain more from [college] education than their white counterparts after statistically controlling for socioeconomic status (SES) and academic characteristics (e.g. proficiency grades)' (Merolla, 2013, pp. 895–896). Merolla (2013) contends that this level of college participation provides black students with a 'net black advantage' and it is an advantage that 'exists across college types and may be stronger for students at lower levels of the SES gradient' (pp. 895–896). The 'net black advantage' Merolla identified is based on a statistical analysis of 5247 white and 701 black students as part of a longitudinal study from 1988 to 2000 undertaken by the US National Center for Educational Statistics. In the study, 30% of the black students' parents had a college degree compared with 37% of white students, and 31% of black students were from low income families compared with 12% of white students. As well as higher college entrance, Tienda (2013) further argues, 'on graduating from college black [students] are *more* likely than white students to enrol in graduate school, and that they do so at a faster rate' (p. 470; emphasis in original).

## Theoretical framework: intersectionality and forms of capital

This section explores the theory of intersectionality alongside a discussion of the notion of 'capital' seen through the prism of critical race theory (CRT) (Yosso, 2005) in relation to the black communities' political mobilisation around racial inequality in education (Wright, 2013).

In essence, intersectional analysis was created by black feminists as an attempt to counter work by white feminists to 'homogenise women's situations' (Yuval-Davis, 2011). Nira Yuval-Davis (2011), reflecting on debates about intersectionality, acknowledges the history of the approach, as exemplified in the work of black women writers. 'Intersectionality' is a term coined by Kimberley Crenshaw (1989). Brah and Phoenix (2004) argue that intersectionality offers a framework whereby race, ethnicity, social class and other social divisions can be theorised as lived realities. Thus, intersectionality signals a departure from the additive multiple models of double or triple jeopardy and the seemingly meaningless list of never-ending hierarchies of multiple positions and identities (Butler, 1990; McCall, 2005). The notion of 'embodied intersectionality' is applied in this article to make sense of what the black males' experiences tells us about the construction of racialised, classed and gendered subjectivity(ties) and identities within the context of education and personal outcomes. Essentially, it provides an understanding of the ways in which markers of social difference, such as race, class, gender, age and so on intersect to create diverse experiences.

Within youth transitions research, it is recognised that as a concept 'social capital' offers a useful analytical framework for capturing how young people negotiate ways out of social disadvantage. As such the arguments presented are located in an understanding, informed by the extension of Bourdieu's (1986) work on social and cultural capital by Yosso (2005). Yosso (2005) takes a CRT perspective in advancing Bourdieu's ideas. The writer attempts to extend the various forms of capital to theoretically reposition or centre the experiences of black people in the discourse of what constitutes social capital. In this regard, the writer 'calls into question white middle class communities as the standard by which all others are judged' (p. 82).

Yosso details the concept of CRT, which is called *Community cultural wealth*. 'Yosso (2005) describes CRT as a framework that can be used to theorize, examine, and change the ways race and racism affect social structures, practices, and discourses' (Schlesinger, 2013, p. 1). Using CRT, Yosso (2005) envisages social and cultural capital as *Community cultural wealth* which she conceptualised as an array of 'knowledge, skills, abilities and contacts possessed by *Communities of Color* to survive and resist macro and micro-forms of oppression' (p. 69). The writer articulates six overlapping forms of capital that comprise community resources: aspirational, navigational, social, resistant, familial and linguistic capital. A brief description of Yosso's forms of capital is presented here: Aspirational capital is to have the desire to be highly ambitious when there are considerable barriers making this almost impossible. Navigational capital is having the skills to see through complex social institutions that systemically disadvantage minorities. Social capital refers to people who can be turned to in order to obtain support. Resistant capital is the ability to not accept negative stereotyping and to assert one's own identity. Familial capital refers to family support. Linguistic capital is the set of communications skills, such as bilingual skills to communicate with a variety of communities.

This article applies an intersectional stratification alongside Yosso's (2005) overlapping forms of capital to a study which analyses the multifaceted, nuanced and complex ways in which postcolonial diasporic young black males resist and work to transform their negative school experience. Essentially, looking at the forms of capital used by black males not only allows us to recognise the system and processes that create school 'failure' but also accounts for the agented strategies they use to create pathways to personal and educational success.

**The study: black male exclusion from school**

This study focuses on black males excluded from school. It documents their post-compulsory school experiences and how they achieved successful personal and educational outcomes.

With respect to the use of the term 'black' to describe the participants of the study, it is noteworthy, that in the UK, the term 'Black has a complex history' (see Warmington, 2014 for debates in this area). 'It can, depending on context, denote either people of African/African-Caribbean descent or, via discourse of "political blackness", the wider assembly of African, African-Caribbean, Asian, Arabic and mixed race peoples constructed in the post-war period of immigration – something akin to the collective referred to in the USA as people of colour' (Warmington, 2014, p. 5). In the article, the term is used to refer to people of African/African-Caribbean descent. The black population in the UK is 5.5% (3.1 million) of the total UK population.

The data were collected as part of a larger project of 33 male and female participants combining quantitative data with qualitative interviewing. Although the study includes male and female participants the concentration here is on male participants. The male participants were considered to exhibit the forms of the capital described previously, such as aspirational, resistant, familial, social and navigational capital.

The data upon which the article is based include 100 narrative interviews conducted with 21 black males between the ages of 14 and 19 all of whom were of African-Caribbean heritage who had experienced permanent school exclusion [1]. The young people were drawn from residents in Nottingham and London [2]. Both cities are known for a disproportionately high level of school exclusions (see Eggleston, Dunn, Anjali, & Wright, 1986; Mirza & Reay, 2000; Mocombe et al., 2014; Wright, Weekes, & Macglauglin, 2000; Wright et al., 2010; Wright, 2015) in the UK, including those who had been excluded from both state and independent schools. The young people were interviewed on a maximum of three occasions over a period of two years. Participants were asked to talk about various aspects of three themes: their view of self, following exclusion, sources of support and coping strategies for transforming school exclusion and their views on current personal circumstances and ambitions/aspiration for the future. Additional data were provided from over 60 interviews with contacts nominated by the young people, including community and social workers, mothers, fathers, grandparents, siblings and friends. Traditionally, these black males are often described as hard to reach (Merton, 1998). Thus, a snowballing sample method was used to access the black males for the study. These included contacts with black community groups, black organisations, supplementary schools and black churches. Meetings with the young men were conducted in a variety of locations including their homes, university and community venues.

Integral to the research design was the desire to both engage and empower the men. In this vein, the use of visual methods was valuable in the following respects. First, we anticipated that traditional one-to-one interviewing would not necessarily be the best way to carry out the research with the excluded men because they were likely to have experienced many interview situations where the aim was to prove their responsibility for the exclusion. After considering other methods, visual research methods, namely participant photography, was chosen to place the men at the centre of the research process. Thus, the empowerment of the research participants was at the core of the research design (see Wright, 2015).

## The findings: how black males in school use different forms of capital [3]

The findings in this article illustrate how the black males traverse and transcend the educational terrain to create successful personal and educational outcomes 'by drawing [on] their community cultural wealth and different forms of capital' (Oropenza, Varghese, & Kanno, 2010, p. 22)

## Aspirational and resistant capital: 'turnaround narrative'

Notably, for Yosso (2005) aspirational capital is to have the desire to be highly ambitious, even in the face of considerable barriers. The desire to achieve educational success, carving out a career path and social mobility was a common theme emanating from the black males narratives.

For the black men, a major source of aspirational capital came from the desire to transform their 'failing' identity through a process of recovery and redemption or what

Harding (2010) refers to as the 'turnaround narrative'. Harding in his study of adolescent boys living in black neighbourhoods in the US context, explains the narrative of 'recovery and redemption' as denoting someone of humble origins who achieves success through hard work and ingenuity. This is considered to be a widespread American idea. It involves recovery from a setback or personal failure. Key elements of the 'turnaround narrative' include recognising previous 'errors' for example, addiction, street crime, juvenile detention (see Toldson, 2011), getting away from people or places that contribute to past problems. Similarly, Merolla (2013) found black parents' high aspirations combined with 'black students high expectations act as a critical buffer against the reproduction of racial inequalities in educational attainment' (p. 919) and create the conditions for future possibilities. The young men became engaged in pursuing the 'turnaround narrative'. The desire for change, overcoming adversity and possibilities for personal and educational success are highlighted in the remarks below by Leon, Roger and Dale:[4]

> I want a decent job ... and anything that pays ... then look for an office job when I get a bit older and wear [a] suit and tie and everything ... it's not like I'm dumb ... I've got plans. I got ideas for the future. (Leon)
> My mum and dad just said, when I was excluded they just said ... the main thing ... was to turn the negative into positive in the long run by what I did, what I achieved, my exam results, which basically [is] like spitting in the head teacher's face. (Roger)
> I need to go back to college, go to school and don't get kicked out. It's not good in the long run ... it's hard to find a decent job without qualifications. (Dale)

The young men are implying that aspirational capital can incorporate resistant capital. For instance, Leon, Roger and Dale talked explicitly about the need to resist and re-negotiate the school 'failure' identity label ascribed to them through the school exclusion process. By re-engaging with education and the subsequent acquisition of educational qualifications, Roger felt able not only to celebrate his educational success but also to dismiss the label ascribed to him by his previous school and the head teacher.

Similarly, for Dale resistance was in the form of his aspiration to go to college for the purpose of acquiring qualifications which would assist in establishing a career pathway. Also, reflected in the men's conversations about the use of resistance and aspiration in negotiating the school 'failure' label is the application of the 'turnaround narrative' connected to resilience and a 'culture of possibility' (Yosso, 2005, p. 78) as a way of responding to personal struggles.

### Family capital: the role of family and parenting in achieving success

Consistent with the literature on the role of family in achieving educational and personal success (Fordham, 1986; Merolla, 2013; Reynolds, 2006; Rollock, Gillborn, Vincent, & Ball, 2011) the black males talked about how their high expectations, inspiration, emotional support and cultural resilience related to the aspirational capital developed through their family, shaped their educational and personal careers.

The cases of Tony and David illustrate how strong bonds within their families in turn helped gain other kinds of capital, such as aspirational and resistant capital. These were essential to their pathways to educational and personal success:

> they (family) kept me up and encouraged me a lot ... they were always there for me and from the beginning they believed in me. (Tony)

ALTERNATIVE EDUCATIONAL PROGRAMMES

David also recalled how his father 'because he cared and wanted to help me out of the situation' had sought legal advice after he was excluded from his mainstream school.

Many of the young men reported that the negative educational experiences and the endeavour to forge success and the family emotional support later offered, had led to an improvement in familial relationships. As Nelson expressed:

> she (mother) believed in me. I think it might have brought us closer together closer because she actually believed me and trusted me ... showed me how to cope ... I was happy that she believed me. I was glad that she was there to support me. (Nelson)

Thus, strong bonds with their families, in turn, helped these black males gain other kinds of capital, such as aspirational and resistant capital which were critical to ensuring educational and personal success. In particular, and consistent with the literature, the family and the role of 'mothers' were considered pivotal to how black males traverse and transcend the educational terrain to ensure a positive outcome. Indeed, Reay (2000) in her study posits that mothers' emotional support of their children's academic success transfers to educational and social prestige (see also Mirza, 2009).

### Social and navigational capital: community, 'diasporic collectives' and social actions

> Cultural action is always a systematic and deliberate form of action which operates upon the social structure, either with the objective of preserving that structure or of transforming it. As a form of deliberate and systematic action, all cultural action has its theory which determines its ends and thereby defines its methods.(Freire, 1972, p. 46)

This quotation from Freire encapsulates the way in which the black diasporic community strives to transform conditions in their communities' and the role of social capital in that transformation (see also Reynolds, 2013).

Several forms of capital used by participants to help them achieve successful personal and educational outcomes. Peter and James talked about using localised community programmes such as those offered by black community organisations, black churches and black supplementary schools (Andrews, 2013; Maylor et al., 2013; Mirza & Reay, 2000). The nature of the navigational capital afforded the black males included advice, mentoring, inspiration, information about accessing education and training opportunities which enabled them to convert their social capital directly into navigational capital. For example:

> the ISSP, they giving me help as well ... they like keeping [me] off the streets like ... more constructive things to do, like more positive things in my mind. (Peter)

Similarly, as James states:

> It made me do a lot of thinking for myself, it made me self-conscious and not so arrogant ... because there are two paths for me, the situation that I was in .... I had to decide which one I had to take, and I took a lot of stick but was given a lot of advice, suggestions. (James)

Both participants' comments illustrate how they sought to re-negotiate their identity as school 'failures' and how this strongly related to aspirational and resistant capital alongside the 'turnaround narrative' developed through their family. Moreover, in addition to the confirmation of the significance of the organisational agents in conferring navigational capital on the participants, they simultaneously mentioned the saliency of the ethos, context and atmosphere in which the resources were delivered. Thus, despite finding engaging with the resources personally challenging as James stated it 'made me self-conscious and not so arrogant . . . took a lot of stick', the participants felt a strong sense of connection to the organisations they utilised.

Further, agents from the organisations utilised by the black men, underlined the participants' strong sense of belonging and the connections to navigational capital afforded them. For instance, staff members discussed the local black community services offered specifically for the purpose of supporting black males excluded from school. The focus of these services would appear to be two-fold. Firstly, navigational capital in the form of practical and emotional support such as advice, career advice, tutoring services, self-affirming classes, access to educational opportunities which were critical to black males pathway to educational and personal success. Secondly, engaging in political activism concerning obstacles to black young people accessing educational opportunities. Indeed, these organisational activities resonated with both Freire's (1972) notion of 'cultural action' mentioned previously and Yosso's (2005) concept of 'community cultural wealth'.

> I just have a team that is trying to support the young people for what they have been through and supposed to get and have been denied of, and try to do the best we can do within the parameters and move the boundaries and knock the door hard and move the doors off the hinges to make changes. (Youth advocate manager, ISSP, London)
>
> Any gaps in society, [we] try and help plug those. (Community development officer, Nottingham)

In essence, these organisations' engagement with the participants, which included activities such as fostering a pro-active approach to accessing educational opportunities, strategies/tactics for social mobility, encouraging constructive racial and cultural identity and a focus on achieving success through personal transformation, in turn, helped the black males gain other capital, such as aspirational and resistant capital.

## Conclusion

This article examined how black males excluded from school employ agentic strategies to create successful personal and educational outcomes. It illuminates the fact that hitherto focus on researching and theorising the problematic experience of education entirely has diverted attention from the creative and dynamic ways black males negotiate barriers and uncertainties endemic in what Beck and Beck-Gernsheim (2009) term the era of 'globalised modernity'. In this regard, the article thus offers a counter-narrative to the discourse relating to black males in the UK.

The article raised the issue of how individuals overcome negative mainstream school experiences and 'succeed'. The dominant notion of 'success' refers to the gaining of educational qualifications and/or 'success' in the job market. It illustrates how black males achieve these, by drawing on different forms of capital they possess. In this regard, the black males incorporated aspirational and resistant capital connected through familial capital. This allowed them to reject the school 'failure' label and pursue further and/or higher education. Additionally, they developed and acquired social and navigational capital through institutional agents, by negotiating the 'failure' label that they were given in school. This helped them re-enter education and later gain employment. Notwithstanding, the increase in youth unemployment in the UK in recent years has resulted in unemployment for many, including black students, who have succeeded in the education system (IPPR, 2010). This has meant that for many black students passing their GCSE examinations does not always translate into positive long term employment outcomes.

Clearly, some black males overcome negative school experiences and they are able to participate in education outside of the mainstream sector. However, we must not focus solely on each individual's attributes, but also focus on what it is that will increase the likelihood of black males as a group being successful. Black male group success warrants further attention with respect to employment possibilities.

Workforce statistics (IPPR, 2010) suggest that not everyone from marginalised groups can necessarily succeed in the labour market. Moreover, the educational system and labour market are structured so that black educational and employment success is not possible (ONS, 2012), and it might be argued that wholesale educational success and employment is unachievable as the labour market needs to have a pool of unemployed labour. Hence, the pathways to social mobility are only possible for limited numbers (Compton, 2008). Can we therefore assume that one million young people currently unemployed in the UK are surplus to requirements?

The change in the UK economy and the reduction in public spending (HM Government, 2010) have had a disproportionate impact on those groups most at risk from exclusion and most at risk of 'failure' educational or otherwise. Following on from this, it can be argued that the propensity for black people to be considered 'failures' has been further exacerbated by the recent Conservative government budget cuts and changes to tax credits and other welfare benefits, which according to a report by the Runnymede Trust (2015), have disproportionately affected black and minority ethnic households as they are more likely to be unemployed, earn less than the minimum wage and have higher poverty rates than white British households. Racial inequality in employment for black people (IPPR, 2010) raises the question as to whether the aspirational and resistance capital infused with 'turnaround narrative' expressed by the young black men here will persist. Will these young black men's aspirations and ambitions be undermined in an era of decreasing employment opportunities? Will the desire to resist and navigate school disadvantage to achieve successful personal and educational outcomes continue? Therefore, perhaps the notion of success could go beyond qualifications and access to the job market but also include developing resilience, self-esteem and resourcefulness. The access of black males to the different forms of capital highlighted in this article becomes ever more vital in an era of increasing uncertainty for post education futures.

**Notes**

1. Within the British education system the most serious sanction that a school can take against a student is to exclude them permanently. This is where a school decides to remove a student from the school role. The local education authority has the duty to ensure that such students receive a basic education elsewhere. However, permanent exclusion is only one form of school exclusion. Most school exclusion is of a fixed term with students readmitted after a period of time.
2. The findings are drawn from a study funded by Joseph Rowntree Foundation, Overcoming school exclusion and achieving successful youth transitions within African-Caribbean Communities, 2003–2005.
3. The form of 'capital' referred to as 'Linguistic capital' is not relevant in this study because English is the first language of all participants.
4. All the names of people are pseudonyms.

# ALTERNATIVE EDUCATIONAL PROGRAMMES

## References

Adams, R. (2015). Number of English schools failing on GCSE targets doubles in a year. *The Education Guardian.*

Andrews, K. (2013). *Resisting racism: Race, inequality, and the Black supplementary school.* Stoke-on-Trent: Trentham Books Limited.

Beck, U., & Beck-Gernsheim, E. (2009). Global generations and the trap of methodological national for a cosmopolitan turn in the sociology of youth and generation. *European Sociological Review, 25*(1), 25–36. doi:10.1093/esr/jcn032

Blair, M. (2001). *Why pick on me? School exclusion and Black youth.* Stoke-on-Trent: Trentham Books Limited.

Bourdieu, P. (1986). The forms of capital. In J.E. Richardson (Ed.), *Handbook of theory for research in the sociology of education.* Westport, CT: Greenwood Press.

Brah, A., & Phoenix, A. (2004). 'Ain't I a woman? Revisiting intersectionality'. *Journal of International Women's Studies, 5*(3), 75–86.

Butler, J. (1990). *Gender trouble: Feminism and the subversion of identity.* London: Routledge.

Byfield, C. (2008). The impact of religion on the educational achievement of Black boys: A UK and USA study. *British Journal of Education, 29*(2), 189–199.

Channer, Y. (1995). *I am a promise: The school achievement of British African-Caribbeans.* Stoke-on-Trent: Trentham Books.

Christian, M. (2005). The politics of black presence in Britain and black male exclusion in the British education system. *Journal of Black Studies, 35*(3), 327–346. doi:10.1177/0021934704268397

Compton, R. (2008). *Class and stratification.* London: Polity Press.

Crenshaw, K. (1989). *Demarginalizing the intersection of race and sex.* Chicago, IL: University of Chicago.

DfE (Department for Education). (2013). *Statistical first release, pupil performance tables* (pp. 04/2013). London: DfE SFR.

DfE (Department for Education). (2015). *School and college performance tables, KS4 2014 results, English schools.* London: DfE. Retrieved from http://www.education.gov.uk/cgi-bin/schools/performance/group.pl?qtype=NAT&superview=sec

DfES (Department for Education and Skills) (2003) *Minority ethnic attainment and participation in education and training: The evidence, research topic paper* RT01-03. London: DFES.

DfES (Department for Education and Skills). (2006). *"Getting it. Getting it right": Exclusion of Black pupils, priority review.* London: Stationery Office, DfES.

Dumas, M. (2014). 'Losing an arm': Schooling as a site of black suffering. *Race Ethnicity and Education, 17*(1), 1–29. doi:10.1080/13613324.2013.850412

ECU (Equality Challenge Unit). (2014). *Equality in higher education 2014: Students statistics.* London: ECU.

Eggleston, J., Dunn, D., Anjali, M., & Wright, C. (1986). *Education for some.* Stoke-on-Trent: Trentham Books.

Eitle, T., & Eitle, J. (2004). Inequality, segregation, and the overrepresentation of African Americans in school suspensions. *Sociological Perspectives, 47*(3), 269–287. doi:10.1525/sop.2004.47.issue-3

Farkas, G. (2003). Racial disparities and discrimination in education: What do we know, how do we know it, and what do we need to know? *Teachers College Record*, *105*, 1119–1146. doi:10.1111/tcre.2003.105.issue-6

Fordham, S. (1986). *Blacked out: Dilemmas of race identity and success at capital high*. Chicago, IL: University of Chicago Press.

Freire, P. (1972). *Pedagogy of the oppressed*. London: Penguin Books.

Gardner, R., Ford, D.Y., & Miranda, A.H. (2001). Education of African American students: The struggle continues. *The Journal of Negro Education, 70, Fall*, 212–224.

Gillborn, D. (2008). *Racism and education: Coincidence or conspiracy?* London: Routledge.

Goff, P.A., Jackson, M.C., Di Leone, B., Culotta, C.M., & DiTomasso, N.A. (2014). The essence of innocence: Consequences of dehumanizing black children. *Journal of Personality and Social Psychology*, *106*(4), 526–545. doi:10.1037/a0035663

Gosai, N. (2009). Educational experiences of black African Caribbean boys. Unpublished Ph.D University of Birmingham,UK

Graham, M., & Robinson, G. (2004). The silent catastrophe: Institutional racism in the British educational system and the underachievement of black boys. *Journal of Black Studies*, *34*(5), 653–671. doi:10.1177/0021934703259347

Gregory, A., & Thompson, A. (2010). African American high school students and variability in behavior across classrooms. *Journal of Community Psychology*, *38*(3), 386–402. doi:10.1002/jcop.v38:3

Harding, D. (2010). *'Living the drama': Community, conflict and culture among inner-city boys*. Chicago, IL: The University of Chicago Press.

HM Government. (2010). *Freedom, fairness, responsibility: the coalition: our programme for government*. London: Cabinet Office.

Hooks, B. (1992). *Black looks: Race and representation*. Boston, MA: South End Press.

House of Commons Home Affairs Committee (2007) "Young black people and the criminal justice system", second report of session 2006–07. Retrieved from http://www.publications.parliament.uk/pa/cm200607/cmselect/cmhaff/181/181i.pdf

Institute for Public Policy Research (IPPR). (2010). *Youth unemployment and recession*. London: IPPR.

King, J. (Ed). 2005. *Black education: a transformative research and action agenda for the new century, pub. American Educational Research Association*. London: Lawrence Erlbaum Associates.

Ladson-Billings, G. (2006). From the achievement gap to education debt: Understanding achievement in U.S. schools. *Educational Researcher*, *35*(7), 3–12.

Leonardo, Z. (2009). *Race, whiteness and education*. Abingdon: Routledge.

Majors, R. (ed.). (2001). *Educating our black children*. London: Routledge.

Maylor, U. (2014). *Teacher training and the education of black children: Bringing color into difference*. London: Routledge.

Maylor, U., Rose, A., Minty, S., Ross, A., Issa, T., & Kuyok, K. (2013). Exploring the impact of supplementary schools on black and minority ethnic pupils mainstream attainment. *British Educational Research Journal*, *39*(1), 107–125.

McCall, L. (2005). The complexity of intersectionality. *Signs: Journal of Women in Culture and Society*, *30*(3), 1771–1800. doi:10.1086/signs.2005.30.issue-3

Merolla, D. (2013). The net black advantage in educational transitions: An education careers approach. *American Educational Research Journal*, *50*(5), 895–924. doi:10.3102/0002831213486511

Merton, B. (1998). *Finding the missing*. Leicester: Youth Work Press.

Mirza, H.S. (2009). *Race, gender and educational desire: Why black women succeed and fail*. London: Routledge.

Mirza, H.S., & Reay, D. (2000). Spaces and places of black educational desire: Rethinking black supplementary schools as a new social movement. *Sociology*, *34*, 521–544. doi:10.1177/S0038038500000328

Mocombe, P., Tomlin, C., & Wright, C. (2014). *Race and class distinctions within black communities-a racial-caste-in-class*. London: Routledge.

National Assessment Education Progress (NCES). (2008). *NAEP 2008 trends in academic progress*. Washington, DC: National Center for Education Statistics, Institute of Education Sciences, U.S.

# ALTERNATIVE EDUCATIONAL PROGRAMMES

Department of Education. Retrieved from. http://nces.ed.gov/nationsreportcard/pdf/main2008/2009479.pdf

National Center for Education Statistics. (2009). *Achievement gaps: How black and white students in public schools perform in mathematics and reading on the national assessment of educational progress, statistical analysis report, NCES 2009-455.* Washington: U.S. Department of Education.

Obama, B. (2014) Remarks by the President on my brother's keeper initiative. Retrieved from https://www.whitehouse.gov/my-brothers-keeper

Office for National Statistics (ONS). (2012). *Labour force survey.* London: ONS.

Office of the Children's Commissioner. (2012). *"They never give up on you", School Exclusions Inquiry.* London: Office of the Children's Commissioner.

Oropenza, M., Varghese, M., & Kanno, V. (2010). Linguistic minority students in higher education: using, resisting, and negotiating multiple labels. *Equity& Excellence in Education*, *43*(2), 216–231. doi:10.1080/10665681003666304

Owen, D. (2006). Demographic profiles and social cohesion of ethnic communities in England and Wales, special issue: ethnicity and social capital. *Journal of Community, Work and Family*, *9*(3), 251–272. doi:10.1080/13668800600743552

Phoenix, A. (1998). Dealing with difference: The recursive and the new. *Ethnic and Racial Studies*, *21*, 859–880. doi:10.1080/014198798329694

REACH (2007) An Independent report to Government on raising the aspirations and attainment of Black boys and young black men. London: DfES.

Reay, D. (2000). A useful extension of Bourdieu's conceptual framework? Emotional capital as a way of understanding mother's involvement in their children's education? *Sociological Review*, *48*(44), 568–585. doi:10.1111/1467-954X.00233

Reynolds, T. (2006). Caribbean families social capital and young people's diasporic identities. *Ethnic Racial Studies*, *29*(6), 1087–1103. doi:10.1080/01419870600960362

Reynolds, T. (2013). 'Them and us': 'Black neighbourhoods' as a social capital resource among black youths living in inner-city London. *Urban Studies*, *50*(3), 484–498. doi:10.1177/0042098012468892

Rhamie, J. (2007). *Eagles who soar: How black learners find the path to success.* Stoke on Trent: Trentham Books.

Richardson, B. (ed.). (2005). *Tell it like it is: How our schools fail black children.* London: Bookmarks.

Rollock, N., Gillborn, D., Vincent, C., & Ball, S. (2011). The public identities of the black middle classes: Managing race in public spaces. *Sociology*, *45*(6), 1078–1093. doi:10.1177/0038038511416167

Runnymede Trust. (2015). *The 2015 budget: Effects on black and ethnic minority people.* London: Runnymede Trust.

Schlesinger, R. (2013) Tag archives: Communities of color – 'looking for students in all the right places'. Retrieved from http://nicole-renee.com/actionresearcheducation/tag/comm

Sewell, T. (1997). *Black masculinities and schooling: How black boys survive modern schooling.* Stoke-on-Trent: Trentham Books.

Skiba, R.J., Trachok, M., Chung, C.G., Baker, T., & Hughes, R. (2012). *Parsing disciplinary disproportionality: Contributions of behavior, student, and school characteristics to suspension and expulsion.* Paper presented at the meeting of the American Educational Research Association, Vancouver, British Columbia, Canada.

Strand, S. (2010). Do some schools narrow the gap? Differential school effectiveness by ethnicity, gender, poverty and prior achievement. *School Effectiveness and School Improvement*, *21*(3), 289–314. doi:10.1080/09243451003732651

Strand, S. (2012). The White British-Black Caribbean achievement gap: Tests, tiers and teacher expectations. *British Educational Research Journal*, *38*(1), 75–101. doi:10.1080/01411926.2010.526702

Strand, S. (2014). School effects and ethnic, gender and socio-economic gaps in educational achievement at age 11. *Oxford Review of Education*, *40*(2), 223–245. doi:10.1080/03054985.2014.891980

Tett, L. (2014). Learning, literacy and identity: 'I don't think I'm a failure any more'. *British Journal of Sociology of Education*, 1–18. doi:10.1080/01425692.2014.939265

## ALTERNATIVE EDUCATIONAL PROGRAMMES

Tienda, M. (2013). Diversity inclusion: Promoting integration in higher education. *Educational Researcher, 42*(9), 467–475. doi:10.3102/0013189X13516164

Toldson, I. (2011). *Breaking barriers 2: Plotting the path away from juvenile detention and toward academic success for school-age African American males*. Washington, DC: Congressional Black Caucus Foundation Inc.

U.S. Department of Education. (2014). Institute of Education Sciences, National Center for Education Statistics, National Assessment of Educational Progress (NAEP), various years, 1992–2013 Mathematics and Reading Assessments.

Warmington, P. (2014). *'Black British intellectuals: Race, education and social justice'*. London: Routledge.

Wright, C.Y. (2013). Understanding black academic attainment policy and discourse, educational aspirations and resistance. *Education Inquiry, 4*(1), 87–102. doi:10.3402/edui.v4i1.22063

Wright, C.Y. (2015). Using cameras to give a 'voice' and to empower socially excluded black youth. In H. McLaughlin (Ed.), *Involving children and young people in practice and research* (pp. 64–75). UK: National Children's Bureau.

Wright, C.Y., Standen, P., & Patel, T. (2010). *Black youth matters: Transitions from school to success*. London: Routledge.

Wright, C.Y., Weekes, D., & Macglauglin, A. (2000). *Race, gender and class in exclusion from school*. London: RoutledgeFalmer.

Yosso, T. (2005). Whose culture has capital? A critical race theory discussion of community cultural wealth. *Race Ethnicity and Education, 8*(1), 69–91. doi:10.1080/1361332052000341006

Youdell, D. (2003). Identity traps or how black students fail: The interactions between biographical, sub-cultural, and learner identities. *British Journal of Sociology of Education, 24*(1), 3–20. doi:10.1080/01425690301912

Yuval-Davis, N. (2011). Beyond the recognition and re-distribution dichotomy: Intersectionality and stratification. In H. Lutz, M. Teresa, H. Vivar, & L. Supik (Eds), *Framing Intersectionality: Debates on multi-faceted concept in gender studies* (pp. 155–182). Farnham: Ashgate.

# Caught between a rock and a hard place: disruptive boys' views on mainstream and special schools in New South Wales, Australia

Linda J. Graham, Penny Van Bergen and Naomi Sweller

Students with disruptive behaviour in the Australian state of New South Wales (NSW) are increasingly being educated in separate 'behaviour' schools. There is however surprisingly little research on how students view these settings, or indeed the mainstream schools from which they were excluded. To better understand excluded students' current and past educational experiences, we interviewed 33 boys, aged between 9 and 16 years of age, who were enrolled in separate special schools for students with disruptive behaviour. Analyses reveal that the majority of participants began disliking school in the early years due to difficulties with schoolwork and teacher conflict. Interestingly, while most indicated that they preferred the behaviour school, more than half still wanted to return to their old school. It is therefore clear that separate special educational settings are not a solution to disruptive behaviour in mainstream schools. Whilst these settings do fulfil a function for some students, the preferences of the majority of boys suggest that 'mainstream' school reform is of first-order importance.

Since the mid-1990s, the use of separate special educational settings has rapidly increased in Australia's largest school system, the New South Wales (NSW) state government school sector (Dempsey & Foreman, 1997; Graham & Sweller, 2011; Sweller, Graham, & Van Bergen, 2012). These settings are varied and include separate support classes, as well as separate special schools. Support classes are housed within mainstream schools and may be situated within the main school campus (as in the case of students with mild intellectual impairment) or behind high fencing elsewhere on the school grounds (as is often the case for students with autism, moderate to severe intellectual disability and/or disruptive behaviour). There are now over 2000 of these classes in the NSW government school sector – almost one for every public school in the state – however, they tend to be concentrated in densely populated areas, particularly those marked by social disadvantage.

Whilst it is unclear how many support classes specialise in disruptive behaviour, more than one-third of the 113 special schools in the NSW government school sector – officially termed 'Schools for Specific Purposes' – are now reserved for students with behavioural problems (Graham, 2012). Not surprisingly, this increase in placement availability corresponds to a significant increase in the exclusion of students from mainstream schools (Graham & Sweller, 2011). Like support classes, the location of these special schools is also associated with urban density and social disadvantage, however, unlike some forms of alternative education provision (Cleaver & Riddle, 2014; Jahnukainen, 2001; McKeown, 2011; McGregor & Mills, 2012; te Riele, 2007; Thomson & Russell, 2009), these 'alternative placement options' are anything but 'alternative', if alternative is taken to represent a progressive, student-centred focus on 'learning choice' (te Riele, 2007, p. 57). It is important therefore to distinguish this particular group of NSW government special schools – colloquially known as 'behaviour schools' – from other more common forms of alternative education, as these sites differ from the settings described elsewhere in this special issue.

There has been very little research on NSW behaviour schools to date; however, in a review aimed at mapping alternative education provision in Australia, te Riele (2007) placed these schools at the 'student' end of a *changing educational provision – changing the student* practice dimension (p. 60). Indeed, NSW behaviour schools are the type of setting that was ruled *out* of McGregor and Mills' (2012) study of alternative schooling, which specifically aimed at researching 'practices in sites deemed non-mainstream' (p. 848). Although there is some diversity within this group of special schools, te Riele's (2007) characterisation would be an accurate portrayal of the behaviour school model itself. Having emerged from Australia's largest parallel special education system, NSW government behaviour schools are underpinned by a 'remove, rehabilitate, return' model (Granite & Graham, 2012); an approach and purpose that McGregor and Mills (2012) describe as '"fixing" students' to fit the mainstream' (p. 848). The history of these schools corresponds closely with their purpose and, despite questions as to their effectiveness dating back some 20 years (1997; Bradshaw, 1994), there has been significant increase in behaviour school placements since these questions were first raised (Graham & Sweller, 2011).

## The emergence of 'behaviour' schools in New South Wales

Historically, separate placements for students with disability in the NSW government school sector were available in what were once known as 'Opportunity Classes' (McRae, 1996).[1] Between the 1950s and 1980s, 14 special schools for the 'emotionally and behaviourally disturbed' (ED/BD) emerged from this disability support model (McRae, 1996). A number of these 'ED/BD' special schools were housed in or affiliated with child and adolescent psychiatric units in major hospitals, but just as many were not. The latter type of ED/BD special school, operating outside the hospital system, catered to disaffected, disruptive and low-attaining young people with relatively severe behavioural issues. Amid growing demands from mainstream schools and professional associations, and in the context of a 'tough on crime' state government agenda (Conway, 2006; Vinson, 2002), the decision was taken to establish more of this type of special school. The first in a new series of what became known as 'behaviour schools' were established in the 1990s, 'as part of the 1989 Special Education Plan to provide appropriate alternate placements for students with Oppositional Defiance Disorder and Conduct Disorder' (Inca Consulting, 2009, p. 8). At that time, it was not considered appropriate to house these students with those already enrolled in ED/BD schools, although research has since found that many students in behaviour schools are indistinguishable from those in ED/BD schools and vice versa (Graham, 2012; Van Bergen, Graham, Sweller, & Dodd, 2015).

Aside from the few child/adolescent psychiatric units, the main difference between the original ED/BD special schools and the more recent behaviour schools is administrative (Graham, 2012). ED/BD schools require a confirmation of disability (within the limited categories eligible for individual funding support) prior to enrolment and are managed by the NSW Department of Education Disability Programs Directorate, whereas behaviour schools do not require a confirmation of disability and are managed by Student Welfare Directorate. This does not mean that students in behaviour schools do not have mental health diagnoses, rather that students whose issues can be framed in terms of disruptive behaviour (rather than disability or mental health) can be placed more quickly and without having to undergo disability verification (Graham, 2012). There are now around 27 behaviour schools, in addition to the 14 original ED/BD schools in the NSW government school sector. Together these schools account for much of the increase in special school enrolments since the late 1990s (Dempsey & Foreman, 1997; Dempsey, 2007; Graham & Sweller, 2011).

**Why research the experiences of students in NSW behaviour schools?**
The use of separate special educational settings or 'alternative placement options' is often couched in a language of support or care. In truth, however, there is no 'option' when it comes to the segregation of students with disruptive behaviour. This is because the NSW Labor government amended the 1990 Education Act in 2010 to allow 'greater powers to enforce the removal of students with potential and/or demonstrated violent behaviour' to 'the education setting which can best eliminate or control the risk posed' (DET, 2010, p. 1). Whilst 'potential... violent behaviour' is not defined within the Act, in practice this terminology has also come to mean students who are persistently disruptive (Van Bergen et al., 2015).

A number of concerns about behaviour schools were raised during the *2010 NSW Parliamentary Inquiry into the Provision of Education to Students with Disability and/ or Special Needs* (NSW Parliament, 2010) following a 2009 appraisal commissioned by the NSW Department of Education. The appraisal found that the duration of enrolments in behaviour schools were much longer than the anticipated 6–12 months and that enrolments of up to four years in length were not uncommon (Inca Consulting, 2009). Further questions were raised about the appropriateness of curriculum, given that behaviour schools are staffed on a primary school model and students tend not to receive instruction by subject specialist teachers (Granite & Graham, 2012). This is concerning, given that the average enrolment age is 13 years (equivalent to Year 8 in secondary school where instruction *is* provided by subject specialist teachers). Whilst concerns were predominantly raised about the duration of enrolments in the context of unmet demand from mainstream schools, the Inquiry final report recommended that the NSW Department of Education conduct a full evaluation to determine why students were not returning to mainstream schools and what the effect of spending extended periods enrolled in a behaviour school might be.

To our knowledge, no such departmental evaluation has been conducted. At the same time, however, we were successful in securing funding from the Australian Research Council (ARC) (DP110103093) to investigate the past and current educational experiences of students referred to special schools for disruptive behaviour and their reintegration to mainstream. The background to this research was another ARC-funded project (DP1093020) which found that enrolments in behaviour schools begin around age 9 and peak at age 13, with an extremely fast drop in enrolments thereafter (Graham, Sweller, & Van Bergen, 2010). Special schools in NSW juvenile detention centres have an almost identical (but time lagged) profile with enrolments gaining speed at age 13 and peaking at age 17, with a similarly fast drop thereafter. As these findings suggested that students may be graduating from behaviour schools to juvenile detention, questions relating to the effectiveness and impact of NSW behaviour schools became critical. The current project was therefore underpinned by four explicit objectives, which were to:

(1) Document how such interventions take form and the ways in which these are perceived by students and school personnel
(2) Trace student memories of their prior schooling experience and what connection, if any, these students make between these experiences and where they are now
(3) Track changes in student attitudes, beliefs and behaviour during and after their enrolment in special schools
(4) Observe and analyse student reintegration to regular schooling to understand what events lead to positive and negative experiences

This article engages with the first, second and fourth of our project aims by presenting views on special and mainstream schooling of a group of boys enrolled in five case-study behaviour schools in NSW. Before we begin however, there are a number of factors that came to light in the process of conducting this research, which are important to note here to contextualise both our approach and the focus of this article. First, our behaviour school sample consists only of boys because gender representation in these schools is affected by Department of Education placement policy. According to participating principals, some of whom have served on placement panels, this policy deliberately diverts girls in order to avoid mixing 'maladjusted' (and, in their words, potentially promiscuous) girls with troubled and/or troubling boys (Van Bergen et al., 2015). For that reason, we do not examine gender as an issue, nor do we make inferences about boys or boys' education.

Second, our project originally aimed to follow reintegrating students back into mainstream settings, in order to understand why there is so little reintegration from NSW behaviour schools. Although a number had attempted reintegration prior to the commencement of our project in 2011, to our knowledge only one of the 33 boys in this project has successfully returned to date, and this was subsequent to the completion of this three-year project. While lack of reintegration contributes to the perception that behaviour schools have become 'long-term holding areas for students that regular schools are either unable or unprepared to work with' (Dempsey, 2007, p. 76), it is important to note that absenteeism is extremely high in some of these schools, particularly amongst older students. Therefore, whilst behaviour schools might be described as 'holding areas', this perception is based on the assumption that enrolments equal attendance, whereas our observations would suggest that they do not (Graham & Buckley, 2014). It is crucial therefore to listen to the views of the boys themselves in regards to their own schooling. No amount of broad-brush analysis of enrolment figures, or indeed of interviewing the staff in schools, will determine the boys' own reasons behind their attitudes towards school.

Given continued pressure from mainstream schools and professional associations to increase the number of placements in behaviour schools against the other factors we have raised, we believe it is critical to learn more about these settings from the young people currently enrolled in them, as well to as understand – from their perspectives – what led to their dislike of and exclusion from mainstream. Students with disruptive behaviour, particularly those enrolled in special schools and units, are among the least heard of all student groups, yet we share Sellman's (2009) view that 'this often ignored group has both useful and challenging messages about what constitutes a relevant curriculum and effective teaching style' (p. 35). Indeed, we found the majority of boys were keen to 'have a say' about something that had such a big influence on their lives. In the following section, we first describe our study methodology. We then present these students' responses to seven questions about their current and past school experiences.


**Research design and methodology**

Thirty three boys, aged between 9 and 16 years of age (mean 13 years) and who were enrolled in special schools for students with disruptive behaviour, each participated in a semi-structured interview. The boys were recruited from five participating case-study special schools, three of which were located in severely disadvantaged communities in NSW, one in an area that is considered moderately disadvantaged and one from an advantaged area (Vinson, 2007). This mix is reflected in each school's score on the Index of Community Socio-Educational Advantage (ICSEA).[2] As shown in Table 1, the majority of participants (84.85%) were from behaviour schools in low socio-economic areas with ICSEA scores below the national mean of 1000 (800–999). Two students transferred to other behaviour schools (Schools 3 and 6) during the project, however, both went to schools of the same ICSEA range (for a full description of recruitment criteria and procedure, see Graham, Van Bergen, & Sweller, 2015).

Project information statements were distributed by each of the schools to their students, some of whom took the forms home to their parent/s. Parent consent was received for 39 students, however, six of those students were not attending school, even irregularly, and only 33 students were interviewed. The purpose of the research was fully explained to each participant and student consent was confirmed prior to the interview commencing. As this was a longitudinal project tracking students over an 18 month period, this process was repeated in each of the three interview rounds. Participants were assured that their views mattered, that the research data would be anonymised, that they could withdraw at any time and that they could say anything they liked. At this point, some students asked if they could swear and all were assured that they could.

Transcribers were instructed to faithfully transcribe exactly what was said and asked not to overlay these students' voices with middle class vernacular by correcting grammar or pronunciation. This was important both for authenticity and to retain the authorial integrity of the speaker (see discussion in Graham & Buckley, 2014). During the interview students were free to move around in ways that made them feel comfortable, such as get a

Table 1.  Participating behaviour schools, distribution of participants and ICSEA range.

| School | ICSEA range | Number of participants | Percentage |
|---|---|---|---|
| 1 | 800–899 | 5 | 15.15% |
| 2 | 1000–1099 | 5 | 15.15% |
| 3 | 900–999 | 1 | 3.03% |
| 4 | 800–899 | 6 | 18.18% |
| 5 | 800–899 | 9 | 27.27% |
| 6 | 800–899 | 1 | 3.03% |
| 7 | 900–999 | 6 | 18.18% |
| Total | | 33 | 100% |

Note: ICSEA score was not available, a composite score comprising participating students' home postcode and the ICSEA score of their local government high school was constructed. Exact ICSEA scores are not reported as these could reveal participating schools' identities.

ALTERNATIVE EDUCATIONAL PROGRAMMES

drink, have a snack, roll on the floor, do push-ups, play chess with the interviewer, teach them to make origami or leave and resume (or not) later if they so wished. At the conclusion of each interview, students were compensated for their time with a double movie voucher (for a full description of interview procedure, see Graham & Buckley, 2014).

Each first round interview lasted approximately 45 minutes and featured up to 75 questions in total. For the purposes of this article, we analyse student responses to seven questions from the section of the interview focusing on attitudes to and experiences of school:

(1) 'Do you like school?'
(2) 'When did you begin disliking school?'
(3) 'What happened to make you start disliking school?'
(4) 'What kind of school is this?'
(5) 'Why do YOU think you were sent to this school?'
(6) 'Are you happier in this school than your previous school/s?'
(7) 'Would you like to go back to your old school or stay in this school?'

Individual responses to each of these questions were coded using inductive content analysis to identify categories of responses arising from the data (Berg, 2001). Categories were established until all response types had been exhausted. For example, in relation to the first question, 'Do you like school?' responses were coded into four categories: (i) No, (ii) Yes, (iii) Equivocal (e.g. 'Sort of', 'Sometimes', 'I like it now but I didn't used to') and (iv) Don't know/No answer. Questions eliciting a broader range of responses, such as 'Why do you think you were sent to this school?' were coded into thematic categories, including (i) my behaviour, (ii) only option available, (iii) need more support/help and (iv) don't know/no answer. Singular responses to any of the interview questions were grouped into the category of 'other', however, the majority of responses to the questions in this article fit within the main categories reported.

This approach to data analysis was chosen for a number of reasons. First, whilst this article focuses on the responses of 33 boys in behaviour schools, this group is a subset in a larger mixed-methods project involving 96 students in total: 33 students in behaviour schools, 21 students with a history of severely disruptive behaviour in mainstream schools, and 42 students with no history of disruptive behaviour enrolled in mainstream. In other analyses using the full dataset, we have converted each response to ordinal variables to enable statistical comparisons between these three participant groups (see Graham et al., 2015). It is important to maintain the same method of data coding for the subset of students involved in this article as for the larger cohort, so that no systematic differences resulting from coding discrepancies could arise between the three student groups. Second, as this was an interdisciplinary project involving both qualitative and quantitative researchers from very different paradigms, we took great care in the process of coding to ensure that each response was accounted for in the shared belief that each student's view was important; in effect, that every student's 'vote' counts. We did this for two main reasons: (i) because not all participants can be quoted in the text and we felt strongly that each participant's response must be 'registered' in a transparent way, and (ii) because we anticipated that some students may not be willing or able to answer all questions and it was important to be clear about how 'strong' or otherwise our analyses were. In the following section, we report our analyses using descriptive statistics and present illustrative quotes for transparency. We begin with the boys' responses to our questions on school liking.

### *'Do you like school?'*

Our interview opened with the question 'Do you like school?' to which the majority of participating students (n = 29) either responded negatively (n = 16) or indicated that they liked (or were ambivalent towards) school now, but that they didn't like school when they were in mainstream (n = 13). The latter type of response is typified by the statements made by 12-year old Zack:

> Interviewer: Do you like school?
> Zack: It's alright.
> Interviewer: Have you always liked school?
> Zack: Nuh.

Each of the 29 boys who said they disliked school was then asked when and why they began disliking school, while all 33 boys were asked what type of school they were now attending, whether they knew why they had changed schools, whether they were happier in the behaviour school and whether they wanted to return to mainstream. Their responses to each of these questions are discussed in turn.

### *'Do you remember when you began to dislike school?'*

When asked when they began to dislike school, the majority of our 29 'school dislikers' said that they began having trouble in the early years (K-2).

> 'I've hated school my entire life. I just can't do it. When I was young I'd think, 'You know all those teachers who are just OLD and you go, I hope I don't get this person next year?' From kindergarten all the way to Year 6, I actually had a whole row of them!' (Ethan, age 15)

The middle years (5–8) were the second most common response (see Figure 1). It should be noted that at the time of the interview, some boys were not yet in the oldest year group noted in Figure 1 (Years 9–10). It is possible that the younger age of our participants

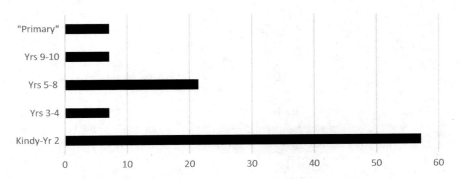

Figure 1. Percentage of participants and the age they recall disliking school.

might contribute to the small number of boys who nominated the older bracket as the time they began to dislike school (Van Bergen et al., 2015).

Nonetheless, our sample is broadly representative of the student population in NSW behaviour schools. Behaviour schools cater for students in Years 5–12 (age 9–17), however, as we mentioned earlier, previous research has found that enrolments peak at age 13 and drop sharply from there (Graham et al., 2010). Therefore, whilst there may be many young people who began disliking school in the secondary years in the general school population, these young people are not typically enrolled in behaviour schools. Further, and in terms of gender, boys are significantly overrepresented in NSW behaviour schools with nine boys for every girl enrolled (Graham et al., 2010). As discussed earlier however, gender representation in behaviour schools is affected by NSW Department of Education placement policy and should not be taken to mean that only boys engage in severely disruptive behaviour. For example, whilst there is still some reluctance to mix genders in behaviour support classes, girls are more visible in these settings with three boys for every girl enrolled (NSW Department of Education and Communities, 2011).[3] Rather than reflect the relative severity of boys' behaviour, the gender representation in NSW behaviour schools (and by virtue our sample) should be interpreted as one effect of an administrative decision-making process that more readily excludes boys.

### *'What happened to make you start disliking school?'*

Each of the 29 boys who said they did not like school was then asked why they started disliking school, however, only 27 were able to answer the question. Responses were coded into five categories including schoolwork, teachers, institutional practices (e.g. discipline/no-smoking policies), peers and 'other' (e.g. having to wake up early).

Almost half of the participants nominated issues relating to 'schoolwork'. Whilst many of these boys referred to a generic sense of boredom, others indicated that their difficulties in school began with an increase in curricular demand, which corresponded with a decrease in enjoyable activities.

> It just got boring and harder. (Michael, age 14)

> Just all the work and the homework and everythin'. I got over it and – when I was in Year 3 just started misbehavin' and everythin'. (Charlie, age 13)

Almost one-third of participants nominated issues to do with 'teachers'. These responses centred on issues relating to teacher power, teacher attitudes and teacher behaviour with these students describing how teachers would treat them because they weren't one of the 'smart kids', or because they had a 'family reputation', or because they didn't have the 'right' uniform.

> . . .just because I wasn't one of the smart kids, they basically just kind of push you off to the side, didn't have anything to do with you and just kind of left you. They didn't care. (Corbin, age 15)

> The teachers. They always target me. Because of my sister and my brother. Because they were always naughty and that. They were always misbehaved. (Cameron, age 13)

> The Principal, like, the deputy always. . . like it was like she was always trying to get me suspended and stuff and the teachers were always. . . like the sport teacher would always pick

# ALTERNATIVE EDUCATIONAL PROGRAMMES

> on me about my shoes and that because they weren't black, and that's when I didn't start going to school. (Jett, age 14)

In some cases, the boys felt baited into behaving poorly, with the teachers' own emotional behaviour leading to an escalation in teacher–student conflict. Twelve-year old Andy, for example, described how battles over schoolwork would escalate to the point where he would erupt in frustration.

> One time I didn't want to do work and the teacher went off at me, and I just, just went off and then I clicked. (Andy, age 12)

This first occurred when Andy was the 'new boy' in Year 2 and was being bullied every day by the other kids because 'everyone picks on the new person'. Andy said he felt sad and depressed because 'no one thought of me as a friend' but also frustrated because he couldn't do the work he was being told to do. Feeling 'like no one was going to help me', Andy said he 'clicked' and 'smashed up the classroom'.

Fifteen-year old Ethan was one of a number of students who believed that he was being targeted by his teachers in an effort to eject him from the classroom.

> They're just *asking* me to do something. And I've actually felt at times that they've wanted me to, just to get me out of the class. All of my friends have felt that. We all agree on that. (Ethan, age 15).

Whilst such statements might sometimes be dismissed as paranoia or an attempt to justify disruption, Ethan's suspicion resonated with the stories told by each of the behaviour school principals. During interviews, and unprompted, each principal noted the tactics that some mainstream schools and teachers use to provoke students so that they can then suspend that child, justify their placement in a separate setting, or prevent their reintegration to mainstream.

In other cases, teachers were nominated as the reason for disliking school simply because they were associated with 'schoolwork': something that the boys found too hard or didn't want to do. Eleven-year old James, for example, described how he began disliking school in Year 1 (around age 6). When asked why he began to dislike school, James replied 'Teachers'. However, further questioning revealed that James disliked his Year 1 teacher, Mr O, because 'He made me do too much work' and James found the work difficult. Mr O was later replaced by Miss J but, according to James, the problem worsened because 'She gave me *harder* work'. Some students' dislike of teachers therefore may be partly associated with the increasing demands of the academic curriculum, although elsewhere in the interview the boys were quite vocal about the harsh tactics that some teachers employ to make students do their work.

Interestingly, although bullying and peer conflict were consistent themes elsewhere in the interviews, only three students cited issues to do with peers as the reason they began to dislike school. Two of these students had experienced sustained bullying and the third had experienced significant difficulties relating to other children and disclosed that he had later been diagnosed with Asperger's Syndrome. These students stated that they liked the behaviour school because it had fewer students and therefore less people to deal with.

## *What kind of school is this?*

We were interested to learn whether the students in these special schools perceived these schools as being different to their previous schools and, if so, in what ways. We were also interested in the language they would draw on to describe or name the type of school. To begin this discussion, we asked participating students to tell us what kind of school they were now attending. Of the 29 students who responded, one student said that it was a special school, and two referred to it as just a 'regular' school. Perhaps misinterpreting the question, another nine students gave general comments as to the school characteristics, like 'It's a good school', 'This one listens to you', and 'It's a guarded school... like, there's always a teacher watching you'. The majority (18) of the boys, however, used the colloquial term 'behaviour school'. The ubiquity of this term is somewhat worrying, and may negatively impact on young peoples' developing sense of self (Tremblay, Saucier, & Tremblay, 2004; Yang, Wonpat-Borja, Opler, & Corcoran, 2010), as well as the ability of behaviour schools to reorient focus on learning. These were both issues that we sought to investigate with a follow-up question.

## *'Why do YOU think you were sent to this school?'*

As the psychological research literature suggests that children and young people with behavioural disorders lack self-awareness and are inclined to positively self-enhance (Colvin, Block, & Funder, 1995; Owens, Goldfine, Evangelista, Hoza, & Kaiser, 2007), we were interested in the reasons (self or other) that these young people attributed to their referral to a behaviour school.[4] Further, and in line with the second objective of our ARC project, we were interested to know whether the young people perceived separate special schools to be a form of support (as they are framed in NSW Department of Education discourse) or whether they viewed being sent to the behaviour school as a consequence of, or punishment for, their past behaviour.

When asked why *they* thought they'd been sent to the behaviour school, 7 of the 33 participants either did not answer or said they did not know. Of the remaining 26 students, four stated that the behaviour school was their only remaining option (e.g. 'Because I'm not allowed to go to any other schools'). Another six participants provided responses that were framed in the language of support. These responses tended to be less focused on what the students were or had been doing in the past and more on their environment and/ or what they needed:

> Because I still need way more help. (Aiden, age 12)

> Uh, because I had problems doing my work. That's what the teachers told me. (Owen, age 12)

Notwithstanding these less common responses however, the majority (n = 16) named their own behaviour as the reason they had been sent to the behaviour school and none blamed 'others' for their referral (see Table 2). Rather than provide evidence for self-enhancement or poor self-awareness theories, the range of responses we received lend more support for the theory – found in both psychological and post-structural analyses – that the labelling and exclusion of students for behavioural reasons may negatively affect developing identities or self-concepts (Graham, 2015a; Tremblay et al., 2004; Yang et al., 2010).

This is an interesting finding given the explicit focus of one of the behaviour schools from which we drew our largest number of participants (n = 9). The teachers and

# ALTERNATIVE EDUCATIONAL PROGRAMMES

Table 2. Behavioural explanations for enrolment in the behaviour school.

| Pseudonym | Age | Reason |
|---|---|---|
| Zack | 12 | Fightin' and swearin'. Got suspended. |
| Andy | 12 | Because of anger. |
| John | 13 | For being bad. |
| Ahi | 13 | Because of my behaviour at [X school] and [Y school] |
| Tom | 15 | Behaviour. Oh, truancy. I truant a lot, at my old school. But I don't truant anymore now, since I came here. |
| Nathan | 13 | Um, (yawn) because of my behaviour. |
| Cooper | 16 | Because of my bad behaviour. Mum just thought it would be a good idea. |
| Darrin | 12 | Ah, being silly. Being silly and stupid. |
| Blake | 12 | Because I'm too wild. |
| George | 15 | 'Cause of my behaviour at [Z school]. Just how I couldn't cope with all of the students. |
| Luke | 13 | Probably because of last year. I was mucking up in class. I was always at the principal's office. (pause) Swearin' at teachers. |
| Nick | 15 | Because I've been truanting a lot. |
| Reuben | 12 | I used to hang with the wrong crowd. |
| Adam | 14 | For my behaviour. |
| Patrick | 10 | Because my naughtiness. |
| Justin | 13 | Because I've got issues, because like, I've been naughty in mainstream. |

leadership team at this school explicitly state to their new students that they have not been sent there because of their behaviour but because their behaviour is 'getting in the way of their learning'. Whilst this may seem to be a subtle play on words, this emphasis is reinforced in the school's responses to student behaviour where the focus is on learning: academic, social *and* emotional. However, 7 of the 16 students listed in Table 2 were attending this particular behaviour school (and had been for considerable time), which suggests that earlier messages about 'bad' behaviour, and perhaps the referral experience itself, may have had a more powerful and indelible effect than the reparation work that is now occurring in the behaviour school.

### *'Have you felt happier in this school than your other schools?'*

Two students in our sample did not provide an answer to this question. Of the 31 students who responded, the majority (n = 25) said that they were happier in the behaviour school. Not all of these students were able to explain why they preferred the behaviour school (n = 6) but there was an interesting pattern in the responses of those who did (n = 19). Whilst one of these students named differences related to the school building and facilities, such as the existence of a 'rec room' with 'a Wii and a Playstation and drinks vouchers' (Harry, age 11), another two raised less obvious differences, such as shorter school hours and differences in curriculum offerings.

Because you get to go home early. (Andy, age 12)

Because I get to do wood burning, woodwork and everything else. (Costa, 12)

ALTERNATIVE EDUCATIONAL PROGRAMMES

Despite the dominance of schoolwork in responses to our previous question asking why they began to dislike school, participants rarely reported feeling happier in the behaviour school for academic reasons alone. Although two students implied that they preferred the behaviour school because it was 'easier' (Grant, age 12) and 'more fun' (Reuben, age 12), possibly referring to the types of curricular activities and lower academic demand reported elsewhere, other aspects of schoolwork and learning were typically referred to in the context of describing a positive and supportive teacher–student relationship.

Indeed, relationships featured prominently in students' descriptions of why they were happier in the behaviour school than their previous school. While there were differences in the types of relationships that mattered, the majority of the 19 students (n = 10) who were able to explain why they were happier in the behaviour school described supportive teachers and positive teacher–student relationships. In tandem with responses outlining why some participants disliked teachers, teacher–student relationships again appeared bound to issues relating to teacher–student interactions, particularly around the completion of schoolwork. This time, however, the relationship was positive. As can be seen from the collection of responses in Table 3, 'teachers' and 'schoolwork' were often raised in the same breath. Potentially influencing these boys' positive perceptions of their behaviour school teachers was the level of support provided, a more democratic approach and differentiation of curriculum to match student ability.

Only four of the 19 students who could explain why they were happier in the behaviour school – Aiden, John, Ahi and Owen – referred to more positive *peer* relationships:

Well, I'm making a bit more friends here. (Aiden, age 12)

'Cause it like, at the other schools everyone torments you and that, making you wanna fight. Makes me wanna fight them and that. (John, age 13)

Table 3. Teacher- and curriculum-related reasons for preferring the behaviour school to previous school/s.

| Pseudonym | Age | Reason |
| --- | --- | --- |
| Ethan | 13 | Just the less work and the possibility of negotiating. (Ethan, age 14) |
| Tom | 15 | I dunno, probably teachers are more laid back, I can get along with these teachers. You can have a mad conversation with them... so that's alright. |
| Cooper | 16 | Because [School X] was all about working, [School Y] was all about commitment. This is about helping you behave, making a fresh start with support and doing school work at the same time. |
| George | 15 | Just got better teachers, better work... better everything. |
| Nick | 15 | All the teachers are, like, really, really nice. Like, they make me feel like, more welcome. Well, whenever I'm working, like, they always know, like, when I need help. Like, they'll come up to me straight away and ask if I need help. |
| Jake | 13 | Because it's helped me out and that's a good thing. |
| James | 11 | Better people. Teachers nicer. |
| Michael | 14 | It's like, it's easier here, because you get more help with work. Like, you learn more because there's more teachers to help you out. |
| Eamon | 12 | That I know I'm getting stuff done. That I know that I can maybe pass. |
| Patrick | 10 | Um, because I get to be much better at my learning. |

# ALTERNATIVE EDUCATIONAL PROGRAMMES

> Because at this school, I get, um... I get, um...the same as all the other kids. I'm not different out of all of them. I don't have my own problems, we've all got the same problems. Yeah. (Ahi, age 13)

> I dunno. Just... people like me here but at my other schools they just don't like me. (Owen, age 12)

Of the six students who said that they were *not* happier in the behaviour school, only three were able to articulate why. The first, Darrin (age 12), said that he felt the same in the behaviour school as he had at his previous school because he had 'moved schools so many times'. The other two participants – Justin and Andreas – reported being happier in their previous (mainstream) schools: one because of his connection to old friends and the other because he missed the 'normality' of mainstream school culture.

> Because I miss my mates. (Justin, age 13)

> I'd prefer to be in a mainstream school and have like – just because, I don't know, like I want to put on a school uniform. I want to wear a backpack, put my books in my bag, take the school laptop. I just want to – like I just want to be at the normal school. (Andreas, age 14)

Interestingly, these two perspectives were also evident in the responses to our next question.

### *'Would you like to go back to your old school or stay in this school?'*

One student did not answer this question and another was equivocal in response. The remaining 31 participants were relatively evenly split with 16 wishing to return to mainstream and 15 wishing to stay in the behaviour school. This was a particularly surprising result given that the majority of participants had told us that they were happier in the behaviour school. Closer analysis of these responses showed that 11 of the 16 students who wished to return to mainstream were ones who had specifically stated that they *were* happier in the behaviour school. In other words, almost half of all the students who earlier said they were happier in the behaviour school *still* wished to return to mainstream. All 5 of the remaining students who stated that they wished to return to mainstream were students who had said they were *not* happier in the behaviour school.

The reasons given by the 15 students who wanted to stay in the behaviour school resonated with the reasons they said they were happier there: 'nicer' and more supportive teachers, easier work, more relevant curriculum, fewer students and better peer relationships. Perhaps more interesting, in the context of this article, are the reasons that the other 16 gave for wishing to return. These responses fell into two main categories: (i) peer relationships and (ii) 'normal' or mainstream school participation. In relation to the latter category, a small number of students alluded to a perception that the mainstream was 'better', referring to rites of passage like Year 12 and other forms of school participation.

> Well, I want, like, a better education. Like, I want to go into Year 12 and that. (Nick, age 15)

> It just upsets – like upsets me because all of my high school year, I was at – I was in a behaviour school. I wanted to at least get one of those jerseys with your name written on the back and all of that? Yeah, I wanted all of that. Just to be in a mainstream school. (Andreas, 14)

# ALTERNATIVE EDUCATIONAL PROGRAMMES

Three students made isolated comments that suggested that they were 'bored' by the behaviour school (Luke, age 13), that their parents were considering other options (Eamon, age 12), or that they felt a sense of 'belonging' to their old school that they didn't feel at the behaviour school (Quade, age 16).

> There's a school that my Mum's been thinking about. It's Saint [X]'s, I believe. It's a Catholic school but I'm not going there for the Catholic stuff. (Eamon, age 12)

> Yeah. I want to – I would have done, I still would do, anything to go back to [X school]. That's just my main school. That's where I want to be. (Quade, age 16)

The most consistent response category (10 students) related to peer relationships. For example, Patrick (age 10) and Ethan (age 14) both reported wanting to leave the behaviour school so they could re-join their friends in mainstream. Although each had stated that they were happier in the behaviour school – Ethan because there was less work and 'the possibility of negotiating' and Patrick 'because I get to be much better at my learning' – neither of these positive aspects of the behaviour school had as much pull as the desire to return to their friends. As discussed previously, 13-year old Justin had never warmed to the behaviour school because he missed his 'best mate' and he reiterated this as the reason for wanting to return.

Conversely, some students wanted to return to their old school to avoid their peers in the behaviour school. Sixteen-year old Quade, for example, said that he liked the behaviour school but that he was not *happier* there and was very angry that his mum had applied for enrolment. Quade had concerns about the other students in the behaviour school and wanted to return to mainstream to be among 'normal' peers.

> I prefer to be normal, so I've got people to talk to at least. (Quade, age 16)

Quade's concerns were echoed by 13-year old Max, who had been equivocal about whether he would like to return to his old school or not. Max was a school refuser whom we initially had to visit at home. When we first met him, Max was enrolled in one of our five participating behaviour schools, but not attending. When we interviewed him a few months later, Max was attending a separate support unit in a mainstream secondary school on a partial enrolment (part-time) basis. When we asked him whether he would like to return to his 'old school' (the behaviour school that he had refused to attend) Max, of course, said no. However, he was adamant that he did *not* want to stay where he was, wishing instead to transfer to a regular classroom on the main (mainstream) school campus. As he was still only able to attend the behaviour support unit for half-day, reintegration to mainstream was very unlikely to occur in the near future. This was a source of great irritation to Max, who believed that the alternative setting and the peers to whom he was exposed in that setting were holding him back.

> But – I want to go in a normal class – because I have autism they stick me in a class with complete arseholes... we have a class pretty much, where all of the baddest kids go in. 'Cause if they stuck one of these kids in a normal class... he'd be walking around doing stuff, never putting their hand up to speak, not even doing their work. They wouldn't last very long in there. It'd mess everyone up. Where we have a small bunch, like eight kids of the worst. They stick the worst with the worst and the best with the best. Me, I'm able to work in those other rooms with the normal kids. I want that, because I can control myself. I like quiet. I just want to do my work in peace.

ALTERNATIVE EDUCATIONAL PROGRAMMES

Students like Max and Quade were in the minority, however. The majority of students in our sample preferred the behaviour school for the positive teacher–student relationships, but judging from the desire to return to their old schools, it seems these relationships were not enough to keep them all there.

## Implications for policy and school practice

The boys in our study demonstrate a troubling, although perhaps not surprising, pattern of school like/dislike. While approximately half indicated that they liked the behaviour school, the vast majority disliked their previous (mainstream) school/s and most began feeling this way in the early years of primary (K-2). More than half of those who reported disliking their previous school cited reasons relating to difficulties with schoolwork, followed by negative and conflictual relationships with mainstream school teachers. Issues included poor or biased treatment and teachers being associated with schoolwork that the boys could not or did not want to do: factors which have been shown to strongly predict poorer-quality teacher–student relationships (see McGrath & Van Bergen, 2015, for a review). Very few students cited reasons involving their peers or institutional issues.

The majority of our participants knew why they had been sent to a behaviour school. Although a fifth of the boys couldn't answer or didn't know why, of those who could, most cited their own behaviour as the primary reason. It is important to note, given prior research attesting to poor self-awareness and self-enhancement, that these boys did not try and sugar-coat or pretend their behaviour was somebody else's fault. Rather, the boys in our study readily acknowledged their behaviour, whilst also taking the opportunity to voice their opinions about contributing factors, including a lack of academic support and hostile teacher behaviours in their formative school years. The boys' responses indicated, however, that the majority viewed the behaviour school as a punishment or consequence of their past behaviour, rather than a means by which they could receive more support. The prevalence of this view suggests that their previous school experiences, and the process of exclusion itself, may have a shaping effect that is difficult to undo once done. The ubiquity of the colloquial term 'behaviour school' (used by the majority of boys when asked 'What kind of school is this?') is certainly unhelpful in this regard and changing the language characterising this type of special school (e.g. to 'Support School' or 'Transition School') would be a simple but positive first step.

Despite the perception that they had been sent to the behaviour school as a punishment or consequence, most students indicated that they felt happier there. The reasons given by the boys suggest that the teachers in the behaviour schools in our study are very good at building positive teacher–student relationships and moderating curriculum demands; thereby mitigating the main issues that the boys had with their previous schools. However, lack of academic rigour and credentials was a drawback for some boys, whilst loss of friends and the lack of potential to make new ones was of greater consequence for others. More than half of the boys who said that they were happier in the behaviour school also said that they wanted to return to mainstream, suggesting that the behaviour schools are not able to fully satisfy the academic and/or social needs of all the students they enrol.

These findings are troubling, but they make more sense if we remember the specific purpose for which behaviour schools were originally designed; that is, 'to fix students to fit the mainstream' (McGregor & Mills, 2012, p. 848). Such an approach is underpinned by the logic of mainstream/special education (Artiles, 2003; Gartner & Lipsky, 1987), however, the problem with this logic is that it assumes the 'mainstream' plays no part in producing the students that the behaviour schools are called in to fix. A related issue – one which underpins the philosophy of inclusive education – is that in providing an 'alternative to' or a 'safety valve' for the mainstream (Tomlinson, 1982), special education ultimately acts as an enabler, forestalling the types of reforms that might otherwise lead to a more inclusive and effective system overall; one in which there is no such thing as a 'mainstream' (Graham & Slee, 2008). In other words, the existence of 'alternative placement options' encourages some schools to continue engaging in practices that fail to meet the needs of all of their students, in the belief that there is and should be somewhere else for those students to go (Graham, 2015b; Slee, 2011). However, judging by the growth in separate special educational settings over time, together with the decline in mainstream enrolments in the NSW government school sector (Sweller et al., 2012), the mainstream has become increasingly exclusive in recent years and, thus, ever harder to 'fit'.

Exclusionary practices appear to be limiting reintegration as well, severely limiting the effectiveness of behaviour schools in the process. As we mentioned earlier, only one of the 33 boys in our study ever managed to return to mainstream during this three-year research project, however, the reasons for this are complex and not simply because behaviour schools fail to 'rehabilitate'. Whilst it is clear that some students make little progress, there are many others whose attitude and behaviour changed completely in a calmer, more respectful and supportive environment. Yet, even these students foundered when attempting to reintegrate. During a separate interview conducted as part of the larger project on which this research is based, one participating behaviour school principal summed up the problem by saying:

> If you're going to force a school to take a student back just because they have to, and the culture hasn't changed and the behaviours of that school haven't changed, the behaviours of the teachers haven't changed, the behaviours of the kids that go there haven't changed, then you're actually going to just send that kid back there to get expelled. He'll lose his place in a school like this and he'll have to start all over again, which will be more destructive to the kids.

For this reason, the behaviour school principals in our study have largely given up on 'reintegration', focusing instead on preparing their students to transition to apprentice-ships or technical/vocational education. While this shift in focus may also help to explain why there is so little reintegration to mainstream, there are serious problems with this approach. First, and as we noted earlier, the average age of students in behaviour schools is 13 years, which means that most students will spend years in the behaviour school before they are old enough to transition to an adult learning environment around the age of 16 or 17. Second, the creation of a competitive vocational education and training market has 'placed a premium upon particular types of courses and particular types of students' (Graham et al., 2015, p. 252), leaving very limited further education opportunities for students with learning and behavioural difficulties. Third, and perhaps most critically, the ability of these young people to successfully engage in further education is highly dependent on the depth and quality of their learning in the behaviour school setting, given that many arrive there at the beginning of the middle years of school (Years 5–7). *But*, if behaviour schools cannot satisfy these students' academic, social, emotional and developmental needs *and* if students subsequently do not attend, their opportunities to learn and to progress into further education and training become extremely limited.

The implication of this research for education policy and practice is that behaviour schools are not the solution to disruptive behaviour in mainstream schools. Whilst these settings do fulfil a function for some, the early school experiences and placement preferences of the majority of the boys in our study suggest that 'mainstream' school reform is of first order importance. Taken together, these boys' accounts suggest that mainstream schools can start by improving the ways in which students with early learning and behavioural difficulties are supported – academically *and* emotionally – and by changing how teachers interact with these students. This may help to limit the flow of excluded students, however, it is also critical that referring schools examine their own culture and practices to enable these students' return following enrolment in a behaviour school.

## Conclusion

This study investigated the current and past educational experiences of 33 boys attending separate 'behaviour' schools. Participants were asked whether they liked school, when and why they began disliking school, what type of school they were now attending, whether they knew why they had changed schools, whether they were happier in the special school and whether they wanted to return to mainstream. The majority of participants began disliking school in the early years due to difficulties with schoolwork and conflictual relationships with teachers. The majority of the boys in our study also stated that they preferred being in the behaviour school, however, perhaps a more important question is why they began disliking school in the first place and why they say they prefer being in the behaviour school. This is critical because our findings indicate that being happier in the behaviour school does not necessarily translate to wanting to remain there.

The desire to return to old friends or a 'normal' environment in which these boys might be able to develop positive emotional connections with their peers exerted a surprisingly strong pull; even for students who stated that they are happier in the behaviour school and who reported very negative mainstream school experiences. Their narratives suggest that an increase in placement availability may satisfy the demands of mainstream schools looking to exclude students with disruptive behaviour, but this is unlikely to lead to improved outcomes for the young people themselves. Fundamentally, their exclusion does not encourage or promote change within the mainstream school system and neither does it seem that the behaviour schools are able to fully satisfy the academic or social, emotional and developmental needs of all of the young people they enrol.

## Acknowledgements

The views expressed herein are those of the authors and are not necessarily those of the Australian Research Council. Ethics approval was obtained from the Macquarie University Ethics Committee (Final Approval No. 5201000654) and the NSW Department of Education (SERAP No. 2011027).

## Funding

This research was supported under the Australian Research Council's Discovery Projects funding scheme [DP110103093].

## Notes

1. Over time the use of the word 'opportunity' was replaced with 'support' for classes for students with disability, but was retained for academically selective classes in flagship primary schools.
2. All schools in Australia are given an ICSEA score: A calculation of the relative affluence of the school community. ICSEA has a mean of 1000 and a standard deviation of 100. Note, as geographic information or single ICSEA scores could reveal the identity of the schools, only ICSEA ranges have been provided here.
3. Similarly, in the larger project from which our behaviour school data is drawn, girls accounted for almost a quarter of students in our mainstream behaviour group nominated by mainstream school principals (see Graham, Van Bergen, Sweller, 2015).
4. Our findings here, as well as others based on analyses of participants' self-characterisations (Graham, 2015a), do not provide support for this hypothesis.

## References

Artiles, A. (2003). Special education's changing identity: Paradoxes and dilemmas in views of culture and space. *Harvard Educational Review, 73*(2), 164–202. doi:10.17763/haer.73.2.j78t573x377j7106

Berg, B. L. (2001). *Qualitative research methods for the social sciences.* Boston, MA: Allyn & Bacon.

Bradshaw, K. (1994). *The integration of children with behaviour disorders: a comparative case study analysis of two Australian states* (Unpublished PhD thesis). University of Western Sydney, New South Wales.

Bradshaw, K. (1997). The integration of children with behaviour disorders: A longitudinal study. *Australasian Journal of Special Education, 21,* 115–123. doi:10.1080/1030011970210206

Cleaver, D., & Riddle, S. (2014). Music as engaging, educational matrix: Exploring the case of marginalised students attending an "alternative" music industry school. *Research Studies in Music Education, 36*(2), 245–256. doi:10.1177/1321103X14556572

Colvin, C. R., Block, J., & Funder, D. C. (1995). Overly positive self-evaluations and personality: Negative implications for mental health. *Journal of Personality and Social Psychology, 68*(6), 1152–1162. doi:10.1037/0022-3514.68.6.1152

Conway, R. (2006). Students with emotional and behavioral disorders: An Australian perspective. *Preventing School Failure: Alternative Education for Children and Youth, 50*(2), 15–20. doi:10.3200/PSFL.50.2.15-20

Dempsey, I. (2007). Trends in the placement of students in segregated settings in NSW government schools. *Australasian Journal of Special Education, 31*(1), 73–78. doi:10.1080/10300110701338710

## ALTERNATIVE EDUCATIONAL PROGRAMMES

Dempsey, I., & Foreman, P. (1997). Trends in the educational placement of students with disabilities in New South Wales. *International Journal of Disability, Development and Education, 44*(3), 207–216. doi:10.1080/0156655970440303

Department of Education and Training (DET). (2010). *Management of health and safety risks posed to schools by a student's violent behaviour guidelines*. Sydney: NSW Department of Education and Training.

Gartner, A., & Lipsky, D. K. (1987). Beyond special education: Toward a quality system for all students. *Harvard Educational Review, 57*(4), 367–396. doi:10.17763/haer.57.4. kj517305m7761218

Graham, L. J. (2012). Disproportionate over-representation of indigenous students in New South Wales government special schools. *Cambridge Journal of Education, 42*(2), 163–176. doi:10.1080/0305764X.2012.676625

Graham, L. J. (2015a). "I'm happy with who I am": A discursive analysis of the self-characterisation practices of boys in behaviour schools. Chapter 28. In M. O'Reilly & J. Lester (Eds.), *The Palgrave handbook of child mental health*. London: Palgrave MacMillan.

Graham, L. J. (2015b). A little learning is a dangerous thing: Factors influencing the increased identification of special educational needs from the perspective of education policy-makers and school practitioners. *International Journal of Disability, Development and Education, 62*(1), 116–132. doi:10.1080/1034912X.2014.955791

Graham, L. J., & Buckley, L. (2014). Ghost hunting with lollies, chess and Lego: Appreciating the 'messy' complexity (and costs) of doing difficult research in education. *The Australian Educational Researcher, 41*(3), 327–347. doi:10.1007/s13384-013-0137-5

Graham, L. J., & Slee, R. (2008). An illusory interiority: Interrogating the discourse/s of inclusion. *Educational Philosophy and Theory, 40*(2), 277–293. doi:10.1111/j.1469-5812.2007.00331.x

Graham, L. J., & Sweller, N. (2011). The inclusion lottery: Who's in and who's out? Tracking inclusion and exclusion in New South Wales government schools. *International Journal of Inclusive Education, 15*(9), 941–953. doi:10.1080/13603110903470046

Graham, L. J., Sweller, N., & Van Bergen, P. (2010). Detaining the usual suspects: Charting the use of segregated settings in New South Wales government schools, Australia. *Contemporary Issues in Early Childhood, 11*(3), 234–248. doi:10.2304/ciec

Graham, L. J., Van Bergen, P., & Sweller, N. (2015). To educate you to be smart': Disaffected students and the purpose of school in the (not so clever) 'lucky country. *Journal of Education Policy, 30*(2), 237–257. doi:10.1080/02680939.2014.953596

Granite, E., & Graham, L. J. (2012). Remove, rehabilitate, return? The use and effectiveness of behaviour schools in New South Wales, Australia. *International Journal on School Disaffection, 9*(1), 39–50.

Inca Consulting (2009). *Behaviour Schools/Learning Centres Appraisal Report, NSW Department of Education and Training 2009*, GIPA-11-145.

Jahnukainen, M. (2001). Experiencing special education: Former students of classes for the emotionally and behaviorally disordered talk about their schooling. *Emotional and Behavioural Difficulties, 6*(3), 150–166.

McGrath, K. F., & Van Bergen, P. (2015). Who, when, why, and to what end? Students at risk of negative student–teacher relationships and their outcomes. *Educational Research Review, 14*, 1–17. doi:10.1016/j.edurev.2014.12.001

McGregor, G., & Mills, M. (2012). Alternative education sites and marginalised young people: 'I wish there were more schools like this one'. *International Journal of Inclusive Education, 16*(8), 843–862. doi:10.1080/13603116.2010.529467

McKeown, A. (2011). Young people speak: Experiences of alternative education. *Developing Practice: The Child, Youth and Family Work Journal, 29*, 68.

McRae, D. (1996). *The integration/inclusion feasibility study*. Sydney, NSW: Department of School Education.

NSW Department of Education and Communities (2011). *Statistical bulletin: Schools and students in New South Wales*. Centre for Education Statistics and Evaluation. Retrieved from http://www.cese.nsw.gov.au/publications/statistical-bulletin

NSW Parliament. (2010). *NSW parliamentary inquiry into the provision of education for students with a disability or special needs*. Sydney, NSW: Parliamentary Library. Retrieved from http://www.parliament.nsw.gov.au/prod/parlment/committee.nsf/0/47F51A782AEABB ABCA25767A000FABEC

Owens, J. S., Goldfine, M. E., Evangelista, N. M., Hoza, B., & Kaiser, N. M. (2007). A critical review of self-perceptions and the positive illusory bias in children with ADHD. *Clinical Child and Family Psychology Review, 10*(4), 335–351. doi:10.1007/s10567-007-0027-3

Sellman, E. (2009). Lessons learned: Student voice at a school for pupils experiencing social, emotional and behavioural difficulties. *Emotional and Behavioural Difficulties, 14*(1), 33–48. doi:10.1080/13632750802655687

Slee, R. (2011). *The irregular school: Exclusion, schooling and inclusive education*. London: Routledge.

Sweller, N., Graham, L. J., & Van Bergen, P. (2012). The Minority report: Disproportionate representation in Australia's largest education system. *Exceptional Children, 79*(1), 107–125.

te Riele, K. (2007). Educational alternatives for marginalised youth. *The Australian Educational Researcher, 34*(3), 53–68. doi:10.1007/BF03216865

Thomson, P., & Russell, L. (2009). Data, data everywhere–but not all the numbers that count? Mapping alternative provisions for students excluded from school. *International Journal of Inclusive Education, 13*(4), 423–438. doi:10.1080/13603110801983264

Tomlinson, S. (1982). *A sociology of special education*. London: Routledge.

Tremblay, G., Saucier, J.-F., & Tremblay, R. E. (2004). Identity and disruptiveness in boys: Longitudinal perspectives. *Child and Adolescent Social Work Journal, 21*(4), 387–406. doi:10.1023/B:CASW.0000035223.61627.08

Van Bergen, P., Graham, L. J., Sweller, N., & Dodd, H. F. (2015). The psychology of containment: (mis)representing emotional and behavioural difficulties in Australian schools. *Emotional and Behavioural Difficulties, 20*(1), 64–81. doi:10.1080/13632752.2014.947101

Vinson, T. (2002). *Second report of the inquiry into public education in New South Wales*. Retrieved from New South Wales Teachers Federation: http://www.nswtf.org.au/files/second_report.pdf

Vinson, T. (2007). *Dropping off the edge: The distribution of disadvantage in Australia*. Melbourne: Jesuit Social Services.

Yang, L. H., Wonpat-Borja, A. J., Opler, M. G., & Corcoran, C. M. (2010). Potential stigma associated with inclusion of the psychosis risk syndrome in the DSM-V: An empirical question. *Schizophrenia Research, 120*(1–3), 42–48. doi:10.1016/j.schres.2010.03.012

# 'It's the best thing I've done in a long while': teenage mothers' experiences of educational alternatives

Kerry Vincent

Pregnant and mothering schoolgirls have been identified as an educationally vulnerable group. Many are not welcomed in their mainstream schools and as a consequence, access a range of educational alternatives. This article presents the views and experiences of 14 young women in the English Midlands, who became pregnant while still of statutory school age, 12 of whom spent time in alternative educational settings. It is based on data gathered from repeat interviews over an 18-month period and shows that all who attended the educational alternatives rated them highly and benefitted from what they had to offer. Using the concept of 'difference' as a central analytic theme, the article examines how and why this was the case. The analysis shows that it was through recognising some differences but not others that the educational alternatives were successful in supporting young women's learning and well-being. Importantly, those that were recognised were done so in non-stigmatising ways. The research also highlights some limitations of the alternatives, alongside the ways in which gender and class continue to impact the educational outcomes and career trajectories of this particular group of students.

## Introduction

Pregnant and mothering schoolgirls are a small but educationally vulnerable group. A consistent finding in research on teenage pregnancy and education is the strong and enduring correlation with poor educational outcomes. Teenage mothers have been found to be more likely to leave school early, less likely to leave with qualifications and less likely to participate in post-compulsory education (Coleman & Dennison, 1998; Wiggins, Oakley, Austerberry, Clemens, & Elbourne, 2005). Keirnan's (1997) analysis of longitudinal data in the United Kingdom showed that at age 23, 61% of teenage mothers had no qualifications compared to only 26% of those who delayed motherhood. Despite a national campaign and associated policy aimed at supporting educational continuity (SEU (Social Exclusion Unit), 1999), more than one-third of the young mothers who participated in the Teenage Pregnancy Strategy Evaluation (TPU, 2005) were found to have left school before the statutory school leaving age and to experience difficulties in returning to education. Similar trends have been documented in the United States, New Zealand, Canada and the United Kingdom – the four OECD countries with the highest teenager pregnancy rates (see Fergusson & Woodward, 1999; Snow Jones, Astone, Keyl, Young, & Alexander, 1999).

ALTERNATIVE EDUCATIONAL PROGRAMMES

Research also sheds some light on the reasons behind these findings. Coleman and Dennison's review (1998, p. 312) found that pregnant teenagers and schoolgirl mothers in the United Kingdom lose out 'because of limited resources, rigid policies or outright prejudice against teenage parenthood'. In the United States, Pillow (2004) suggests that lack of clarity within policy leaves local practice open to interpretation and therefore variable. Similarly, practices in the United Kingdom have been found to be variable and to not necessarily reflect the inclusive intent of policy. Teenagers have reported being excluded from school, or 'strongly encouraged' not to attend because of health and safety reasons, while others stop attending because of bullying (Dawson & Hosie, 2005; Osler & Vincent, 2003). This, for many, marks the beginning of a more permanent detachment from education. Of those who are not lost to formal education altogether, a good number access some form of educational alternative – some because they choose it and others, because it appears to be the only alternative (Pillow, 2004; Vincent & Thomson, 2010). Understandings about the extent to which such alternatives support better educational outcomes for this vulnerable group of learners are therefore important.

Research that focuses on educational alternatives for pregnant or mothering teenagers is limited but the themes that emerge reflect those found in the wider literate on educational alternatives – namely, that they offer some unique benefits but there are also some limitations. In the United Kingdom, Dawson and Hosie's (2005) research in 10 local authorities, and Rudoe's (2014) ethnographic study of a programme in London, found that alternative provision was successful in re-engaging young women, many of whom had experienced disaffection in their mainstream settings. Rudoe highlights the relaxed and informal environment, as well as attention to students' emotional and practical needs as important factors in this re-engagement. She noted, however, that academic provision was limited and students did not have access to higher level academic study.

In educational alternatives not specifically for pregnant or mothering teenagers, successful outcomes have been attributed to environments that support students emotionally and socially as well as academically (McGregor & Mills, 2012). The smaller, less formal settings, tailored programmes of study and more respectful relationships between staff and students have all been identified as important contributing factors (Fuller & Macfadyen, 2012; Mills, Renshaw, & Zipin, 2013). However, educational alternatives have also been criticised for offering only low-level qualifications that do not necessarily support higher level academic study (Fuller & Macfadyen, 2012; Simmons, Thompson, & Russell, 2014), for overlooking the needs of girls where they are outnumbered by boys (Fuller & Macfadyen, 2012; Osler & Vincent, 2003), and for providing schools with an easy opt-out that removes the need to examine the systemic and institutional barriers that lead to disaffection among some students (Mills et al., 2013).

In their work in educational alternatives for schoolgirl mothers in America, researchers Luttrell (2003) and Pillow (2004) acknowledge the positive aspects of the special provision but are critical of the limited resourcing of separate provision as well as a curriculum that focuses more on the moral and vocational redemption of students than the academic curriculum to which they are entitled. Pillow (2004) rejects rhetoric about the pregnant teenager being removed from the mainstream for her own benefit and safety as instead being primarily for the benefit of the mainstream. This is related to the stigmatised status of teenage pregnancy. Analyses such as those provided by Kelly (2000) suggest that removal from the mainstream is a convenient way of addressing concerns about the moral contamination of other students. Pillow (2004) additionally argues that while educational alternatives may be helpful, they ignore larger questions of equal opportunity and 'do not

## ALTERNATIVE EDUCATIONAL PROGRAMMES

address the structural barriers in schools and society that girls face' (p. 222). These are issues that require further attention.

Through examining the views and experiences of 14 young women in the English Midlands, 12 of whom became pregnant while still of statutory school age, this article explores the merits and limitations of educational alternatives for pregnant and mothering teenagers and in doing so, contributes to understandings about a specific group of marginalised learners whose experiences of education have been under-represented in the wider literatures. The concept of 'difference' is used as a central analytic theme. Difference is generally identified through comparison with an accepted norm – a socially constructed norm that is based on the perceptions and unquestioned assumptions of the dominant culture (Minow, 1990). This creates an identified 'other' who is invariably recognised in ways which devalue, marginalise or stigmatise (de Beauvoir, 1953). For example, in the United Kingdom, pregnant and mothering teenagers have widely been recognised as feckless, irresponsible individuals whose ignorance and poor choices are costly both to themselves and society (see SEU, 1999). This contributes to the stigma and oppression experienced by this group. By focusing on institutional responses to pupil 'difference', the article provides insights into how and why the educational alternatives worked for the young women in this study as well the limitations of what they offered. It concludes that it is only by ignoring some differences while simultaneously attending to others that educational participation can sensibly and fairly be supported. Whether in mainstream or alternative education, this approach may equally be applied to other groups of pupils with other 'differences'.

### The research

The data on which this article is based is drawn from a larger doctoral study of the educational experiences of pregnant schoolgirls and schoolgirl mothers. It aimed to explore how the national policy of supporting pregnant and mothering teenagers to stay in education was experienced by young women themselves. Consistent with the research outlined above, the educational achievements of the young women were modest. Seven completed Year 11 (the final year of compulsory schooling) with no A–C GCSE (General Certificate of Secondary Education) grades and a further five achieved between two and four A–C grades. Another student had just started Year 11 while the remaining student stood out as exceptional for her 14 A–C grades.

This article focuses on students' perceptions of the educational alternatives they attended. They are derived from in-depth, semi-structured repeat interviews undertaken over an 18-month period in 2007/2008 and supplemented by the views of some of the professionals that worked with them. Over the course of the study, 12 of the 14 young women in the research attended programmes that catered specifically for pregnant and mothering teenagers. A pupil referral unit (PRU) catered for a number of students while they were still of statutory school age and two entry-to-employment (E2E) programmes supported transition to post-compulsory education. A brief description of each setting is provided below. With the exception of *Young Mums To Be* (YMTB), which was offered nationally, all names used for institutions and individuals are fictional.

### *The PRU: Phoenix*

PRUs are government-funded educational alternatives for those who 'because of exclusion, illness or other reasons, would not otherwise receive suitable education' (DfE, 2013,

p. 3). The statutory guidance (DfE, 2013) does not define 'suitable' and the exact programme on offer varies widely from centre to centre, however, the main focus is educational alongside an expectation to address pupils' personal and social needs. PRUs typically cater for pupils, mainly boys, who are excluded from school but the local authority within which the research took place provided a PRU for pregnant schoolgirls and school-aged mothers. Phoenix catered for around 18 pupils at a time, was well-staffed and incorporated an on-site nursery and two nursery staff. Its primary aim was to support educational continuity during pregnancy and after childbirth by offering students core subjects for the GCSE alongside some vocational qualifications.

### *Entry-to-employment*

E2E was a national post-16 work-based programme that focused on the development of knowledge and skills for young people deemed not yet ready for employment or other forms of education or training. It was replaced in 2010 by Foundation Learning which caters for 14–19 year olds. Like PRUs, E2E programmes varied from centre to centre. Programmes of study were expected to be tailored to the individual but to include opportunities to gain nationally recognised qualifications, including those in English, Maths and IT, as well as vocational qualifications.

*YMTB* was an E2E programme designed specifically for pregnant teenagers. It offered an NVQ (National Vocational Qualification) Level 1 award comprised of 12 units of study that focused primarily on the skills and knowledge required to manage pregnancy, childbirth and motherhood. It also supported the development of literacy, numeracy and IT skills. *Stepping Stones* was also an E2E programme exclusively for pregnant and mothering teenagers. The exact programme offered was determined by the two staff members who ran it and by the needs and interests of students but in accordance with national guidance, the focus was on improving basic literacy, numeracy and IT skills. Students were encouraged to work towards nationally recognised qualifications such as OCN (Open College Network) or ALaN (Adult Literacy and Numeracy) awards.

## Young women's views and experiences

### *Benefits*

Across all three settings, and without exception, the young women spoke highly of the centres and they appreciated and benefited from what they had to offer. Much of what they valued echoes research undertaken in other educational alternatives, both those specifically for pregnant schoolgirls (Dawson & Hosie, 2005) and those that cater for other students (McGregor & Mills, 2012). Student experiences in these centres contrast almost point for point with the secondary school experiences they had found most difficult and which, for some, contributed to their disaffection with school. Students valued the greater range of teaching and learning strategies that were used and enjoyed the combination of small-group and individual work, practical-based activities and computer-based activities. Having programmes tailored to their individual needs and interests and being able to work at their own pace were other recurring themes. Better academic support compared to their school experiences and being educated in smaller classes with less formal structures and relationships with staff were also noted as positive features. These are commonly recurring themes in terms of what works with disaffected young people and are not further illustrated here. Instead, this article focuses on issues specific to students' pregnant or mothering status.

Being able to continue in education and to gain qualifications despite being pregnant or a young mother, was highly valued. This was particularly important given that most of their schools had been unwilling to support their mainstream education. Those who attended Phoenix were able to continue working towards their GCSE in some subjects. Aimee, who had been 'strongly encouraged' to attend Phoenix from very early in her pregnancy, explained:

> I really enjoy it here better than school. And I was just really pleased that I could carry on with my GCSEs ... get the same education as I would at school. (Aimee)

Those who attended Stepping Stones and YMTB did not have access to GCSEs but were able to work towards other nationally recognised qualifications. This was especially valued by those students who did not have the necessary credentials to embark on their preferred college programme. As staff at Stepping Stones noted:

> The majority have no qualifications, no GCSEs. They've been excluded. Some have been formally excluded and others just haven't been engaged ... low attendance or didn't take their GCSEs for various reasons.

However, it was not just the tangible outcomes such as qualifications that were helpful, but also less tangible factors such as the development of personal confidence. Several students spoke about attempting but failing college courses before attending Stepping Stones but were successful in managing college courses afterwards. Sonia illustrates how it was not only the literacy and numeracy qualifications she gained while at Stepping Stones but also greater personal confidence that had been crucial in supporting her eventual successful transition to college.

> S: I think I jumped into it [college] too soon cause I hadn't been in school for about two years. I came back [to Stepping Stones] cause I weren't ready for college.
> K: [pause] So what's different for you, going to college now from that first time?
> S: I'm more confident now.

She attributed her growing confidence to close and supportive relationships with staff. Other students verified the importance of the strong pastoral dimension in their successful outcomes. What appeared to be important was staff recognising all aspects of student identities in non-stigmatising ways, including the fact that they were pregnant or young mothers. They also conveyed an expectation and belief that they could succeed in education. Sonia's negative school experiences during her pregnancy and after the birth of her child meant that she left school with no qualifications and feeling like an academic and a personal failure. By positively embracing all aspects of their students, including their different choices and circumstances, staff affirmed their students as both capable learners and mothers.

> A: I don't mean to sound big headed, but maybe we are the first adult in their lives that's told them that they can achieve, and that we think they are bright ... and that they are good mothers.
> J: The conclusion we come to is it's about confidence. They don't get that positive input during their education that actually validates who they are ... and that it's OK to have different choices. (Stepping Stones staff)

ALTERNATIVE EDUCATIONAL PROGRAMMES

This approach helped counteract the sense of failure and educational alienation students had experienced in their secondary schools and helped them feel academically and socially more confident and ready to re-engage in formal education.

Spending time with other people of a similar age and in the same position as them was identified as a key benefit. This was attributed to the centres providing an emotionally safe place where their youthful pregnancies were accepted rather than condemned. Tracy explained:

> There's people here in the same situation as you, whereas at the other schools, if you go there and you're pregnant you'll get called a slag and everything and they'll all be looking at you and stuff.

Schools are not necessarily emotionally or physically safe places for pregnant pupils. Research shows that basic needs such as ready access to a toilet are sometimes refused (Alldred & David, 2007), and that other forms of fair and respectful treatment cannot be assumed (Vincent, 2012). The less rigid structures of the alternatives made accessing toilets, food and water easier than when they were in school, but students also valued their shared experience of pregnancy and knowing they would not be negatively judged by classmates or staff. Belonging to a group where their circumstances and choices were not met with condemnation or disapproval but rather with understanding and acceptance provided a refreshing change. This was a way of recognising the oppression that each of them had experienced as a result of their youthful pregnancies.

A closely related benefit that featured prominently in student accounts was the importance of social contact. Other research with young mothers has attributed motivation to pursue educational outlets to their being bored at home and needing social contact (MacDonald & Marsh, 2005). My work supports this. Reasons for attending these programmes included: 'I was on my own a lot of the time' (Sonia) and 'I wanted to do something. I didn't want to just be at home' (Lisa). Sarina explained:

> If I can get some skills while I am pregnant then that's better than sitting at home doing nothing ... sitting there thinking that the world is crashing down. You get depressed when you're sitting at home on your own.

And as noted by staff.

> A: To be honest, a lot of them join us because they want something to do.
> J: Yeah, they come because they want to be out of the house and they want to meet some other mothers. And they want to be in a group where they feel they are not judged for being a mother or pregnant. (Stepping Stones staff)

The PRU offered an on-site nursery. This was valued because it allowed young mothers to continue their education, but their babies were also close to hand so they could feed and change them during the day. Having the nursery on-site made it easy for students to get to know the nursery staff and as a result, they had few worries about being judged as inadequate mothers by these professionals. Anxieties about leaving their babies with someone they do not know and about being judged as inadequate mothers because they are young has been found to act as a barrier to accessing childcare and therefore also education (Dench, Bellis, & Tuohy, 2007). The on-site nursery at Phoenix appeared to be a good way of recognising this barrier.

60

The nursery, that's a big thing. I don't think a school would be able to have a nursery. Like here ... we can see them at dinner time, give them dinner cause it's in the same building ... and we know the nursery nurses quite well.

Issues of identity and changing identities emerged as an important outcome of attending one of the educational alternatives. Seeing themselves as competent and capable mothers, and developing a mother identity which did not mutually exclude other and additional possibilities, were changes noted by students at Stepping Stones.

It's given us all faith in ourselves that we can do both [motherhood and education] and that just because you're young doesn't mean your life has to be based on being a mum all the time. Here [at Stepping Stones] they are telling you that you can also do other things for yourself. (Megan)

Staff achieved this by continuously encouraging but not pressuring young women to undertake qualifications and consider further educational routes. In doing so they conveyed an expectation that gaining additional educational qualifications at Stepping Stones, and then later at college, was both desirable and possible. Equally important, Clare found that attending YMTB helped her re-evaluated popular stigmatised representations and to develop a more positive identity as a pregnant teenager.

I came out with a different attitude ... [before] I was so embarrassed ... I just completely degraded myself when I found out I was pregnant ... and it made me feel a lot better being there.

Other changes in thinking were also noted. Mia spoke about being influenced by peers in a way that adults may have been less successful. Her initial unwillingness to extract herself from a violent relationship with the father of her child resulted in social services involvement. It seemed that it was not so much the two broken ribs she sustained, or even the realisation that she was physically unable to protect her child at that point, but also the subsequent processing with classmates that led her to eventually end that relationship. Discussions with people her own age rather than those in positions of power were instrumental in this. Speaking of Stepping Stones she said:

It's the best thing I've done in a long while. We get to talk about all sorts of things. Like with the domestic violence stuff, most of the girls, they would give me advice, and although they feel like they're telling me off, I don't mind. And adults are constantly telling me things ... and that makes me sort of rebel against them but when I hear it coming from my friends, like what it's doing to my child ... [it is different]. (Mia)

Staff verified Mia's account and highlighted their intentional 'no direct advice' stance.

No matter how we may feel about it, we don't say 'you've got to finish with him' or anything like that but we'll give clues or suggestions, 'oh, have you tried it this way' or 'have you thought about this or that?' Our focus is giving them the ability to think for themselves and decide for themselves what they want. And if at the end of that, they get rid of that bloke who's been kicking shit out of them then it's their choice. (Stepping Stones staff)

Their non-authoritarian approach and the more equal relationships between teacher and learner represents a different power dynamic than that typically found in students' mainstream schools. This has been highlighted as an important component in the success of other educational alternatives (Connell, 2013; Mills et al., 2013). This approach conveyed messages about competence and was a way of recognising the young women's abilities to assume greater control and responsibility in their lives.

Megan suggested that an additional advantage of this form of specialist provision was that staff have an understanding of their broader lives and the ways in which the responsibilities of motherhood may complicate a smooth educational passage. She explained:

> They're understanding here. You're all here because you're either pregnant or a young mum and you're all going through the same experiences whereas a normal college, the fact that people don't understand that you've got a baby at home, so if she's teething and you've had a really rough night of it ... or she's got chicken pox and she can't go to nursery, they're not going to be ... well they might be understanding but I think that it's a lot easier at a place like this.

An inflexible stance towards pregnant and mothering students was noted by staff at Stepping Stones and has been highlighted in other research (Alldred & David, 2007; Vincent, 2012). A teacher at Stepping Stones spoke with some frustration about this lack of flexibility. She observed that schools often do not recognise that being a mother has obvious implications for what else can reasonably be expected, but she and her colleague pointed out that this was equally true of some further education colleges.

> It seems to be very inflexible ... just from what the girls have said when they've come to us. If they did have their baby when they were 14 or 15, there just doesn't seem to be that much flexibility within the school system. They seem to have a five day or no day approach rather than saying let's do three days with you where you do this, this and this and see how it goes. (teacher at Stepping Stones)

Several mainstream teachers spoke about the need for a flexible approach and this was reflected in their school practice, as illustrated by the part-time arrangements made for one student who returned to her mainstream school after having her baby. All three educational alternatives accepted late arrivals or early departures from class when a medical appointment could not be scheduled out of class time, alongside non-attendance when a child was ill. Unfortunately such practices do not seem to be widespread. The flexible approach to attendance and progression rates adopted by the educational alternatives was an effective way of recognising the additional demands resulting from being heavily pregnant or the mother of a young child.

### *Limitations*

As well as benefits, the young women identified some limitations of the educational alternatives. These related to restricted curricula access and uncertainties about the relative merit of alternative qualifications.

Shae explained that she was unable to continue with all her school subjects when she moved to Phoenix, and the extra-curricular activities she had enjoyed were unavailable. She did not frame this aspect of her new educational setting as a disadvantage but rather, spoke about it in a matter of fact way, and appeared to be grateful to continue her education there, even if the curriculum was limited. Interestingly, within the local authority, Phoenix was promoted as a centre that offered individually tailored programmes and encouraged the completion of nationally recognised qualifications. In reality, the limited staff numbers and expertise understandably placed considerable restriction on the breadth of the curriculum to which students had access. Although not explicit, one reading of Shae's words is that the student is made to fit the system rather than the other way round.

> I didn't have many because [at school] I was doing loads of things … maths and history and science. [At Phoenix] They had to fit me a timetable that was more up to them. So I had to finish expressive arts. I couldn't do that anymore because they don't have that. I was doing PE … and I couldn't do that anymore [laughter]. And I was doing the choir at school and they don't have that sort of thing … so just little things like that.

So Shae's educational experiences became more restricted once she began attending Phoenix. Both Luttrell (2003) and Pillow (2004) highlight this as a problematic aspect of the American educational alternatives they studied. In the United Kingdom, two of the higher achieving teenage mothers in Simmons et al. (2014) research on youth transitions found that the educational alternatives they attended only offered qualifications at a lower level than those that the students had already attained. Access to these alternatives kept them in education but did little to support their future employability. Rebecca, who chose not to go to Phoenix, was the only participant who perceived the limited curriculum as a major disadvantage.

> I was talking to some of the girls that went there, and they were doing like a maths and an English GCSE. I was doing manufacturing and French and history and geography, as well as maths, English and science. You can't do the GCSEs you want to do.

She was also the only student to remain in mainstream education throughout her pregnancy. She insightfully suggested that her status as a high achieving pupil who would make a positive contribution to her school's league table results was influential in her school's willingness to accommodate her desire to stay in mainstream education.

> Yeah, but I think part of that was because I was going to get good exam results and everybody knew that … so it's good for him [the headteacher] because his league tables look higher.

The pressure on schools to perform in particular ways makes them less willing to work with particular pupils. The high-stakes testing regimes associated with neoliberal reforms have rightly been criticised for working against inclusive education (Connell, 2013).

A related issue was the type of qualifications to which students had access. All three centres offered NVQ, OCN and ALaN awards. Almost all students were working towards one of these, and as noted earlier, valued the opportunity to acquire qualifications while they were pregnant or alongside their mothering responsibilities. In some respects, this is a positive outcome. These qualifications are nationally recognised and thus offer a constructive way of supporting educational continuity. They enable students who have difficulty with mainstream school, or whose strengths are not academic, to demonstrate skills in other areas and to gain a sense of achievement as well as formal qualifications. Gutherson, Davies, and Daszkiewicz (2011) international review of educational alternatives found that accreditation can give a sense of achievement and thus help raise student self-esteem and motivation. In my research, the qualifications that some of the young women gained also provided an alternative route to further education for those without GCSEs. However, student accounts highlighted some important issues with regard to these.

## ALTERNATIVE EDUCATIONAL PROGRAMMES

One emerging theme was that of confusion about qualifications and the progression routes they offered. Seven participants expressed uncertainty about what qualifications they had gained and at what level. Many were also unclear about the equivalence of what they had achieved to other nationally recognised qualifications. This exemplifies an issue raised by Thomson and Russell (2007). Alternative education providers in their research offered GCSEs (but not usually many) alongside a range of vocational qualifications. As the authors noted, 'young people were often left to themselves to try to manage the complexities of getting equivalencies of qualifications sorted out' (Thomson & Russell, 2007, p. 23). They found, as did some of the young women in my study, that some OCNs or GCSEs were not enough to access preferred their college programme. Although Shae had some GCSEs, her college choices were limited because they did not include English and Maths. She was unable to access an A Level course and so started a lower level business course instead.

> Cause of my four GCSEs, there weren't many courses going that I could do ... and when he said [what about] Business, I thought I'm fine with that.

Several of the young women were influenced by other people's views of what is appropriate for them. Clare and Lisa were directed into hairdressing NVQs when their pregnancies resulted in them discontinuing their mainstream education. This influenced their subsequent college choices. As Lisa explained:

> I would like to do other stuff, but like that's all I know really ... hairdressing. I was gonna try and do midwifery, but that's a long course, and I've always liked interior design and that sort of thing ... I can see myself going more down the hairdressing line though. (Lisa)

Some of the professionals expressed frustration about the students' gendered college course choices.

> They all want to be nursery nurses, hairdressers and beauticians' (teacher at Stepping Stones)

This is a long-standing issue that has been highlighted in numerous feminist studies (Leathwood, 2006; Tinklin, Croxford, Ducklin, & Frame, 2005) but seems resistant to change.

Two participants reflected on the relative value of the alternative qualifications to which they had access. Sarina, who was attending Stepping Stones when I first met her, was sceptical about the value of the OCNs and ALaNs she had completed, particularly with regard to how future employers might view them. She was also clear in her view that those students who were still of statutory school age (admittedly, a small minority at Stepping Stones), should really be studying for GCSEs. And as a student with only two A–C GCSEs, she would like to have had an opportunity to retake her GCSEs while at Stepping Stones but staff were not qualified to offer this.

> You can do an English OCN. It's not a GCSE but it's equivalent ... but I don't think an OCN stands for very much. When people ask you how many GCSEs you've got, you can't say 'well I've got one in English because I've got an OCN' because it's not the full course. And here, like, they do OCNs on yoga. You couldn't go like to a yoga place and say I've got my level one OCN, I'd like a job. (Sarina)

Other participants also placed particular value on GCSEs or thought that not having them would limit their college options. These accounts resonate with those offered by the young people in Fuller and Macfadyen (2012) study who viewed the vocational qualifications they were working towards as second best. The authors make an important point when they conclude that, 'Only when traditional and non-traditional educational routes have parity can vocational courses be seen as an option that is not just for educational under-achievers' (p. 99). This issue was recognised in a major review of vocational education in the United Kingdom which noted that while many students benefit from vocational education, 'between a quarter and a third of the post-16 cohort is fed a diet of low-level qualifications, most of which have little or no market value' (Wolf, 2011, p. 7).

**Making sense of benefits and limitations: the recognition and non-recognition of difference**

The research found that all who attended the educational alternatives rated them highly and the accounts above illustrate aspects of the provision that young women believed enhanced their academic achievements, and for those who were disaffected, made it possible for them to re-engage in education. Important insights into how these positive outcomes were achieved can be gained by considering which differences were recognised in the educational alternatives, and which were not. The noted limitations of the educational alternatives can similarly be understood through an analysis of which differences were recognised and which were not.

A crucial factor underpinning the positive experiences of participants was that staff adopted a positive (non-stigmatising) recognition of the difference of teenage pregnancy/motherhood. That is, there was no judgement conveyed about how they came to be pregnant or about their decisions to continue with a pregnancy at their age. This contrasted with many of the responses received from participants' schools, medical professionals and the general public. Finding themselves in the company of other young women who had similar experiences of oppression was also important and seemed to work as an antidote to the shameful and shaming ways that pregnancy had been responded to in other parts of their lives. Within these institutions, expectations about regular attendance and about working towards nationally recognised qualifications were the same as for any other student and conveyed the message 'you are a pregnant/mothering teenager but you can still complete your education'. In this respect, pregnancy or motherhood per sae was irrelevant (non-recognised).

At the same time, each of these institutions adopted a flexible response to differences related to the embodied nature of pregnancy or the additional responsibilities of mother-hood. In contrast to their mainstream schooling experiences, students in all three educational alternatives had ready and unquestioned access to toilet facilities. This recognised the need to use a toilet more frequently during pregnancy. The on-site nursery at Phoenix made it easier for young mothers who may have been reluctant to leave their baby for long periods of time or with someone they did not know, to do so. At Stepping Stones, staff encouraged regular attendance but simultaneously accepted non-attendance or late arrival when the demands of motherhood had meant a sleepless night or when another engage-ment, such as a medical appointment, took priority. The recognition of these differences helped support educational continuity by conveying feelings of respect and care that had largely been absent in young women's mainstream schools.

In addition, there were some non-pregnancy/motherhood-related differences that were also recognised in these institutions in non-stigmatising ways. Again, these contrasted with participants' school experiences. All three specialist alternatives had a low teacher to student ratio and provided flexible, tailored programmes of learning with additional academic support available if needed. These learning environments were also characterised by closer, less formal and more trusting relationships with staff. These factors have long been recognised as integral to successful outcomes in educational alternatives (Thomson & Russell, 2007). The messages conveyed through these arrangements included 'we recognise that past educational experiences may not have been positive', 'we recognise that some of you may have learning gaps or need additional support with your learning' and 'we recognise that not all students learn and progress at the same pace'. Implicit within these messages was the assumption of academic success and progression for all students. The effect of these non-stigmatising forms of recognition and non-recognition was an increase in educational confidence and motivation. This may go some way to explaining why the young women rated them highly with most suggesting that they achieved more at these alternatives than they would have if they had stayed at school.

At the same time there were other differences that remained largely unrecognised within these institutions and which, albeit not necessarily immediately, may well have a detrimental impact on young women in the future and in the meantime, unintentionally reinforce rather than challenge stigmatising individualistic discourses. Like the educational alternatives in Luttrell (2003) and Pillow's (2004) research, all three institutions were characterised by an uncritical and primary focus on educational qualifications and future employment. Few questions were asked about the type or level of qualification gained or the extent to which this would support or inhibit subsequent life chances and choices. Such non-recognition reinforces the assumption implicit within policy (see SEU, 1999), that for young women in their position, qualifications and employment are the route to social and economic salvation and also that motherhood on its own is not a real or valued occupation. This stance fails to recognise the unpaid labour associated with the domestic and caring responsibilities undertaken primarily by women (Gillies, 2007) or any representation of this work as socially useful (Duncan, 2007).

Similarly, this perspective also fails to recognise the intertwined and deeply rooted relationships between gender, class, educational outcomes and the labour market. The hairdressing, beauty therapy and social care courses that participants invariably undertook (or planned to undertake) were unmistakeably gendered while the OCNs and NVQs they acquired will facilitate access to further education, but not higher education. Both of these outcomes will tend to lead these young women into lower paying and less secure employment with limited opportunities for progression. Lisa could not have been clearer in her statement about her choice of hairdressing: 'I mean, I would like to do other stuff, but like that's all I know really'. While Stepping Stones stood out as unique in at least broaching some wider social issues, the non-recognition of issues of class and gender meant that the PRU and YMTB continued to perform the same normalising function as participants' schools by supporting meritocratic myths that locate success or failure within the individual. These issues are, of course, not limited to educational alternatives but operate across the education system.

## Conclusions

This article began by highlighting the poor educational outcomes experienced by pregnant and mothering teenagers and has aimed to provide insights into how three educational alternatives supported educational continuity for this vulnerable group. This is important because many mainstream schools remain reluctant or unwilling to do so. In line with previous research with teenage mothers in the United Kingdom (Dawson & Hosie, 2005; Rudoe, 2014), the research found that the educational alternatives were rated highly by young women and offered some unique benefits. They provided supportive, nurturing learning environments that were successful in rebuilding students' academic confidence and achievement levels. This was particularly valued by those who had left school with few academic qualification or feeling like academic failures. The educational alternatives also helped rebuild young women's moral integrity and to help them feel better about themselves as pregnant or mothering teenagers. They offered an antidote to the shame that many of them had internalised on becoming pregnant at a young age. Identities were shaped and young women were supported in assuming greater control and responsibility in their lives. These findings support a case for maintaining educational alternatives such as those described here.

The analytical focus on institutional responses to student 'difference' showed how these outcomes were achieved. By recognising (responding to) some differences while not recognising (responding to) others, the educational alternatives were able to support students' personal circumstances. Differences that were recognised, such as those to do with the embodied nature of pregnancy, were done so in non-stigmatising ways; a student's status as a pregnant or mothering teenagers was not seen as a problem. This analytical approach has wider application. Parallels may be drawn between institutional responses to pupils who become pregnant and pupils with other differences. Those who do not fit, for whatever reason, are seen as not belonging and are effectively excluded from mainstream education in one way or another. Little thought is given to changing institutional structures or systems to accommodate difference and individual deficit discourses are used to define those who do not fit as a troubled or troublesome 'other'. Whether in mainstream or alternative education, more affirming educational experiences will be supported through considering which differences institutions need to respond to and which to leave unrecognised. This requires examining taken-for-granted assumptions that construct particular students or groups of students in stigmatised ways.

The limitations identified by the young women in this study in relation to the curriculum and qualifications they were offered, mirror concerns raised in other research with young mothers as well as those with other learners who find themselves in educational alternatives. Educational pathways matter and the type and level of qualifications gained can have negative future consequences for young people (Simmons et al., 2014). If the social justice imperatives underpinning educational alternatives are to be achieved, then current structures would need to be changed so that educational alternatives offer pathways that are valued by all young people as well as prospective employers. It is also important to recognise that what is most helpful for one pupil might not be most helpful for another. At Stepping Stones, Sarina wanted to be able to do the GCSEs she missed through her disrupted schooling but this option was not available. Other students there were glad to undertake vocationally orientated qualifications. So whether in mainstream or alternative education, better outcomes will be promoted if students are offered viable alternatives of equal value and given access to a range of curricula, qualifications and support. Better long-term outcomes would also be achieved through greater recognition of broader social issues, such as those related to class and gender, and the impact these have on educational trajectories and outcomes.

## ALTERNATIVE EDUCATIONAL PROGRAMMES

### References

Alldred, P., & David, M. (2007). *Get real about sex: The politics and practice of sex education.* Milton Keynes: Open University Press.

Coleman, J., & Dennison, C. (1998). Teenage parenthood research review. *Children and Society, 12* (4), 306–314. doi:10.1111/j.1099-0860.1998.tb00084.x

Connell, R. (2013). The neoliberal cascade and education: An essay on the market agenda and its consequences. *Critical Studies in Education, 54*(2), 99–112. doi:10.1080/17508487.2013.776990

Dawson, N., & Hosie, A. (2005). *The education of pregnant young women and young mothers in England.* Bristol: University of Bristol.

de Beauvoir, S. (1953). *The second sex.* London: Random House.

Dench, S., Bellis, A., & Tuohy, S. (2007). *Young mothers not in learning: A qualitative study of barriers and attitudes.* University of Sussex, Brighton: Institute for Employment Studies.

DfE. (2013). *Alternative provision. Statutory guidance for local authorities.* Department of Education. Retrieved from www.education.gov.uk/aboutdfe/statutory/g00211923/alternative-provision

Duncan, S. (2007). What's the problem with teenage parents? And what's the problem with policy? *Critical Social Policy, 27*(3), 307–334. doi:10.1177/0261018307078845

Fergusson, D., & Woodward, L. (1999). Maternal age and educational and psychosocial outcomes in early adulthood. *Journal of Child Psychology and Psychiatry, 40*(3), 479–489. doi:10.1111/jcpp.1999.40.issue-3

Fuller, C., & Macfadyen, T. (2012). 'What with your grades?' Students' motivation for and experiences of vocational courses in further education. *Journal of Vocational Education & Training, 64*(1), 87–101. doi:10.1080/13636820.2011.622447

Gillies, V. (2007). *Marginalised mothers. Exploring working class experiences of parenting.* Abington: Routledge.

Gutherson, P., Davies, H., & Daszkiewicz, T. (2011). *Achieving successful outcomes through alternative education provision: An international literature review.* Berkshire: DfBT Education Trust.

Kelly, D. (2000). *Pregnant with meaning. Teen mothers and the politics of inclusive schooling.* New York, NY: Peter Lang.

Kiernan, K. (1997). Becoming a young parent: A longitudinal study of associated factors. *British Journal of Sociology, 48*(3), 406–428. doi:10.2307/591138

Leathwood, C. (2006). Gender equity in post-secondary education. In C. Skelton, B. Fransis, & L. Smulyan (Eds.), *The SAGE handbook of gender and education.* London: Sage.

Luttrell, W. (2003). *Pregnant bodies, fertile minds. Gender, race, and the schooling of pregnant teens.* London: Routledge.

MacDonald, R., & Marsh, J. (2005). *Disconnected youth? Growing up in Britain's poor neighbour-hoods.* Basingstoke: Palgrave MacMillan.

McGregor, G., & Mills, M. (2012). Alternative education sites and marginalised young people: 'I wish there were more schools like this one'. *International Journal of Inclusive Education, 16*(8), 843–862. doi:10.1080/13603116.2010.529467

Mills, M., Renshaw, P., & Zipin, L. (2013). Alternative education provision: A dumping ground for 'wasted lives' or a challenge to the mainstream. *Social Alternatives, 32*(2), 13–18.

Minow, M. (1990). *Making all the difference.* New York, NY: Cornell University Press.

Osler, A., & Vincent, K. (2003). *Girls and exclusion. Rethinking the agenda.* London: RoutlegeFalmer.

Pillow, W. (2004). *Unfit subjects. Educational policy and the teen mother.* New York, NY: RoutledgeFalmer.

Rudoe, N. (2014). School exclusion and educational inclusion of pregnant young women. *Ethnography and Education, 9*(1), 66–80. doi:10.1080/17457823.2013.828477

SEU (Social Exclusion Unit). (1999). *Teenage pregnancy.* London: SEU.

Simmons, R., Thompson, R., & Russell, L. (2014). *Education, work and social change.* New York, NY: Palgrave Macmillan.

Snow Jones, A., Astone, N., Keyl, P., Young, K., & Alexander, C. (1999). Teen childbearing and educational attainment: A comparison of methods. *Journal of Family and Economic Issues, 20* (4), 387–418. doi:10.1023/A:1022932305898

Thomson, P., & Russell, L. (2007). *Mapping the alternatives to permanent exclusion*. York: Joseph Rowntree Foundation.

Tinklin, T., Croxford, L., Ducklin, A., & Frame, B. (2005). Gender and attitudes to work and family roles: The views of young people at the millennium. *Gender and Education, 17*(2), 129–142. doi:10.1080/0954025042000301429

TPU (Teenage Pregnancy Unit). (2005). *Teenage pregnancy strategy evaluation: final report and synthesis*. London: Author.

Vincent, K. (2012). *Schoolgirl pregnancy, motherhood and education: Dealing with difference*. Stoke-on-Trent: Trentham.

Vincent, K., & Thomson, P. (2010). 'Slappers like you don't belong in this school': The educational inclusion/exclusion of pregnant schoolgirls. *International Journal of Inclusive Education, 14*(4), 371–385. doi:10.1080/13603110802504580

Wiggins, M., Oakley, A., Austerberry, H., Clemens, F., & Elbourne, D. (2005). *Teenage parenthood and social exclusion: A multi-method study*. London: Social Science Research Unit, Institute of Education, University of London.

Wolf, A. (2011) *Review of vocational education – The wolf report*. Retrieved from www.gov.uk/government/uploads/system/uploads/attachment_data/file/180504/DFE-00031-2011.pdf

# Meaningful education for returning-to-school students in a comprehensive upper secondary school in Iceland

Ingólfur Ásgeir Jóhannesson and Valgerður S. Bjarnadóttir

Dropout from upper secondary education in Iceland is higher than in the neighboring countries, but varied options to re-enter school have also been on offer. This article focuses on how students, who had returned to a selected upper secondary school after having quit in one or more other schools, benefited from an innovative pedagogical approach used in the school. The article draws upon interviews, in which the interviewees expressed their pleasure with the school, reporting three main assets of its pedagogy: firstly, a supportive school ethos and student–teacher relationships expressed by the ways in which teachers worked, and also in teachers' views towards students; secondly, an online learning platform, used by all teachers, which the students could use to structure their studies; and thirdly, the use of formative assessment and no final end-of-term examinations. This pedagogy comprises a whole school approach, and the article concludes that such a school culture and practice enables teenagers and young adults to exercise their right to re-enter academic upper secondary education, which prepares for college, rather than directing them to an industry vocational or practical study program they take little or no interest in.

## Introduction

All around the world, the phenomenon called dropout from school is of concern. Teenagers' reasons for leaving upper secondary school are diverse (e.g., Frostad, Pijl, & Mjaavatn, 2015; Jónasson & Blöndal, 2002; Ministry of Education, Science, and Culture, 2014b), and much effort is directed, internationally, as well as in Iceland, at studying how students could be engaged with their studies so they would choose not to leave school (e.g., Blöndal, 2014; Rumberger & Lim, 2008; Rumberger, 2011). Less frequent but important in this literature are studies on what is often called 'second chance education' for those who wish to re-enter upper secondary education, either within the ordinary school system or outside it (e.g., McGregor, Mills, Te Riele, & Hayes, 2015; Mills & McGregor, 2014; Nordlund, Stehlik, & Strandh, 2013; Ross & Gray, 2005).

We commonly hear from the public, politicians, and employers that those who leave upper secondary school must have done so because they did not have access to good industry vocational, technical, or practical study programs. We also hear the myth that students, who do not succeed in academic studies belong to industry-based vocational education. While the former may be true, regarding lack of access to such quality programs, the latter supposition is a myth, which devalues the dreams of many young people for success in academic studies and preparation for college education.

Therefore, in this article, we consider the experience of those teenagers and young adults, who choose to re-enter academic upper secondary education, because we think their experiences are not well represented in education debates. The article draws upon interviews with eight Icelandic students, aged 20–24 years, who had left school and re-entered an upper secondary school known for its appeal to students leaving other upper secondary schools. We asked them about their experience of the pedagogy in an academic program in the new school and how it met their needs. At the outset, we had no preconception of the future dreams of these students, but soon it became apparent that college preparation was high on the list of almost every student we spoke with. Therefore, the question we aim to answer in this article is: How do students, who have returned to upper secondary school for academic education, benefit from an innovative pedagogical approach relying on an online learning platform and formative assessment? The article is a contribution to an understanding of how pedagogical strategies can help teenagers and young adults to re-engage with education.

## Background

Iceland is a 103 thousand square kilometer large, sparsely populated island in the middle of the Atlantic Ocean and a republic since 1944. Only about 330 thousand people live in Iceland, thereof about two-thirds in the capital city area of Reykjavík.

The education system in Iceland consists of different school levels: the pre-school level for 1–6-year old children, compulsory level for 6–16-year old children and teenagers, the upper secondary level, and the tertiary level. The Icelandic upper secondary school is free of charge, noncompulsory, and primarily designed for 16–20-year old students (The Upper Secondary School Act, 2008). From autumn 2015, all but two schools will offer a three-year program in accordance with a decision by the minister of education, science, and culture (Tveir bjóða ekki upp á þriggja ára nám [Two do not offer a three year education program], 2015).

The upper secondary schools are divided between those confining themselves to academic study programs, comprehensive schools offering academic and vocational programs, and vocational schools, which in some cases also offer practical academic programs such as computer science and design. Most of the schools are organized around a credit-unit system, but a few of the academic schools have age-cohort classes. Altogether, in the spring of 2015, there were 35 different upper secondary schools, as well as several other educational institutions, offering programs at upper secondary school level. The upper secondary schools are state-run, with four exceptions.

### *Dropout rates from the Icelandic upper secondary schools and return-to-school options*

In the early and mid-1900s, the upper secondary school system in Iceland developed in a somewhat disorganized manner, with specific legislation on vocational education and *ad hoc* legislation about many other different schools, including any new academic school. In the 1970s and 1980s, many comprehensive credit-unit schools were founded. The system developed flexibly, in contrast to the earlier academic and vocational schools, and it provided access for many more teenagers to upper secondary education, especially academic programs. The first overall legislation on upper secondary education dates from 1988 where it was confirmed that the system should remain flexible so that students would be able to move between different study programs (The Upper Secondary School Act, 1988). This has been emphasized in subsequent Acts (The Upper Secondary School Act, 1996; The Upper Secondary School Act, 2008). The Icelandic system is flexible in this regard by international comparison as well as Nordic systems in general where 'students can leave the education system relatively easily and re-enter it later on' (OECD, 2012b, p. 42; see also, Blöndal, 2014).

In a recent Governmental White Paper, one of two major goals is to reduce dropout from the upper secondary school to the extent that 60% of the age cohort would complete their upper secondary education at the defined time, compared to the current 44% (Ministry of Education, Science, and Culture, 2014a). This is considerably lower than the OECD average of 68% (OECD, 2012a). Many factors may contribute to Iceland's situation, including the structure or quality of upper secondary education, the availability of lifelong learning for completion of studies, and employment opportunities for youth (Blöndal, Jónasson, & Tannhäuser, 2011; OECD, 2012a). A recent OECD report suggests that high dropout rates in Iceland may, in part, be caused by 'lack of relevant curricula, or a system that is not addressing well enough the students' needs of choice of studies and guidance at the upper secondary level' (OECD, 2012a, p. 7). It further suggests that 'their great ease of transfer between upper secondary programs and schools, can lead students to a sense of confusion and irrelevance in the education received' (OECD, 2012a, p. 7).

In contrast to other OECD countries, it is common in Iceland to study later in life; a significant number of Icelandic upper secondary school graduates are older than 25 (e.g., Blöndal et al., 2011; OECD, 2012a, 2013). More than 30% of women in Iceland graduate from tertiary level after the age of 30, while the OECD average is 10% (OECD, 2013). The government has now planned to limit access of those older than 25 years to free-of-charge upper secondary education (Alþingi, 2014).

To give a sense of the number of young people, who have changed schools through the years, we note that in autumn 2005, about 36% of the almost 6000 upper secondary school students, who had dropped out during the school years of 2002–2003 and 2003–2004, had returned (Alþingi, 2006–2007), that is, over 2000 returning students. Out of those who left a particular upper secondary school in autumn of 2013, 16% (170) immediately attended another school (Ministry of Education, Science, and Culture, 2014b). Comparable figures in an Australian study are that about 32% of 15–24-year olds, who enrolled in upper secondary education from May 2000 to May 2001 were 'noncompleters' (Ross & Gray, 2005).

As mentioned, some research has focused on students, who change schools. For instance, Jónasson (1994) studied the transfer between three different types of programs, that is, academic studies, traditional programs involving authorized branches of industry (I. löggiltar iðngreinar), and other vocational programs. He found that in 1991, less than 10% of the students had transferred to another study program after having completed one half-year school term. Guðmundsson and Daníelsdóttir (2013) studied the experience of young adults, who re-registered for a vocational program after dropping out of academic studies. They interviewed 10 individuals, aged 27–37 years, about leaving school and returning to school, and stressed the importance of the upper secondary school being open at all times to those who want to return to it.

### *Pedagogy – teaching methods and assessment*

The pedagogy of the upper secondary school in Iceland is traditionally subject-based. This is probably due to its origins in the academic tradition of elite schools, preparing their

# ALTERNATIVE EDUCATIONAL PROGRAMMES

candidates for college or university, and industry vocational schools, preparing their graduates for registered crafts. In the above-mentioned OECD report from 2012, a subject-based curriculum is defined as an obstacle to dropout prevention, stating that teachers in the upper secondary schools 'receive an initial education that focuses less on pedagogical training than for teachers at other levels' and that 'in-service teacher training seems to be *ad hoc* and not systematically planned' (OECD 2012a, p. 7).

Among others, Lingard and Mills (2007), Lupton and Hempel-Jorgensen (2012), McGregor and Mills (2012), McGregor et al. (2015), and Mills and McGregor (2014) direct our attention to the importance of pedagogical issues, such as teaching and learning, assessment, and student–teacher relationships, with regard to student dropout and engagement at upper secondary school level. These authors emphasize that 'alternative pedagogies' are characterized by a number of features 'designed to promote greater recognitive and distributive justices' (Lupton & Hempel-Jorgensen, 2012, p. 603). Such pedagogies make less use of prescriptive external resources, relying instead on the professional judgment of teachers; besides, teachers take more 'risks' in their teaching approaches as processes where students are able to have an input. These alternative approaches to pedagogy are inclusive in the sense that student–teacher relationships are based on trust and a sense of community, attempting to include connections to the outside lives of the students and the communities they live in. The classroom context focuses on questioning and problematizing the curriculum. And, not least importantly, the alternative approaches to pedagogy are based on the capability of students to transform not only themselves but also things around them. In accordance with these descriptions, assessment needs to be not only diverse in methods but also democratic in the sense that students have a say in how it is constructed and delivered.

O'Donovan, Berman, and Wierenge (2015) researched a hands-on-learning program as an enabling space, built on respectful relationships that foster 'a sense of belonging and tangible links' (p. 64). They argue that it is important to students to find meaning, connection, and control over their lives. Meaning is having a sense of purpose in activities and being able to relate them to their identities and future plans. Connection is about how students perceive the links to others in the school. Control is about feeling safe and having a voice.

The above is by no means a comprehensive description of what, for instance, McGregor et al. (2015) term as a 'meaningful' education in their studies of alternative sites of upper secondary education. But it draws attention to issues relevant to the study of the experiences and views of students, who have returned to a 'regular' school in the upper secondary school system where they exercise their rights to academic studies despite having made attempts in other academic or vocational schools.

## The research setting

While almost all upper secondary schools in Iceland receive students, who have previously left another school, some do more of it than others. We wanted a site where there would be a concentration of returning students, and we also wanted a site, which maintained a policy of using innovative pedagogies.

By selecting one school, rather than two or even more, we thought we would gain a deeper understanding of the ways in which its pedagogy (teaching, assessment methods, and student–teacher relationships) would be perceived by the students and how they would benefit from such an approach. Our selected site is both known for accepting returning-to-school students (nearly half of the students at the time had previously been in another upper secondary school), as well as for developing pedagogies which, among other things, rely on an online learning platform and formative and continuous assessment, considered innovative in the Icelandic upper secondary school context. The school is located in the capital city area of south west Iceland and is relatively small (an exact number might reveal its identity). We have given the school the pseudonym Long Hill Upper Secondary School.[1]

### *Participants*

The authors visited the school twice in February and March 2015. We met with four student groups the assistant principal of the school had found for us, comprising quite a few students, who had transferred from another school. We presented our study, and volunteers registered for an interview, which took place in the school building on the same day. Many were willing to speak with us, but the final sample of participants in the study consisted of six boys and two girls; six were 20–21 years old and two were 23–24 years old. Our interviewees had attended one or two other schools prior to being accepted to Long Hill; three of them had at some point attended Long Hill before registering for another secondary school, either begun at Long Hill or had a stop there between other schools; thus, two of our interviewees had left three schools. All participants had attended comprehensive or vocational schools, based on a credit-unit system. None of them had attended age-cohort schools or the schools considered most prestigious.

### *The interviews*

An interview frame had been developed by the authors in cooperation with researchers, who had performed several similar studies in another country (e.g., Mills & McGregor, 2014). The frame was developed by writing topics and questions in Icelandic and English, side-by-side, in two different columns.

The interview frame focused on how the students experienced their new school and why they did not want to continue their studies at their old school. We first asked about the school(s) they had been to prior to Long Hill. We continued by asking them what it was that Long Hill did well and subsequently we suggested that they compare Long Hill to their previous school(s). Then we encouraged them to elaborate on what they were currently doing in the school, for instance by asking what was easy and what was difficult and why. We inquired whether they thought the school was helpful in preparing them for their future goals. Finally, we asked them about their friends, relationships to other students, especially to the younger students, and to their teachers.

The length of the interviews varied from 11 to 21 minutes except for the one which lasted 33 minutes. The interviews were recorded and transcribed verbatim by one of the researchers.

### *Analysis*

The analysis of data corresponds roughly to Braun and Clarke's (2006) phases of thematic analysis. We carefully read the interviews and wrote notes. This we did separately, and then we discussed our first ideas of what was most significant before coding the data in a systematic way. Subsequently codes were organized into the themes that appear in the next section and a thematic map was created and revised, after reviewing the data again. Information was gathered from the interviews to form stories to tell of the experiences of the participants. The name of each theme and subtheme was determined during the writing, as the details of each theme developed during the phases of the analysis. After drafting the stories, we read all the interviews once more, to further ensure that we would not miss anything important and to make certain that we adhered to the voices of the interviewees.

### Notes on ethical issues and value of the research

We have made all regular precautions to ensure that our participants' identities and that of the school could not be traced. After the interviews were transcribed, the recordings were destroyed, and the school and the participants were given pseudonyms.

There is a certain dilemma in only using the stories of interviewees aged 20 or over, as if the experiences of younger students did not count. Using only materials relating to students aged 20 and above, however, meant that the interviewees had gained more experience, not only of Long Hill, since some of them had been working at a variety of jobs in the interval between attending schools. We do not know whether the views presented by our participants correspond to the views of those who entered the selected school at 16 and remained there. However, given the high proportion of returning-to-school students in the school we selected, their experiences are highly valuable in also mirroring some comparison to other types of pedagogy.

### The experience of eight returning students

This chapter is structured in such a way that we first present why our interviewees left the previous school(s) and why they selected Long Hill. We then proceed to discuss the pedagogy of Long Hill, and lastly we look at the way in which students' level of maturity might be reflected in their perceptions.

### The journey to Long Hill

The most common reasons for choosing the first upper secondary school had to do with location and accompanying classmates from the compulsory school up to the next school level. Three of the participants had attended vocational or technical studies in a specified school, and one individual had been in a school outside the capital city area.

Most of the interviewees had selected Long Hill because they lived relatively close to the school and had also heard good things about the organization of teaching and assessment, of which the main attraction was no final end-of-term examination. Among other attractive issues they mentioned was the school's online learning platform, where for example, teaching materials, assignment descriptions, and practical information are provided. One of the participants selected Long Hill because of a new study program combining practical and academic studies (naming the exact nature of that program would reveal which school this is). Apparently, Long Hill had also been gaining reputation, which further served to attract these young people.

### What did not work out in their previous school?

The participants had different reasons for leaving their previous school or schools. After a while, most of them realized they were not satisfied with their choice. While the reasons for leaving the previous school(s) were many and not always related to their academic competence, almost all interviewees had not been doing well in terms of grades or general engagement with their studies, or social life.

Lárus (21), Leifur (21), Katla (21) and Lúðvík (24), after graduating from compulsory school, all chose schools not far away from their homes. They emphasized how impersonal these schools were, and how little support they received from their teachers. Lárus and Katla, who had attended the same school, said that teachers in their school had not cared about them. Lúðvík, who had attended a different school, experienced the same:

> You were simply in a group and the teacher did not know your name ... after one or two weeks, then he just stopped trying ... it was obviously just a policy, not to spend time on students that would not study, or whom they did not find smart enough. (All translations of excerpts from the interviews are those of the authors.)

Ketill (20) and Knútur (20) both thought they were interested in computers and information technology and chose a school that offered programs within that field. However, they soon found out that neither the programs nor the school appealed to their interests and moved to Long Hill. Kristín (20) reported that the previous school was good in performing slide shows but such a teaching method did not attracted her.

Our interviewees were usually dissatisfied with the atmosphere and social relations in the previous school. Kári (23) was feeling bored, even though his school offered a study path he was really interested in. But the worst thing about his old school, according to him, was the student–teacher relationships: 'You felt like these teachers did not care'. Katla (21) said that the previous school was 'a very good school' but if 'one was not doing well, no one was bothering about it'. In general, however, the interviewees were rather careful in their judgments of the previous schools; even considered themselves responsible for not doing well there.

### *The pedagogy of Long Hill*

Long Hill prides itself in using pedagogical approaches different from the majority of the upper secondary schools. Here we are not focusing on the official policy of the school, although we were well aware of this, but rather on what the interviewees told us.

### *School ethos and student–teacher relationships*

All interviewees were pleased to have chosen Long Hill. Evidently, according to the students' perceptions, the school had managed to shape a culture where students felt engaged and connected with their studies. Most of the students felt that they had opportunities to influence their studies and express their opinions concerning their school experience.

All participants reported that the student–teacher relationships were pleasant and characterized by respectful attitudes. Furthermore, they described how students and staff regularly discussed possible improvements and ideas, and they felt that consideration was given to the opinions of the students. Lárus (20) noted that the best thing about Long Hill was 'kind of just the atmosphere in the school, or like, you know, how everybody is ...'. Other interviewees seconded this perception of the school. Lúðvík (24) said about the constructive school culture of Long Hill: 'They clearly have some policy ... they obviously have some kind of staff meetings or something, where they agree on this'.

# ALTERNATIVE EDUCATIONAL PROGRAMMES

We further explore two issues that appeared particularly prominent in the interviews as helping the students re-engage with their education; that is, the assessment policy and how the teachers approached their work.

## *The assessment policy*

According to the perceptions of our interviewees, the school policy of Long Hill crystallizes in a more relaxed learning environment than they were used to from their previous schools. The main reason for this is the school's assessment policy, in which the abandonment of end-of-term examinations weighs the most, combined with good access to teachers outside regular classes, limited homework, and an effective online learning platform.

Our interviewees maintained that they learned more by not having tests at the end of the term, since they needed to work constantly during the whole semester. They argued that this kind of assessment was fairer. For instance, Kári (23) argued: 'There are no end-of term exams, more of continuous assessment, and that suits me better'. The reason why it suited Kári better was that, according to him, he usually forgets everything he has just learnt, right after the examinations. He continued: 'This system is more convenient. You are always working in your education, and it requires better planning on your behalf'.

Test anxiety also came up in the interviews as a reason for liking the assessment practices, but not often. Kristín (20) described how much more she learns if there is a steady flow of assignments during the term. For her this is also related to test anxiety:

> And because I have so much test anxiety, the final the end-of-term examinations always failed me. ... Thus I decided to check it out here.

In accordance with the emphasis on students' responsibility and continuous assessment, the school organizes regular working lessons for students, where they have access to their teachers, but attendance is not mandatory. Nearly all of the interviewees talked about the advantage of this arrangement, resulting in good access to the teachers, when needed, as well as the possibility of completing homework within school hours. They had all used this opportunity, and because of this procedure, they hardly seemed to experience assignments as being too difficult or unmanageable.

News of the online learning platform was a reason why some of the participants selected the school, and they also told us how much they liked it. Some reported specifically how they used the platform to structure their studies and to locate information, for example, about assignments and due dates. Also importantly, the use of the online learning platform seemed to be integrated with assessment practices in such a way that our interviewees experienced teachers using the platform consistently to structure and perform the courses.

## *The teachers*

The participants talked about their teachers as an important factor in their satisfaction with Long Hill. They were described in general as cheerful, helpful, encouraging, supporting, and enthusiastic about their own work and students' achievement. For instance, Kristín (20) argued:

ALTERNATIVE EDUCATIONAL PROGRAMMES

> I just think this school really is amazing. And you know, the distinction between this school and other schools, are especially the teachers, because they are just somewhat so cheerful and alert and are interested in teaching. And I just find it really unusual in other schools ... [Long Hill is her third upper secondary school].

She further pointed out that the teachers 'make the syllabus fun'. Lúðvík (24) added that

> student–teacher relationships are ... really good here. Teachers really work hard, even though some students are, not all as interested, then they are really encouraging ... they obviously put great effort in [trying to ensure] that everyone succeeds.

Furthermore, Katla (21) noted that all her teachers knew her name and that it helped her to know that she is not just anybody.

Lárus (20) emphasized how hard the teachers tried to reach out to their students. He had done poorly in school and failed some of his courses, before he came to Long Hill. The number one reason for his success now is because 'here, the teachers believe in you'. Lárus described how he felt that the teachers in his old school did not care as much about him. And Lena (20) noted about the teachers:

> The sooner you get the opportunity to [understand that] someone believes in you in education ... the sooner you are ready to be willing to learn ... if they say, 'yes, you can do it', just try harder, try more ...

We were told, for example, by Kári (23), that 'the teachers are interested in hearing what you think'. Ketill (20) pulled the same strings; he said that his teachers have encouraged him to express his opinions and reflect on his reading in the social science program. That made him interested in the field and increased his courage in the school setting, or, as he put it: 'I felt more comfortable sharing my input and there is a lot of conversation in many of the classes'.

The teachers not only seem to be interested in encouraging students to reflect on the subject content, but also on the teaching methods. This is, for example, reflected in the words of Knútur (20): 'I feel like the teachers listen to you and many of their decisions are based on what we, the students, think'. Ketill (20) and Leifur (21) explained how the students sometimes were invited to write course syllabi with the teachers.

While the teachers are not all alike, their methods that lead to these judgments of their qualities are a whole school approach. All interviewees described their teachers in this way. It seemed common that teachers sat down with their students at the end of every semester to discuss students' objectives, strengths, and weaknesses. In that way, teachers showed students that their achievement and well-being matters to them and found ways to support them to continue working hard towards their aims.

### *The mature returning-to-school student*

Most of the interviewees described how they had matured since they first started upper secondary school. Some of them spoke at length about how they had been ready to work hard to re-engage in education when they were admitted to Long Hill. For instance, Leifur (20), devoted '18 months to work and [getting] some money and to realizing [what I wanted] ... and then I decided to complete this'. He especially noted his attitude had not been oriented to learning.

This may in part appear contrary to our investigation of the pedagogical practices that seem to engage students in their learning, because there is the possibility that for some of the oldest in the group various other types of pedagogy would be suitable. But it also seems reasonable to believe that because of their maturity, our participants appreciated the solid structure of the online learning platform and continuous assessment more than they would have done while they were younger.

We asked the participants what they felt about learning with the younger students. They did not complain about it, although in some instances they said that some of the younger students approached their studies more carelessly, but it did not disturb them because they seemed to be too mature to let the disengagement of others affect them.

We also asked about the participants' future plans for studies and how the school helped them approach these. We were surprised how ambitious some of the plans were; they mentioned anthropology, biology, computer science, medical science, physics, and psychology. Only two of the interviewees did not mention specific future disciplines, yet these two had plans to study at a specific university or in a specific country.

## Summary and conclusions

The purpose of this article is to understand how upper secondary school students, who had left one or more schools and returned to another school, which we purposefully selected, perceived the ways in which their current school met their needs in an academic program. We aim to answer the question whether they benefited from the pedagogical approach that relied, among other things, on an online learning platform and formative assessment.

At Long Hill, according to the perceptions of students, the faculty and staff seem to have developed a comfortable and constructive school ethos, which helps to make education meaningful and ambitious. Without an exception, the interviewees described the teachers in a positive way and their good qualities identified as being supportive, warm, and friendly. Practically none of the participants, having attended other schools before Long Hill, had ever experienced such a supportive learning environment. This emphasizes the impact of what takes place within the classrooms, the importance of a constructive pedagogy and a supportive school ethos, backed up by the attitudes of the teachers. This experience of the participants is in agreement with OECD's (2012a) contention that the lack of pedagogic training by Icelandic upper secondary school teachers hinders successful dropout prevention, and underpins the view that more pedagogical training should be given to teaching candidates and in-service teachers.

Not only the assessment policy and the online learning platform seem to be a whole school approach; our interviewees told us nothing critical at all about the teachers and reported, as we interpret it, excellent student–teacher relationships. This strongly agrees with what Mills and McGregor (2014) have maintained that 'works' well in alternative schools and is also in line with the argument by O'Donovan et al. (2015) emphasizing how important it is for students to experience meaning, control, and respect within the school setting. The student–teacher relationships, portrayed as respectful, seem a highly important aspect of the way our interviewees had re-engaged with their education. In the previous schools, almost none of them had experienced positive student–teacher relationships. The end result is that all our participants seemed to be content with their studies at Long Hill and planned to graduate from there.

Long Hill is rather small so it has in part the same features as the Australian alternative schools, described by, for instance, Mills and McGregor (2014). Our participants had in most cases transferred from schools with 1000–2000 students and the relatively small size of Long Hill apparently helped; here every one can know each other by name and it is also easier for administrators to maintain an overview of school activities. It should be emphasized, however, that features such as innovative teaching approaches by using the online learning platform and relying on continuous assessment have nothing to do with the size of the school.

While, as we believe this study indicates, the pedagogy used in upper secondary schools is important, it is, however, not the only aspect that matters. Ease of returning to school is another significant issue. Our participants reported various reasons for leaving one or more schools and returning to upper secondary education through Long Hill. While the stories we were told are usually not without difficulties somewhere along the way, our participants, however, seem to have been able to return to upper secondary school with relative ease. On this issue, we disagree with the OECD (2012a, see above), which suggested it should not be so easy to transfer between schools as it has been in Iceland. On the contrary, the stories of our interviewees support the importance of a flexible upper secondary school level.

School location is another salient circumstance. All participants but one lived relatively near Long Hill when the interviews were conducted. It surprised us how much weight location had in the choice of a school to re-enter, since we had thought the school's reputation for welcoming returning-to-school students would rank higher in students' selective priorities. However, this is in line with Jónasson & Blöndal's (2002) findings, that the largest groups re-entering school, chose a nearby upper secondary school. The location is of significance, probably not least because of students' financial and social circumstances, underlining how important it is for young people to be able to choose a school close to their homes. And the location may be even more relevant in the rural parts of Iceland than within the capital city area.

The study indicates the importance of academic upper secondary programs being available for all teenagers or young adults, who want to attend such programs. The online learning platform and formative assessment, approved of by the students, who had re-entered Long Hill after studying in other schools, seem to work well as technical procedures in support of a whole school approach where teachers develop good working relationships with students. This arrangement was apparently beneficial to the students, since they might not otherwise have been able to attend an academic program that re-engaged them in education they found meaningful and useful. This form of schooling opens 'access for all' to a wider extent and in some instances provides training in decision-making, for instance regarding the organization of course material.

The stories our interviewees told us suggest that educators, the public, and especially policy makers, should re-consider how dropout is viewed as a problem of school ineffectiveness (Ministry of Education, Science, and Culture, 2014a). We suggest viewing dropout and the right of teenagers and adults to return to free-of-charge upper secondary education as practical issues to be solved. The answers range from technical matters, for instance finding ways in which students can transfer credits for courses they have completed successfully in a previous school, to more demanding tasks, such as educating teachers in innovative pedagogies of the kinds that seem to work at Long Hill.

### *Final words*

In light of what we consider success at Long Hill in teaching re-entering students, we are worried about political complaints focusing on the low proportions of upper secondary school students, who enter vocational studies. Currently, for instance, the

ALTERNATIVE EDUCATIONAL PROGRAMMES

Federation of Icelandic Industries has defined it as an objective to increase the proportion of upper secondary school students, who select industry vocational and other practical studies from 12% to 25% within 10 years (e.g., Hafsteinsdóttir, 2015). While there should of course be ample access to quality vocational education across the country, we emphasize that it is also an issue of social justice that teenagers and young adults are able to attend any program they want, including traditional academic programs emphasizing natural or social sciences or the humanities, as well as less established study lines in the arts or programs with an emphasis on design or media. It is a democratic right that the students themselves should decide what kind of study program – academic, college-preparatory, industry-oriented, practical – suits their interests and future plans.

**Funding**

This study is supported by the Nordic Center of Excellence Justice Through Education (a NordForsk) project 2013–2018. It comprises a part of a research project conducted in cooperation with Glenda McGregor, Griffith University, Brisbane, Australia, and Martin Mills, The University of Queensland, Brisbane, Australia.

**Note**

1. The research is registered with the Icelandic Data Protection Agency with a report no. S7413/ 2015.

**References**

Alþingi [The Parliament]. (2006–2007). *Svar menntamálaráðherra við fyrirspurn Björgvins G. Sigurðssonar um brottfall úr framhaldsskólum* [The education minister's answer to a parliament member's inquiry about dropout from upper secondary schools]. Retrieved 9 April from http:// www.althingi.is/altext/130/s/pdf/1406.pdf

Alþingi [The Parliament]. (2014). *Frumvarp til fjárlaga fyrir árið 2015* [Governmental fiscal budget proposal for 2015]. Retrieved 24 March 2015 from http://www.althingi.is/altext/pdf/144/s/ 0001.pdf

Blöndal, K. B. (2014). *Student disengagement and school dropout: Parenting practices as context* (Doctoral dissertation). The University of Iceland, School of Education, Reykjavík.

Blöndal, K. S., Jónasson, J. T., & Tannhäuser, A.-C. (2011). Dropout in a small society: Is the Icelandic case somehow different?. In S. Lamb, E. Markussen, R. Teese, N. Sandberg, & J. Polosel (Eds.), *School dropout and completion: International comparative studies in theory and policy.* Dordrecht: Springer. doi:10.1007/978-90-481-9763-7_13

Braun, V., & Clarke, V. (2006). Using thematic analysis in psychology. *Qualitative Research in Psychology, 3,* 77–101. doi:10.1191/1478088706qp063oa

Frostad, P., Pijl, S. J., & Mjaavatn, P. E. (2015). Losing all interest in school: Social participation as a predictor of the intention to leave upper secondary school early. *Scandinavian Journal of Educational Research, 59*(1), 110–122. doi:10.1080/ 00313831.2014.904420

# ALTERNATIVE EDUCATIONAL PROGRAMMES

Guðmundsson, G., & Daníelsdóttir, H. K. (2013). Brotthvarf og endurkoma fullorðinna í nám á framhaldsskólastigi [Dropout and return of young adults to upper secondary education]. *Tímarit Um Menntarannsóknir* [*Journal of Educational Research (Iceland)*], *10*, 61–77.

Hafsteinsdóttir, G. (2015). *Hvernig kveikjum við áhuga fleiri nemenda? Getum við leitað á ný mið og jafnað kynjahlutfall? Er jafnara kynjahlutfall leiðin?* [How do we increase the interest of more students? Can we attract more women to selecting vocational education?] Talk at the Education Day of SA-Business-Iceland, 19 February 2015. Retrieved 11 April 2015 from http://www.si.is/malaflokkar/menntamal-og-fraedsla/menntafrettir/menntastofa-si-fjallad-um-fjolgun-nemenda-i-idnnam-med-aherslu-a-kynjahlutfall

Jónasson, J. T. (1994). Skipt um skoðun. Um flutning nemenda á milli þrenns konar námsbrauta í framhaldsskóla [Changing one's mind. On the transfer of students between three types of study programs in upper secondary school]. *Uppeldi Og Menntun*, *3*, 63–81.

Jónasson, J. T., & Blöndal, K. S. (2002). *Ungt fólk og framhaldsskólinn. Rannsókn á námsgengi og afstöðu '75 árgangsins til náms* [Young people and the upper secondary school. Research on learning progress and attitudes to learning of people born in 1975]. Reykjavík: University of Iceland Social Science Research Institute and the University of Iceland Press.

Lingard, B., & Mills, M. (2007). Pedagogies making a difference: Issues of social justice and inclusion. *International Journal of Inclusive Education*, *11*(3), 233–244. doi:10.1080/13603110701237472

Lupton, R., & Hempel-Jorgensen, A. (2012). The importance of teaching: Pedagogical constraints and possibilities in working-class schools. *Journal of Education Policy*, *27*(5), 601–620. doi:10.1080/02680939.2012.710016

McGregor, G., & Mills, M. (2012). Alternative education sites and marginalised young people: 'I wish there were more schools like this one'. *International Journal of Inclusive Education*, *16*(8), 843–862. doi:10.1080/13603116.2010.529467

McGregor, G., Mills, M., Te Riele, K., & Hayes, D. (2015). Excluded from school: Getting a second chance at a 'meaningful' education. *International Journal of Inclusive Education*, *19*(6), 608–625. doi:10.1080/13603116.2014.961684

Mills, M., & McGregor, G. (2014). *Re-engaging young people in education. Learning from alternative schools.* London: Routledge.

Ministry of Education, Science, and Culture. (2014a). *Hvítbók um umbætur í menntun* [White Paper on education reform]. Reykjavík: Author.

Ministry of Education, Science, and Culture. (2014b). *Brotthvarf úr framhaldsskólum haustið 2013* [Dropout from upper secondary schools, autumn 2013]. Reykjavík: Author. Retrieved 21 April 2015 from http://brunnur.stjr.is/mrn/utgafuskra/utgafa.nsf/RSSPage.xsp?documentId=8D1741F0B80D62F000257CC9004C90A8&action=openDocument

Nordlund, M., Stehlik, T., & Strandh, M. (2013). Investment in second-chance education for adults and income development in Sweden. *Journal of Education and Work*, *26*(5), 514–538. doi:10.1080/13639080.2012.664633

O'Donovan, R., Berman, N., & Wierenge, A. (2015). How schools can move beyond inclusion. *International Journal of Inclusive Education*, *19*(6), 645–658. doi:10.1080/13603116.2014.961686

OECD (Organization for Economic Co-operation and Development). (2012a). *Towards a strategy to prevent dropout in Iceland. Result of the OECD-Iceland workshop preventing dropout in upper secondary schools in Iceland.* Retrieved 24 March 2015 from http://www.oecd.org/iceland/49451462.pdf

OECD (Organization for Economic Co-operation and Development). (2012b). *Education at a glance 2012. OECD indicators.* Paris: OECD Publications. Retrieved 8 September 2015 from http://www.oecd.org/edu/EAG%202012_e-book_EN_200912.pdf

OECD (Organization for Economic Co-operation and Development). (2013). *Education at a glance, 2013. Country note.* Retrieved 29 April 2015 from http://www.oecd.org/edu/Iceland_EAG2013%20Country%20Note.pdf

Ross, S., & Gray, J. (2005). Transitions and re-engagement through second chance education. *The Australian Educational Researcher*, *32*(3), 103–140. doi:10.1007/BF03216829

Rumberger, R. W. (2011). *Dropping out: Why students drop out of high school and what can be done about it.* Cambridge, MA: Harvard Educational Press.

The Upper Secondary School Act No. 57/1988. (1988).

The Upper Secondary School Act No. 80/1996. (1996).

# ALTERNATIVE EDUCATIONAL PROGRAMMES

The Upper Secondary School Act No. 92/2008. (2008).

Rumberger, R. W., & Lim, S. A. (2008). *Why Students Drop Out of School: A Review of 25 Years of Research. California Dropout Research Project Report #15*. Santa Barbara: University of California, Santa Barbara.

Tveir bjóða ekki upp á þriggja ára nám [Two do not offer a three year education program]. (2015, April 18th). *Ruv.is*. Retrieved 29 April 2015 from http://www.ruv.is/frett/tveir-bjoda-ekki-upp-a-thriggja-ara-nam

# Disciplinary regimes of 'care' and complementary alternative education

Pat Thomson and Jodie Pennacchia

In schools, the notion of 'care is often synonymous with welfare and disciplinary regimes. Drawing on Foucault, and a study of alternative education (AE) across the UK, and looking in depth at two cases of complementary AE, we identify three types of disciplinary regimes at work in schools: (1) dominant performative reward and punishment, (2) team-building and (3) therapeutic. We argue that while all three regimes aim to steer identified students back to the norm, the two complementary approaches that we saw avoided the narrow instrumental behaviourist approaches of the dominant pattern. In so doing, they also opened up wider horizons of possibility and ways to be and become.

The notion of care is ubiquitous to alternative education (AE), as well as to what Roger Slee helpfully calls 'regular schools' (Slee, 2011). Researchers around the world, and working across disciplines, regularly report that young people in AE settings experience far greater levels of care than in their former school (Aron, 2006; Denny, Fleming, Clark, & Wall, 2004; Guerin & Denti, 1999; Kim & Taylor, 2008; Raywid, 1994). Noddings (1992) and Fielding (2006) see care in contemporary schooling operating in support of either instrumentalism or person-centred-ness. We share their concern about instrumentalist uses of care, but seek to trouble a binary view. Our paper examines the ways in which care is manifest in complementary AE provision, as part of the organisation of welfare and discipline in a school. Our interest is primarily in differences in alternative educational organisational regimes and what this might suggest about, and for, both regular and alternative schooling.

We draw on a Foucauldian conceptual frame in order to consider how schools keep order, and outline the dominant mode of performative reward and punishment discipline that we saw in AE in a recent national study. We then present two short-term alternative programmes – one 'team-building and training' and the other therapeutic in approach. We suggest that these two programmes appear to suffer less from the performative push that dominates both regular schools and AE. We speculate on the implications of these differences. We begin with a brief discussion of alternative and complementary education.

## Alternative and complementary education

AE is defined in English law not by its pedagogy but by its enrolment. AE is designated specifically

ALTERNATIVE EDUCATIONAL PROGRAMMES

... for pupils who, because of exclusion, illness or other reasons, would not otherwise receive suitable education; education arranged by schools for pupils on a fixed period exclusion; and pupils being directed by schools to off-site provision to improve their behaviour. (http://www.education.gov.uk/aboutdfe/statutory/)

A vast array of sites and services offer AE. Some are full-time and long term, some full-time and shorter-term (one to three terms), and there is also part-time provision of various durations. Part-time provision is intended to contribute to a young person's educational programme and is thus known as 'complementary'.

Complementary AE varies enormously, ranging from short-term interventions geared to change behaviour to the provision of vocational education, which offers specific training and qualifications. Complementary programmes are offered both on and off the school site, and by a range of providers, including charities, further education and schools themselves. Schools might for instance purchase places in complementary programmes provided by others, commission a programme for their students, or establish and run programmes in-house.

In England, the allocation of 'pupil premium' funding to schools, specific funding designed to allow them to provide additional support and services to young people they deem at risk of failure, has created both incentive for and increased interest in complementary programmes. Cuts to local authority provision, the development of school-run collaborative processes for young people excluded from school, the growth of 'managed moves' programmes (Abdelnoor, 2007; Harris, Vincent, Thomson, & Toalster, 2006; Vincent, Harris, Thomson, & Toalster, 2007) and a recent trial to test out schools' capacity to commission all of their own AE provision (Institute of Education (University of London) and the National Foundation for Educational Research (NFER), 2013) have all contributed to a significant increase in complementary AE. This expanded AE is run either by schools themselves or with a small group of 'preferred providers' (Institute of Education (University of London) and the National Foundation for Educational Research (NFER), 2014). In this paper, we focus on complementary AE run by external providers for schools that serve populations facing ongoing poverty in 'austerity Britain'.

## Our orientation to care

In the famous text *Discipline and Punish (1977)*, Foucault differentiated between types of discipline, which operated to maintain social order. He delineated an historical shift from violent punishment to ever more self-disciplining practices. Foucault's later work, on technologies of the self and the ethic of care of the self, elaborated the ways in which individuals might, on their own or with the help of others, discipline and groom their bodies and their conduct. Through the ethic and practice of 'caring' for the mind, body and soul, the individual strove to produce happiness, purity and wisdom (Foucault, 1982/1997, 1988). Nevertheless, incarceration and violence of various kinds always remain a possibility for the recalcitrant who refuse self-discipline. Foucault nominated schools as quintessential sites of disciplinary practice, pointing to the ways in which various regimes of surveillance, normalisation and categorisation operated via punishment and reward, assessment and pedagogical approaches.

Foucauldian school studies by Ian Hunter (1994) and Slee (1995, 2011) both show the ways in which reward and punishment systems produce overt and covert resistances, with more pastoral approaches being more conducive to the production of self-managing

85

students. John Devine's (1996) ethnography in one New York school showed how the shift to external policing produced a degree of sullen compliance but considerable alienation, truancy and failure. Kathleen Nolan (2011) came to similar conclusions in her study of the negative consequences of police in a Bronx school.

Drawing on this body of work, we identify three school disciplinary regimes at work in English schools and in AE:

- reward and punishment systems that use continued surveillance and isolation
- team-building regimes in which both bodies and minds are apparently voluntarily 're-educated' and
- the therapeutic management of the psyche and the body.

We discuss these in detail later in the paper.

Foucault argued that discipline works to create norms that (re)produce what it is possible to be, see, say and know. Significant bodies of expertise and experts are created around norming disciplinary practices. School discipline for instance has its own experts and expertise, routinely included in teacher education programmes. The work of discipline 'gurus' – Bill Rogers, Sue Cowley and the like – is largely geared to the production of internalised self-discipline through the setting of rules, the creation of a positive environment, the judicious use of praise, reward and punishment and the avoidance of confrontation. However, this 'common-sense' approach allows non-conforming students to be identified – see for example Maclure and colleagues on the production of students as 'problems' (Maclure, Jones, Holmes, & Macrae, 2012) and Simon Bailey on the diagnosis of students 'with ADHD' (Bailey, 2013).

Once the variously disorderly have been identified, different bodies of expertise are deployed. Medicalised discourse practices are now synonymous with 'special education' (Harwood & Allan, 2014; Harwood, 2005). Therapeutic approaches, often reliant on talking and various ways of 'facing reality' (Glasser, 1990), are commonly used, particularly for students who have been identified as having more generalised emotional/behavioural conduct disorders (Besley, 2002). There are also versions of training/conditioning regimes solely based on reward and punishment (Lewis, 2011) that emanate from the work of Skinner (1968).

The literatures on AE suggest that versions of the therapeutic largely dominate provision, with researchers frequently referring to the value that students place on having someone to talk to and a caring environment (see published literature review by Thomson, 2014). Researchers (e.g. Allan, 1996; Caulkins, 2011) also note that access to AE is, for the majority of young people, via processes that both pathologise and quasi-medicalise; these processes make young people available for a range of specialised interventions.

Our paper uses and builds on this body of work. We begin with the notion that the school, as an institution, has a disciplinary regime. Our question is not whether the school has a disciplinary regime or not, nor whether the disciplinary regime is 'good' or 'bad', but rather what kind of disciplinary regime operates, and what work it does (c.f. Gore, 1993). Key to our argument is the Foucauldian understanding that power circulates and is not top down, and that subjects have some (limited) power to choose how to be and become within disciplinary regimes (Foucault, 1982). The harsher the disciplinary regime, the less room there is to exercise choice. The Foucauldian notion of power as positive and constitutive allows for differentiated readings of what AE programme affords different students.

## The research

This paper draws on data from a 2014 UK-wide study of alternative provision (Thomson & Pennacchia, 2014). This was funded by The Prince's Trust and explored how quality is understood, ensured and challenged in the AE sector. The data consisted of 17 case studies of a range of types of AE, including full time and long term, as well as complementary provisions (see the 17 case studies on http://www.princes-trust.org.uk/delivery_partners_for_xl/xlmicrosite/results/whats_the_alternative.aspx). We saw programmes with a range of specialisms designed to engage young people with diverse interests; we sought quality providers that were rated well by commissioners and auditors (discussed in full in the 2014 report).

We used a common set of questions to guide both data generation and analysis across all of our sites (Yin, 1994). We wanted for example to understand how young people arrived at the provision, the everyday routines, the curriculum on offer, relations with referring schools and with families. Data generation was based on visits to sites that lasted 1–3 days, and included observation, interviews and conversations with staff and young people, photographs, and the collection of a range of documentary materials. Young people were engaged through informal conversations and focus groups, during which we sought their views on the experience of attending AE.

We discuss here two of the English complementary provisions that we visited. We selected these because they were exceptions to the dominant pattern we observed and which we discuss next.

## The dominant disciplinary regime in AE provision

Schools in many parts of the world are now subject to a policy agenda that compels them to focus on performance. This policy agenda is particularly advanced in England and Wales, where tests and exam results are augmented by regular external inspections. Schools are compelled to compile and keep updated a range of school data, which shows how continued improvement is occurring in student learning, teaching and leadership and management. Standardised computing systems support an audit architecture, which now dominates the ways in which everyday life in school proceeds (Ball, Maguire, & Braun, 2011; Gillborn & Youdell, 2000; Ozga, 2009).

The same accountability and audit agenda applies to AE, particularly that which is intended as a full-time school experience on either a short- or longer-term basis. These AE provisions are regularly inspected, as are schools, with judgments about their success/failure drawn from a combination of some observation of practices, and a thorough perusal of paperwork.

Our study showed that the disciplinary regimes that operated in full-time AE followed the same performative pattern. As we have reported in detail elsewhere (Thomson & Pennacchia, 2015), AE disciplinary approaches are now strongly framed by the need to 'show' what is happening to, with and for students. This has led to student attendance and conduct being monitored, graded and graphed across lessons, days, weeks and terms. Charts and folders, both hard copy and digital, are easily/readily available for inspectors – as evidence of systematic monitoring and intervention – and for parents/regular school – as evidence of progress (of lack of it). There has also been a shift to the use of textbooks and worksheets, which can be similarly charted and graphed to show that alternative providers are attending to learning.

ALTERNATIVE EDUCATIONAL PROGRAMMES

The swing to the auditable and performative has meant that AE, particularly but not exclusively in England, has become largely dominated by behaviourist approaches to discipline. Regimes of reward and punishment lend themselves to straightforward forms of representation in ways that talking therapeutic approaches do not. Contrary to the research literatures on AE, we saw a swing away from the therapeutic to reward and punishment, with talking therapies largely confined to supplementary interventions to support, and legitimate the overarching behaviourist regime. We suggest that this shift serves the interests of the AE institutions first and foremost, but does however align with the increasingly carceral approach taken to young people in welfare, employment and justice systems.

These dominant 'brownie points' systems, as we have dubbed them, offer restricted choices to students. Young people can elect to conform and be rewarded, or resist and be subject to more extreme punishments, which range from isolation to permanent exclusion. And where young people are in the youth justice system, refusal to comply in AE can contribute to actual incarceration.

A very small proportion of young people from full-time AE provision return to their referring schools. Staff that we interviewed suggested that young people were not able to adjust to the regular school environment. We interpret this to mean that the AE disciplinary regimes failed to help young people manage themselves any differently in regular school than they had before their referral. The Skinnerian regimes designed to show good AE performance did not afford the kinds of self-discipline that are the expected norm in the regular school.

Some of the complementary provisions that we saw also tended to this kind of behaviourist disciplinary regime. We did however see two other disciplinary regimes at work – team-building and therapeutic approaches. We now discuss each of these in turn, and in some detail.

### Major Tom's team-builders

Major Tom's is a 'fun and fitness' programme. Run by former military personnel, it is commissioned by schools to work with groups of selected young people. Major Tom's is generally engaged by a school to work with young people who are seen to need additional support with educational outcomes, engagement and well-being. All activities take place at the commissioning school site.

We observed the programme in one 'struggling' secondary school in the Midlands – a school whose GCSE results are below expectation and where there was considerable external pressure to show dramatic improvements in a short space of time. The school was one where we had previously researched alternative provision, at that time in an off-site annexe (Russell & Thomson, 2011; Thomson & Russell, 2007, 2009). The head teacher had been involved in a postgraduate programme in the university and had conducted practitioner action research into disciplinary practices. The school had had no permanent exclusions for over two years (at the time we conducted this research), and was often a receiver of students who were formally excluded from other schools.

We saw the Major Tom's programme in its first year of operation in the school. The nature of the programme to be offered was negotiated by the head and placed under the supervision of the senior of two deputy heads. While the school did have a staff complement devoted to learning support, discipline was largely the responsibility of class teachers with some additional support from year level and more senior staff.

# ALTERNATIVE EDUCATIONAL PROGRAMMES

Major Tom's ran several groups within the school, all of them for students deemed likely to benefit from improvements to motivation, attendance, social interaction and so on. We were particularly interested in one group of nine year 11 girls. The school decided to have a single-sex group because these were girls were seen by teachers and senior staff as underperforming and possessing 'a range of social, emotional, behavioural and academic needs'. The school felt that the programme would be 'in the best interests of quickly building rapport' (Deputy Head).

Participation was not compulsory. The Deputy Head told us

> The way we pitched it was: we think this will be really good for your son or daughter because ... Now it's not mandatory because it's a rewards based programme but we feel that your child, both socially, academically and emotionally they will get something out of it.

The girls we met chose to be in the programme when it was offered to them and they worked with Major Tom's for 2–3 hours each week. Their programme emphasised teamwork and peer relationships, and activities were intended to develop collaborative working, comradeship and trust. The Major Tom's instructor told us that the military ethos provided different ways of teaching, with an emphasis on 'problem solving, fun, fitness and resilience'. In a focus group, the girls told us that they were 'probably more comfortable around girls', because they were doing strenuous physical activities such as circuit training and working together to move very heavy objects.

The head teacher, inspired by a programme for 'naughty girls' in Australia that he had read about (Thomson, McQuade, & Rochford, 2005a, 2005b), allowed the girls to design a uniform variation to signal their particular 'identity' – they wore jungle pants and army boots on the days in which they were involved in the programme. They also had a space within the school that they could call their own. In addition to working with Major Tom's, the school trained the girls to be cross-age tutors, and they worked in the local primary school helping their younger peers with basic literacy difficulties, and in their school breakfast and after-school clubs.

The girls made the most of the opportunity on offer to them and they did indeed 'turn around'. 'I've calmed down a lot', one participant told us, and that made it easier for her to cope in relatively unchanged classrooms and the demands of exams. Initially apparently destined to leave school early to join the swelling ranks of local unemployed youth, the girls grew committed to finishing their time at the school and then going on to sixth form or to vocational education. As the Deputy Head put it,

> ... eight from nine have improved their attendance to an average for the course of ninety-two per cent. Some of those girls' average was as low as eighty-five per cent. And five of those girls, at the moment, are predicted to get five A to C including English and Maths. Some are slightly lower but they are all on track to hit targets now.

The programme could thus be seen to be a highly successful intervention in the trajectories of 'troubled and troublesome' girls (Lloyd, 2005).

In separate conversations with the girls, we were told that the Major Tom's instructor was:

- accepting – 'We get on with him.' 'He knows what we're like.'
- fair – 'He treats us the same way as we treat him so we realise that if we didn't treat him with respect he won't do the same with us.'

- encouraging – 'He always says encouraging things.'
- challenging – 'When we, like, say we are not doing stuff he says "yes you are doing it!"'
- flexible – 'Like if we can't do something on our own they make us do it together.'
- committed – 'He won't give up on us.' 'We don't give up.'

We see here the quality of relationships that are discussed in the AE literatures (Thomson, 2014). The girls 'get on' with the Major Tom's instructor. However, the quality of relationships is not seen as an end in themselves. The programme is not directed towards 'having someone to talk to'. Having a good relationship within the group and with the instructor is integral to the development of 'stickability' and learning the value of interdependent behaviour. Keeping at something, and doing it with others, was seen to pay off more generally, including in schooling and future life.

Major Tom's was presented as an offer, which the girls and their families could choose to take up. There was of course some individualising of the behavioural and academic issues facing the girls, but the programme was offered to many more than just their group of nine. The girls were not isolated and ghettoised. There was official school interest in their progress – the Deputy Head took a close interest in what was happening. The school expected the girls to 'put back' for the special programme they were enjoying, and offered the additional privileges of space and clothing. Through this, the girls were made responsible and trusted rather than being seen as deficient and incapable.

The school saw the Major Tom's programme as being about more than improving exam results and thus being of primary benefit for the school itself. The young people's participation in the programme was directed to improving life chances. As the Deputy Head put it:

> Some schools unfortunately have treated it (the funding that paid for Major Tom's) as merely an extra resource just to deal with certain individuals. To some extent to lion-tame them a little bit and we're not about that…

The girls understood this commitment, as evidenced by the ways in which their positive feelings about the Major Tom's programme extended to the school itself.

> … we think of it (school) as a positive thing rather than a negative thing.

This was despite nothing about the remainder of their school programme having changed. Participation in Major Tom's and the associated tutoring activities were enough to make school a place worth being, and further education more possible and desirable.

We had one nagging concern about the programme. Major Tom's is not an army recruitment programme and its staff are very clear that this is not on their agenda. Yet, in promoting 'team work, fun and fitness' as a key benefit of military service, the realities of contemporary foreign policies played out in and as war games are left unexamined. We worried about the potential for the programme to glamorise military service, and make it more desirable and achievable. At the time of writing, none of the girls had elected for a military vocation and we have no information about their attitudes to defence policy and personnel more generally.

## ALTERNATIVE EDUCATIONAL PROGRAMMES

*Major Tom's as a disciplinary regime*

Major Tom's programme worked to defuse and reframe the girls' overt resistance to schooling. Importantly, it did not work by coercion. The programme offered a real choice. Rather than exercise their power against the school, the girls could choose to be involved or not, with no apparent consequences for refusal.

We wondered why the programme appeared to be an attractive choice.

On the surface, Major Tom's offered the girls something rather unattractive – involvement in a physical training regime. We were curious about why girls for whom PE lessons were normally a site of resistance would apparently choose to engage so enthusiastically. We also noted that they appeared unconcerned about what we saw as heightened levels of surveillance – they worked in a small group under the watchful gaze of the instructor with a senior leader never too far away.

It could be argued that participation in the programme served some of the same purposes as resistance – the girls 'got out of' some lessons. And they had already been singled out as 'different' by the school's ordinary discipline regime, and the programme did not change this position. However, participation in the programme allowed the girls to simultaneously fit in *and* stand out. In choosing their own uniform variant – camouflage pants and military-style boots – they were able to visibly, but legitimately, be other than the unattractive school uniform. Their appearance was quasi-masculinised, but referenced dress codes outside school, and in popular culture. They still stood out, but in a way that was 'on trend' but not posh/pretentious.

We also suspect that the boot-camp-style training appeal brought a discourse practice often seen on television into the school. Young people are now immersed in celebrity cultures, and routinely see famous women (and men) engaged in the same kind of physically testing routines that they were offered. While this activity was abnormal in school terms, strenuous physical training is normal in popular culture and in high-profile sports such as football. Engaging in boot camp routines within the school sutured a practice that is possibly more desirable into the school assemblage. The programme allowed the girls a way to demonstrate that they were capable of hard work, a norm that many young people see as important (Allen & Mendick, 2012). In so doing, the programme additionally expanded the ways in which it was possible to 'be' a girl in the school. The group could become 'good girls', when they worked with younger peers. Up until this time, the only way they could occupy this position was through compliance with expected school rules. This new 'responsibilising' activity showed the girls as 'deserving' of the special treatment they had received.

However, as noted, the girls were not isolated by their participation and sequestered off from the rest of the school. They were not the only group in the school engaging in the programme. Major Tom's was an 'othering' through which it was possible for the girls, and peers, to gain official approval (a reward) as well as the pleasure of seeing embodied self-improvement in levels of fitness (a disciplining of the self to provide its own internalised reward system) (c.f. Kelly & Harrison, 2009). Importantly, the girls were not offered a whole-scale alternative curriculum. They were still expected to participate in sufficient classes to achieve their complement of GCSE subjects. They were thus still part of the overall school assemblage and not removed from its most important practice.

We understand the Major Tom's programme to have worked to expand the girls' horizons of possibility, winning their 'souls' (Rose, 1999) by offering ways in which they could become part of the norm, while still being 'different'. This was accomplished via an imbrication of a technology of care – physical training of the body – and an ethic of care –

an opportunity for the girls to do morally approved 'good work' in the form of tutoring as well as exhibiting care for themselves. As the school expanded its disciplinary regime and brought in aspects of popular cultures as part of a practice of embodied physical and ethical retraining, the girls no longer had to exercise power against the school in order to 'become somebody' (Wexler, Crichlow, Kern, & Martusewicz, 1992).

### Thursday's Child Farm

Thursday's Child Farm provides a one-week residential programme for groups of secondary-aged pupils from across England. The young people live on the farm from Monday until Friday, accompanied by members of staff from their school. They engage in all aspects of farm life, including feeding the animals, cleaning out the enclosures, milking and horse grooming. They help cook all of the meals, and go for night-time walks, play board games and watch films. The young people engage in a level of physical activity that would not normally be a part of their day. Alongside this increased physical exertion, the farm has dietary rules – no processed foods, sugar and fizzy or caffeinated drinks. On the farm, young people do not have access to electronic equipment, including mobile phones.

The combination of these elements is summed up by farm staff as a 'life swap' experience for the young people. They exchange their lives back in their neighbourhoods and school for something completely different. Farm staff are sure that eliminating some of the trappings of everyday life ensures that the young people are positioned to be open to the therapeutic components of the programme, the farm's key emphasis. Young people have one-to-one time with a therapist and with other members of farm staff, and engage in a range of group counselling sessions with their peers and school staff. Meal times are crucial to the therapeutic experience and each day begins with the group eating together and reflecting on their experiences. The physical space in the farm building is designed to facilitate a 'family-living' environment, with a large table and comfortable 'lived-in' sofas.

Thursday's Child Farm aims to establish long-term relationships with schools. Their preference is for schools to nominate young people for a week on the farm in consultation with farm staff so that the aims of, and planning for, the week are shared and agreed. Thursday's Child staff attend a meeting with parents and students to explain what is on offer; participation in the programme is voluntary. School staff come to the farm with their students, and farm staff ideally also have the opportunity to brief them on the programme, its aims and processes and to debrief afterwards. Parents are invited to the fifth and last day on the farm to hear about what their children have done, and to see the farm for themselves. A farm staff member goes back to the school to pass on information about what the students have done during their week away.

This process is something more substantial than just good information flow and communication. The school and the farm share a common goal for a particular group of young people. The teachers who also live on the farm with their students share experiences and they have changed interaction patterns and common memories that they can talk about later, thus recreating the different relationship associated with the farm. Parents too have seen for themselves something of the farm and have some new reference points for conversation. This is more than simply the provision of respite from everyday life; there are threads weaving the experience into the young people's biographies.

However, Thursday's Farm is a one-week experience and the farm staff do not want to over-claim its benefits. The resident therapist on the farm maintains that the farm

# ALTERNATIVE EDUCATIONAL PROGRAMMES

experience does have an immediate impact. However, this does not carry simply and seamlessly back at school. As one staff member told us, tracking their young people suggests that

> ...after they leave us there is a dip, but then they improve in the medium term... that is why the schools are happy with us and we didn't lose a single school last year which is great but one of the things that you've got to manage is the expectations because the fact is that the schools expect these kids to go away and come back transformed. They are transformed when they are here, but when they go back into school they will have a lapse sometimes. One kid who has been to the farm and then struggles when they go back into school is enough for teachers to say 'well that didn't work'. But if you look around now there is no way that anyone who sees the kids could say that this hasn't had an impact on them.

The group of students we met was on the farm to improve their confidence, self-esteem, behaviour and peer relationships. Many of the 12 were very withdrawn, including two young people who rarely spoke (selective mutes). We observed the young people in the mainstream school setting at a meeting before the programme, as well as on the farm itself. The farm appeared to be a particularly potent experience for the very withdrawn.

Young people were required to 'care for' animals as soon as they arrived. Staff saw this as establishing the lived experience of caring not only for the self but also for the natural world. Animal husbandry established the interdependence of nature/people. A farm staff member explained this to us as

> ...attending holistically to a child in the sense that you are allowing a completely new experience for their mind, body and spirit and they are living in a community and a setting where nature and animals play a really big part in reconnecting the children to who they are.

As the young people were engaged with farm staff in everyday farm tasks, they talked one to one and in small groups about the things that they found interesting. Conversations beginning with horse grooming or gardening typically meandered but often included the young people's concerns, fears and worries about school, home and neighbourhood. All staff on the farm were able to engage young people in conversations that also mattered to them – topics were of mutual interest and not manufactured for the purpose of covert counselling. We were told and saw for ourselves that the starting point for conversations was the young person's own 'narrative'; the purpose of dialogue was so that young people might learn to

> ...trust in themselves that they can talk honestly about how they feel... And we start with the children: where are they from; what do they enjoy most? It's not starting with pathology.

We did not interview the young people at the farm in the same way as we had in the Major Tom's programme. It would have been a disruption to the carefully structured programme of activities. We did however see the kinds of conversations and interactions that the young people had with both farm staff and their teachers. These were often what farm staff would describe as 'parental' and 'loving', in that the staff were genuinely interested in the young person and their current and future lives.

Farm staff worked to support school staff to carry these kinds of practices back to school.

# ALTERNATIVE EDUCATIONAL PROGRAMMES

> So there is a lot of shared values between the school and us, and when their teachers come to see us they seem to be inspired by what they see and they take that back to the school (therapist)

The resident therapist meets one to one with each young person during their stay. Drawing on this meeting she offers new information to the school that they can use to modify the students' regular programmes.

> I write a brief report on every child from the session that I've had with them and then we do a thing called 'school report' and that will include the celebration notes; my experience of the child in the session and a general picture of the child at the farm with any recommendations that we might make to the school. So we might say that a child's actual level of intellect is way above where she is performing and if you put her in a new environment she'll show real curiosity and interest and ability (therapist).

In optimal conditions, such as the situation we observed, there was an option not only for the young person to change but also for their school to change what they did for the young person.

## Thursday's Child Farm as a disciplinary regime

Thursday's Child Farm, a 'psy' provision, aims to change young people. It claims most success with young people who are apparently compliant in school, but resist by refusing to speak or actively participate. Their choice is to withdraw their voice. But the formation of educated subjects requires more of students than simply being present; it requires social and verbal interaction. So these young people are identified, not by their infractions of rules, but through welfare systems that see this form of behaviour as worryingly ab-norm-al. The school's aim in nominating young people to Thursday's Child Farm is to exercise care by 'helping' young people make more of theirselves available to school regimes.

Thursday's Farm aims not to establish new physical routines but to disrupt established patterns of embodied activity. Away from the school and home, a dawn-to-dusk routine of physical labour combines with group activities to provide opportunities for young people to experiment with and experience another way of living, and being.

The programme's emphasis is not on learning but on everyday management and nurture. Farm workers stress health and responsibility for others – care for the self and also for animals and the land. An overt connection is made to environmental issues and the moral importance of 'care' is seen as a key to sustainability. This is an environmental discourse with which students would be familiar, but perhaps Thursday's Farm offered a unique opportunity to experience what this means as an everyday regime. Surveillance routines appear to be secondary to getting the work done. The farm's emphasis is on responsibilisation – if the cow is not milked it will suffer, if you do not eat breakfast you won't be able to work for the day. There is of course surveillance as students work individually and in small groups with farm staff: this is however framed as a learning and self-managing practice.

Young people are invited to rethink and to re-narrativise themselves. It is possible for young people to engage in many farm activities without speaking a great deal. They are not under pressure when physically working to talk, and they choose how much they say and about what. Students are offered a way to think about social interaction that is different from that of the school – they mix with others not in order to obey school rules and become 'teachable', but to accomplish a series of morally 'good' tasks.

The therapeutic confessional is the opportunity for young people to begin to reframe theirselves in and through conversation. Young people can talk about any aspect of their home, peer and school lives, but the therapist's major focus is on the young person's sense of self and well-being. Using a classic talking therapies approach, she seeks to ascertain and promote self-disciplining strategies that will help young people care for themselves as well as to adhere to school expectations and norms.

Thursday's Farm offers much the same range of opportunities to the school staff that accompany the students. They have no session with the therapist of course, but they are expected to work alongside students and establish new patterns of interaction. As teachers reveal hitherto unseen aspects of themselves, the assumption is that students will see them differently, not just as representatives of the school's disciplinary and pedagogical regimes. This allows for the possibility, together with some adjustment to student's individual school programmes, for students to 'take back' some of their relearnt self-managing behaviours into the school – and home – setting.

Thursday's Farm might be seen as the furtive hand of the 'happiness industry' infiltrating schooling, taking away the focus from learning and knowledge (Ecclestone & Hayes, 2008). However, in our view, it is part of a longer history of psy interventions that seek to bring back into the fold those who do not conform to established ways of behaving. The practice is to talk your way into a new, more norm-al life choice.

Talking as a means of steering people to 'choose' to behave differently is, in the case of Thursday's Farm, offered in conjunction with the embodied experience of acting differently for a short period of time. This might simply be a respite from school, or it might in fact be the beginning of a trigger for a more conforming self. The girls involved in Major Tom's faced overtly punitive regimes – expulsion, transfer to full-time AE – if they chose not to participate and continued to misbehave. But students in the Thursday's Farm programme were more likely to become medicalised if they continued to exercise their power as withdrawal of participation.

As is the case with Major Tom's team-building, the farm offered both a physical regime and an ethic of care. However, much more than Major Tom's Thursday's Child Farm sought to work on the 'soul' and on the ethic of caring for the self.

**In sum**

We began this paper with the suggestion that care was generally strongly tied to both instrumental learning and disciplinary regimes in schools. We suggested that the dominant disciplinary regimes in schools, and in AE, were now largely geared to instrumental ends, and worked in the interests of the school. Our research showed that in AE there had been a strong swing back to behaviourist reward and punishment regimes, which supported this instrumentalised push.

Our analysis of two complementary AE programmes showed how they operated differently. For a start, the students were not offered a reduced curriculum, as is the case in most full-time AE. They maintained access to the national curriculum that currently counts for success and thus to the usual range of further educational options. This is certainly important, but it is not all that matters.

For us, the prime difference between Major Tom's and Thursday's Child Farm and the dominant regular school/AE regimes is in the nature of the care on offer, that is, in the choices that young people were able to make and the ways in which they could exercise power. Care in most AE is highly individualised and reductively focused on obedience and performing well in set tasks. There is a relatively simple binary choice of conform/resist. By contrast, the two complementary programmes we examined offered different choices. There was no penalty for choosing not to participate. And the choice was not to simply conform but also to care – for others (the group, nature, children) and the self. New narratives were also on offer to explain why these choices were moral and good.

The AE programmes steered, not coerced and punished. The key to these complementary programmes, we suggest, is that the major target of student resistance – the everyday, ordinary disciplinary workings of the school – was temporarily displaced. Students were able to choose to exercise their power differently and opt into alternative ways of being and becoming. Their options were connected with wider positive moral and cultural norms and offered different potential trajectories for the future. While these were certainly not the 'emancipation' that some might advocate, they were nevertheless more than students might have anticipated before their involvement. Whether they chose or were able to choose these futures is not the responsibility of these AE programmes, but is the job of their schools, communities and, indeed, the society to which they belong.

Of course, the Foucauldian notion that 'everything is dangerous' certainly rings true. We have no desire to over-claim the benefits of the programmes. On the other hand, we cannot say that we saw no positives associated with the two programmes. Both Major Tom's and Thursday's Child Farm did seem to be somewhat different from the dominant norm, directed towards a more generous vision of education. They were not solely concerned with students achieving designated test targets, coordinating health and welfare agencies, and stopping bullying. We have no doubt that the young people themselves experienced these interventions as being 'cared for'; they were not simply performing outcomes, liabilities needing only triage to allow them to achieve better in tests. They were in schools where more humane and humanistic approaches to schooling remained strong.

Strategies and interventions, which are geared to bring students back into the mainstream of schooling, can be seen as the development of a more generous school ethos. Schools become, as Manchester and Bragg (2013) argue, more capacious, in that they are able to 'hold' many more young people within them. The capacity to enfold larger numbers of young people is integral to efforts to ensure that more of them do engage and reengage with the learning that counts towards employment, training and further study. However, this is not necessarily the same as an instrumental approach that primarily aims to meet school targets and ward off inspection sanctions.

We suggest that our analysis points to a potentially helpful way to reconsider the notion of a 'caring school' and AE. It is easy to suggest that schools must abandon performative disciplinary regimes where the choice is to conform or not. However, they still have to keep order and students still need to learn and be taught. It is less easy to suggest what they might do instead. It is not, we have argued, a question of schools abandoning discipline, but rather what kind of disciplinary regime might be on offer. The examples of Major Tom's and Thursday's Child Farm suggest that schools might look to expand the range of choices open to their students. Rather than simply offering one way to choose to be part of the school, there might be more than one pattern of participation.

In moving away from thinking about whether a school is good/bad, liberatory/repressive, we propose that it might be more generative for schools – and those who research them – to consider what horizons of possibility and what possible selves are on offer to young people, and what this might allow them to be and become. This does mean looking to build a more generous and inclusive norm. It may well also mean working to combine physical as well as cognitive and affective experiences with the opportunity to act responsibly not simply for the self but for others. This is a more expansive notion of 'care' than is now often the case.

## Funding

The Prince's Trust funded the project.

## References

Abdelnoor, A. (2007). *Managed moves. A complete guide to managed moves as an alternative to permanent exclusion.* London: Gulbenkian Foundation.

Allan, J. (1996). Foucault and special educational needs: A 'box of tools' for analysing children's experiences of mainstreaming. *Disability & Society, 11*(2), 219–234. doi:10.1080/09687599650023245

Allen, K., & Mendick, H. (2012). Young people's use of celebrity: Class, gender and 'improper' celebrity. *Discourse, 34*(1), 77–93. doi:10.1080/01596306.2012.698865

Aron, L. Y. (2006). *An overview of alternative education.* Washington, DC: Urban Institute.

Bailey, S. (2013). *Exploring ADHD: An ethnography of disorcder in early childhood.* London: Routledge.

Ball, S., Maguire, M., & Braun, A. (2011). *How schools do policy. Policy enactments in secondary schools.* London: Routledge.

Besley, T. (2002). *Counseling youth. Foucault, power and the ethcis of subjectivity.* Westport, CT: Bergin & Garvey.

Caulkins, M. (2011). *Pathways of pathology and promise in alternative education.* (PhD). Simon Fraser University.

Denny, S., Fleming, T., Clark, T. C., & Wall, M. (2004). Emotional resilience: Risk and protective factors for depression among alternative education students in New Zealand. *American Journal of Orthopsychiatry, 74*(2), 137–149. doi:10.1037/0002-9432.74.2.137

Devine, J. (1996). *Maximum security. The culture of violence in inner-city schools.* Chicago: University of Chicago Press.

Ecclestone, K., & Hayes, D. (2008). *The dangerous rise of therapeutic education. How teaching is becoming therapy.* London: Routledge.

Fielding, M. (2006). Leadership, radical student engagement and the necessity of person-centred education. *International Journal of Leadership in Education, 9*(4), 299–313. doi:10.1080/13603120600895411

Foucault, M. (1977). *Discipline and punish. The birth of the prison.* (A. Sheridan, Trans. 1991 ed.). London: Penguin.

Foucault, M. (1982). The subject and power. In H. L. Dreyfus & P. Rabinow (Eds.), *Michel Foucault: Beyond structuralism and hermeneutics* (pp. 208–226). Chicago: University of Chicago Press.

Foucault, M. (1982/1997). Technologies of the self. In P. Rabinow (Ed.), *Ethics. Subjectivity and truth. Essential works of Foucault 1954-1984* (Vol. 1, pp. 223–252). New York, NY: New Press.

Foucault, M. (1988). *Technologies of the self: A seminar with Michel Foucault.* (L. Martin, Trans.). Tavistock: London.

Gillborn, D., & Youdell, D. (2000). *Rationing education. Policy, practice, reform and equity.* Buckingham: Open University Press.

Glasser, W. (1990). *Quality school. Managing students without Coercion.* New York, NY: Harper Perennial.

Gore, J. (1993). *The struggle for pedagogies. Critical and feminist discourses as regimes of truth.* New York, NY: Routledge.

Guerin, G., & Denti, L. (1999). Alternative education support for youth at-risk. *The Clearing House: A Journal of Educational Strategies, Issues and Ideas, 73*(2), 76–78. doi:10.1080/00098659909600151

Harris, B., Vincent, K., Thomson, P., & Toalster, R. (2006). Does every child know they matter? Pupils' views of one alternative to exclusion. *Pastoral Care in Education, 24*(2), 28–38. doi:10.1111/past.2006.24.issue-2

Harwood, V. (2005). *Diagnosing 'disorderly' children. A critique of behaviour disorder discourses.* London: Routledge.

Harwood, V., & Allan, J. (2014). *Psychopathology at school: Theorizing mental disorder in schools.* London: Routledge.

Hunter, I. (1994). *Rethinking the school. Subjectivity, bureaucracy, criticism.* Sydney: Allen & Unwin.

Institute of Education (University of London) and the National Foundation for Educational Research (NFER). (2013). *Evaluation of the school exclusion trial (responsibility for alternative provision for permanently excluded children).* London: Department for Education.

Institute of Education (University of London) and the National Foundation for Educational Research (NFER). (2014). *School exclusion trial evaluation.* London: Department for Education.

Kelly, P., & Harrison, L. (2009). *Working in Jamie's kitchen. Salvation, passion and young workers.* Basingstoke: Palgrave Macmillan.

Kim, J.-H., & Taylor, K. A. (2008). Rethinking alternative education to break the cycle of educational inequality and inequity. *The Journal of Educational Research, 101*(4), 207–219. doi:10.3200/JOER.101.4.207-219

Lewis, C. (2011). *Poststructuralism at work with marginalised children.* Oak Park, UAE: Bentham Science Publishers.

Lloyd, G. (Ed.). (2005). *Problem girls. Understanding and supporting troubled and troublesome girls and young women.* London: Routledge.

Maclure, M., Jones, L., Holmes, R., & Macrae, C. (2012). Becoming a problem: Behaviour and reputation in the early years classroom. *British Educational Research Journal, 38*(3), 447–471. doi:10.1080/01411926.2011.552709

Manchester, H., & Bragg, S. (2013). 'School ethos and the spatial turn: 'Capacious' approaches to research and practice. *Qualitative Inquiry, 19*(10), 818–827. doi:10.1177/1077800413503800

Noddings, N. (1992). *The challenge to care in schools.* New York, NY: Teachers College Press.

Nolan, K. (2011). *Police in the hallways. Discipline in an urban high school.* Minneapolis, MN: University of Minnesota Press.

Ozga, J. (2009). Governing education through data in England: From regulation to self evaluation. *Journal of Education Policy, 24*(2), 149–162. doi:10.1080/02680930902733121

Raywid, M. A. (1994). Alternative schools. The state of the art. *Educational Leadership, 52*(1), 26–31.

Rose, N. (1999). *Governing the soul. The shaping of the private self* (2nd ed.). London: Free Association Books.

Russell, L., & Thomson, P. (2011). Girls and gender in alternative education provision. *Ethnography and Education, 6*(3), 293–308. doi:10.1080/17457823.2011.610581

Skinner, B. F. (1968). *The technology of teaching.* Englewood Cliffs, NJ: Prentice Hall.

Slee, R. (1995). *Changing theories and practices of discipline.* London: Falmer.

Slee, R. (2011). *The irregular school. Exclusion, schooling and inclusive education.* London: Routledge.

Thomson, P. (2014). Literature review. What's the alternatice? Effective support for young people disengaging from the mainstream. The Prince's Trust. Retrieved from http://www.princes-trust.org.uk/pdf/Literature/Review/FINAL/15/10/14.pdf

# ALTERNATIVE EDUCATIONAL PROGRAMMES

Thomson, P., McQuade, V., & Rochford, K. (2005a). 'My little special house': Re-forming the risky geographies of middle school girls at Clifftop College. In G. Lloyd (Ed.), *Problem girls. Understanding and supporting troubled and troublesome girls and young women* (pp. 172–189). London: RoutledgeFalmer.

Thomson, P., McQuade, V., & Rochford, K. (2005b). 'No-one's a good or bad student here': An active citizenship project as 'doing justice'. *The International Journal of Learning*. Retrieved from http://ijl.cgpublisher.com/

Thomson, P., & Pennacchia, J. (2014). *What's the alternative? Effective support for young people disengaging from mainstream education*. The Prince's Trust. Retrieved from http://www. princes-trust.org.uk/pdf/whats-the-alternative-effective-support-for-young-people.pdf

Thomson, P., & Pennacchia, J. (2015). Hugs and behaviour points: Alternative education and the regulation of 'excluded' youth. *International Journal of Inclusive Education*, 1–19. doi:10.1080/13603116.2015.1102340

Thomson, P., & Russell, L. (2007). *Mapping the provision of alternatives to school exclusion*. York: Joseph Rowntree Foundation.

Thomson, P., & Russell, L. (2009). Data, data everywhere – but not all the numbers that count? Mapping alternative provisions for students excluded from school. *International Journal of Inclusive Education*, *13*, 423–438. doi:10.1080/13603110801983264

Vincent, K., Harris, B., Thomson, P., & Toalster, R. (2007). Managed moves: Schools collaborating for collective gain. *Emotional and Behavioural Difficulties*, *12*(4), 283–298. doi:10.1080/ 13632750701664277

Wexler, P., Crichlow, W., Kern, J., & Martusewicz, R. (1992). *Becoming somebody. Toward a social psychology of school*. London: Falmer Press.

Yin, R. (1994). *Case study research. Design and methods*. Sage: London.

# Alternative education and social justice: considering issues of affective and contributive justice

Martin Mills, Glenda McGregor, Aspa Baroutsis, Kitty Te Riele and Debra Hayes

This article considers the ways in which three alternative education sites in Australia support socially just education for their students and how injustice is addressed within these schools. The article begins with recognition of the importance of Nancy Fraser's work to understandings of social justice. It then goes on to argue that her framework is insufficient for understanding the particularly complex set of injustices that are faced by many highly marginalised young people who have rejected or been rejected by mainstream education systems. We argue here for the need to consider the importance of 'affective' and 'contributive' aspects of justice in schools. Using interview data from the alternative schools, we highlight issues of affective justice raised by students in relation to their educational journeys, as well as foregrounding teachers' affective work in schools. We also consider curricular choices and pedagogical practices in respect of matters of contributive justice. Our contention is that the affective and contributive fields are central to the achievement of social justice for the young people attending these sites. Whilst mainstream schools are not the focus of this article, we suggest that the lessons here have salience for all forms of schooling.

## Introduction

This article has evolved from a project exploring the types of learning occurring in flexible learning sites/alternative[1] education in Australia during the period 2012–2014. The project was concerned with the ways in which such sites supported a socially just education for their students. Our concerns were framed around Nancy Fraser's (1997, 2009) conceptions of social justice in that we were interested in the ways in which such schools took account of: issues of distribution, or the economic injustices faced by the young people attending the schools; issues of recognition, that is, the cultural injustices faced by these young people; and issues of representation, with regard to the political injustices experienced by young people.

In the main, we have been impressed by what these schools do in relation to addressing all of these forms of injustice (see for example, McGregor, Mills, Te Riele, & Hayes, 2015; Mills, McGregor, Hayes, & Te Riele, 2015). However, to us there was something missing in the analysis when it came to describing the types of relationships

---

This article was originally published with errors. This version has been corrected. Please see Erratum (http://dx.doi.org/10.1080/17508487.2016.1123079).

that support young people's engagement in schooling, as well as those that disrupt this engagement. We have come to the conclusion that social justice is a complex and multi-faceted concept that is inadequately explained by Nancy Fraser's framework and we suggest here that there are other elements that need to be considered when addressing issues to do with socially just education. In so doing, we are drawn to the work of both Kathleen Lynch (2012) and Andrew Sayer (2009, 2011). Lynch (2012) in her critique of Fraser's theory suggests that 'it does not recognize the affective domain of life as a discrete site of social practice' (p. 49). In terms of schooling, the affective sphere is concerned with the quality of relationships, care and support available to students. Interrelated with this is Sayer's qualitative understanding of 'contributive justice' and its relationship to meaningful work. Based on our own observations of multiple alternative schooling sites in Australia and England (see for example, Baroutsis, McGregor, & Mills, 2015; Hayes, 2013; McGregor et al., 2015; Mills & McGregor, 2010, 2014; Mills, McGregor, & Muspratt, 2013; Mills, McGregor, Martin, Tomaszewski, & Waters, 2014; Te Riele, 2012, 2014; Te Riele, Davies, & Baker, 2015), and drawing on notions of contributive justice we suggest that 'care' needs to be taken in the provision of flexible education to ensure that students do not receive a watered down curriculum that fails to engage them intellectually and that damages their sense of self-respect.

This article begins with an outline of the research project and its relationship to the work of Nancy Fraser; we then move on to discuss concepts of affective justice and contributive justice and their relevance to schooling, contextualising our theories with interview data collected from teachers and students in flexible learning sites situated in three different Australian jurisdictions. We highlight those issues of affective justice raised by students both in relation to their former and current schools, and we foreground teachers' affective work in schools. A consideration of the types of curricula and pedagogical practices present in these schools and their relationship to contributive justice supports our contention that such approaches are central to the achievement of social justice for the young people attending these sites. Whilst our focus is on young people in alternative forms of education, we suggest that the lessons here have salience for all forms of schooling.

## Flexible learning and social justice

We, like others (see for example, Cribb & Gewirtz, 2003; Keddie, 2012a, 2012b; Lipman, 2008; Power & Frandji, 2010), have found the work of Nancy Fraser useful in considering what a socially just school might look like. Her work has focussed on considering how the sometimes competing demands of economic justice and cultural justice can be worked together to provide a comprehensive theory of justice. In more recent times, she has embedded a concern with political justice into her theoretical framework.

Within Fraser's framework, economic injustice refers to an inequitable distribution of resources and the damaging effects of this 'maldistribution'. Cultural injustice refers to the ways in which various groups have become 'despised', for example, on the grounds of sexuality, gender, or race/ethnicity. This 'misrecognition' occurs when people are forced to suppress their own cultural ways of being and communicating to the (often hostile) norms of the dominant culture, are rendered invisible or are disrespected as a result of belonging to a particular cultural group. Political injustice, which Fraser refers to as 'misrepresentation', occurs in those instances when people are denied an opportunity to make justice claims when they are experiencing economic or cultural injustice or when they are unable to contribute to the decisions that have an impact on their lives. She contends that misrepresentation can occur (although unlikely) in the absence of economic and cultural injustices. Fraser argues that all such aspects of injustice have to be attended to in order to achieve a socially just society where there is 'parity of participation'. Her work has not been without its critics (see for example, Olsen, 2008). However, we have found this framework a useful device for considering how economic, cultural and political injustices, and their respective solutions of distribution, recognition and representation, relate to contemporary schooling, both in the mainstream and alternative sectors (see for example, McGregor et al., 2015; Mills et al., 2015).

Mainstream schools have a long history of not serving particular groups of young people well. Students who come from low socioeconomic backgrounds are disproportionately represented in the lower bands of achievement and attendance data and in the upper bands of data on exclusion, suspension and 'special needs'(see for example, Abrams, 2010; Evans, Meyer, Pinney, & Robinson, 2009; Gale & Densmore, 2000; Kane, 2011; Mills & Gale, 2010; Mosen-Lowe, Vidovich, & Chapman, 2009). Multiple reasons for this have been suggested to us by participants in our study. These include, students' access to particular forms of cultural capital, lack of fit between the middle class expectations of schooling and (non)working class culture, teacher prejudices, lack of resources and even diet. Whilst we have very definite understandings of our own as to why this is the case, we would also suggest that whatever the reason, there is no doubt that an injustice is being perpetrated against the children of the poor. This economic injustice works to ensure that the benefits of schooling are unfairly distributed amongst young people according to their family's economic circumstances, and given the strong relationship between educational success and social mobility (OECD, 2012) reproduces the existing patterns of wealth and poverty. In many of the schools we have visited, this injustice has been addressed through, for example, the provision of food, accommodation support for homeless young people, transportation, basic services (for example, showers) and free excursions (see for example, Mills & McGregor, 2014).

Defining 'culture' in its broadest sense to include gender, sexuality, race/ethnicity, religion, language background and so on, it is clear that young people who belong to marginalised 'cultures' often encounter schooling as a less than positive experience. This 'cultural injustice' can be shaped by a lack of academic reward, but also by harassment and violence, by being ignored, silenced or having one's existence denied, by active and hidden discrimination at multiple levels, and it can be perpetrated by teachers and students alike (Smyth, 2006). In many of the flexible schools we have visited, this injustice has been addressed by a strong commitment to recognising and valuing difference. This has been demonstrated through, for example, seeking input from local Indigenous Elders into organisational and curriculum content, the provision of crèches for those students who have children, ensuring that homophobia or racism is never ignored and providing support around domestic violence issues.

It is also apparent that many young people experience schooling as oppressive because they have no forum in which to express their opinions or challenge the injustices they have experienced (Black, 2011). The importance of student voice in schools has been well documented (see Beane & Apple, 1999; Dewey, 1916; Fielding & Moss, 2011), however its presence is often lacking. The absence of voice, or political injustice, may be apparent in the ways in which students, especially those from marginalised backgrounds, can be summarily suspended from school, given detentions and other forms of punishment without options to challenge those decisions. It is apparent in dress codes, in timetabling restrictions, in the appointment of teachers and in curriculum decisions. It is perhaps not surprising, as Teese and Polesel (2003) indicated, that for many young people who are not achieving well at school, their most common descriptor of school is as a prison. In the schools that we have visited as part of this project, we have seen attempts to give students a voice through regular community meetings (Baroutsis et al., 2015), through consultations on renovations, even in one case working closely with architects to design new premises, and by including them on teacher interview panels.

Whilst in the main, we have been highly supportive of these alternative schools and the various ways in which they have worked to challenge injustice (see for example, Hayes, 2012; Mills & McGregor, 2014; Te Riele, 2006, 2007, 2011), we are of the view that as a matter of social justice these schools also have to consider the types of learning that students do in the classroom. It has been noted in many studies, and compounded by an era of high stakes testing (Darling-Hammond, 2010; Hardy, 2013; Lingard, Martino, & Rezai-Rashti, 2013; Lingard & Sellar, 2013), that many classrooms in mainstream schools are devoid of curriculum, pedagogy and assessment that inspire, challenge and provoke all students (Hayes, Mills, Christie, & Lingard, 2006; Smyth, McInerney, & Fish, 2013). However, whilst concerned about this current state of affairs, we are of the view that such an absence in flexible learning centres is particularly damaging to those students who have already been disenfranchised from learning. We are not alone here.

There have been some concerns raised about the alternative education sector being constructed as a dumping ground for students 'unwanted' by the education system where there is then little academic challenge (Kim, 2011; Kim & Taylor, 2008; Mills, Renshaw, & Zipin, 2013; Smyth et al., 2013). de Jong and Griffiths (2006), for instance, have expressed concerns that the increased use of alternative education programmes for younger and younger students can lead to them being separated from the mainstream and its benefits, and that 'poorly constructed and resourced' programmes will reinforce students' poor outcomes from schooling (p. 37). Thus, in highlighting the necessity for elements of affective justice and contributive justice to be significant considerations when working with disenfranchised young people, we are not suggesting that 'care' *by itself* is sufficient to address all their needs. Our intention is to tease out the complexity inherent in notions of a 'socially just' education as explained in the following sections.

## Multi-sited ethnography

This study represents a 'multi-sited ethnography' of alternative schools (Falzon, 2009; Kraftl, 2013; Marcus, 1995; Pierides, 2010). Marcus (1995) explained that this mode of ethnographic research 'moves out from the single sites and local situations of conventional ethnographic research designs to examine the circulation of cultural meanings, objects, and identities in diffuse time-space' (p. 96). The strength of multi-sited ethnography is that it enables the researchers to 'make connections between sites' (Pierides, 2010, p. 186) in a 'spatially dispersed field through which the ethnographer moves' (Falzon, 2009, p. 2). In this research project, we used ethnographic observations and semi-structured interviews with students, teachers and other workers in three flexible learning schools across three Australian states and one territory during multiple visits over a period of 18 months in 2013 and 2014. We sought to explore a range of themes that included the following broad areas, as relevant to teachers, workers and students: previous experiences; a pathway into the alternative site; reasons for staying; what works (relational, material, pedagogical and curricular elements) and why; and, resourcing and sustainability issues. In this article, we draw upon data from three of these sites, identified using the pseudonyms: Elkhorn Community College in Queensland; Banksia College in the Australian Capital Territory (ACT) and Boronia Flexi School in Victoria, in order to explore concepts of affective and contributive justice that emerged as significant concerns within these schools.

Elkhorn Community College is a non-government and non-fee paying school providing educational programmes for young people in years 10, 11 and 12, the final 3 years of secondary education in Australia. At the time when the researchers were at the College, there was an enrolment of approximately 60 young people and 5 staff, comprising a principal, 2 teachers and 2 youth and community development workers (one of whom was completing teaching qualifications). Banksia College is a mainstream government senior high school in a major Australian city that runs two alternative programmes (now both operating out of the main campus) for students who have difficulties fitting into the mainstream and usually come from very difficult personal circumstances: one is a flexible learning centre for approximately 100 pregnant girls and young parents (mostly mothers) who attended both part and full-time; the other is a 'Big Picture'[2] inspired offering with a focus on flexibility of delivery and project-work for approximately 35 students. Staffed by small teams of dedicated teachers, both programmes provide significant levels of material and personal support to the young people in their care. Boronia Flexi School is a metropolitan year 7–12 alternative school and is part of the Edmund Rice Education Australia (EREA) Youth + network, which 'seeks to respond to the needs of young people disenfranchised and disengaged from education. This non-fee paying school caters to approximately 130 students, and as with Elkhorn and Banksia, their life experiences have been challenging – including poverty, mental illness, out-of-home care, drug dependency, juvenile justice and settlement as recent migrants. Boronia Flexi School offers year 7–12 formal junior and senior secondary credentials.

In the following sections of this article, we consider affective and contributive injustice. Affective justice relates very much to the relationship and supportive structures that are in place within a school, which indicate to young people that they are cared about. We would suggest that learning approaches which appear to have no purpose to the student and provide little by way of satisfaction and serve to demoralise them, not only represent an affective injustice, a lack of care, but also constitute a contributive injustice. Such learning would include, for example, routinised test skilling, worksheets and form filling with an emphasis on basic skills. This does not mean that some rote learning or developing of skills has no place in the delivery of meaningful learning, but that they need to be part of a broader approach to learning and not an end in themselves. We then provide examples of affective and contributive justice, where all students are engaged in meaningful work in a caring and supportive environment. This has particular salience given the context of where these justice acts are taking place. The schools that form the basis of our case study sites are those whose students, in the most part, have not been previously engaged in learning, have been labelled as academically and socially deficit and yet are now willing to come to school. We would suggest that this emphasises the importance of all schools demonstrating a commitment to affective and contributive justice.

## Affective justice and learning environments

The relational and caring dimensions of schooling have been widely recognised (Bingham & Sidorkin, 2004; Noddings, 1988) and these are arguably particularly important when working with students who have experienced marginalisation in school and society (Beck & Cassidy, 2009; Smyth, Angus, Down, & McInerney, 2008; Te Riele, 2006). Additionally, many feminist writers have stressed the political importance of emotions

# ALTERNATIVE EDUCATIONAL PROGRAMMES

and understandings of 'affective justice' (Blackmore, 1999, 2006; Boler, 1999; Hochschild, 1983). As Lynch (2012) has indicated it is often feminist scholars who 'have drawn attention to the salience of care and love as goods of public significance' (p. 47). Her work informs our concern with social justice and alternative education. Those schools deemed alternative, as all schools, are communities where their success, in terms of being a place where both workers and students want to attend, is dependent upon the quality of relationships for all. As with Lynch, we recognise that the care provided by members of that community to each other is a matter of social justice both in relation to who gives it and who receives it (Lynch, 2012, p. 49). She argues that what she refers to as 'affective equality' is focussed on two issues: 'securing equality in the distribution of the nurturing through love, care and solidarity relationships and securing equality in the doing of emotional and other work involved in creating love, care and solidarity relations' (p. 50).

Whilst we are concerned with the issue of who is responsible for 'caring', and recognise the mutuality of such caring, our focus here is on who gets the 'caring'. Many of the young people in our study, when asked to outline the strengths of their current schools suggested that it was the relationships that mattered, that they felt that the teachers and other workers cared for them. This was often contrasted with previous experiences of schooling, for example Audrey, a Boronia Flexi School student, said the following about her current school:

> They care, they care a lot about the students. No matter who you are they care ... Because they're so sweet, they do so much for the students here and more than what other schools would do because the way I've seen in other mainstream schools is you're a teacher, you teach, that's it. They're more caring. Like I say, it's like a community, it's like a family. So the teachers really care about the students and they're also youth workers as well so they deal with the children. If you have something on your mind you talk to a teacher and they're full open with you and they're so nice, they're just the most nicest people here.

Lynch outlines three sets of relations that constitute affective justice: love, care and solidarity. In the first instance, love is said to be related to relationships of high inter-dependency and intense engagement; she suggests that even when such relationships are absent they often have great significance (for example the parent–child relationship even in abusive situations). Care relations are viewed as having a lower order of dependency and obligations, but are significant nonetheless; she suggested that friends, work colleagues and some distant relations fall into this category. Solidarity relations do not involve intimacy, but are, Lynch (2012) suggested 'the more political or public face of affective relations' (p. 52). Here, we can think of advocate groups (for example, refugee support groups), unions and government departments. Lynch suggested that these three categories are not mutually exclusive and that they are interdependent. She also argued that these systems of 'affective equality' are all interrelated with Fraser's framework. She argues that 'it is not possible to address problems of inequality or social justice in one social system therefore without addressing those in related social systems' (p. 53). We contend that it is the relational sets of 'care' and 'solidarity' that construct the affective domain within schools and that these elements are especially important for achieving socially just outcomes for marginalised young people.

Applying Lynch's (2012) conceptualisation of 'relational care work' (p. 56) in alternative settings suggests that teachers play an important mediating role in the nexus of these relationships: supporting and working with students and their families or caregivers; developing flexible structures and processes that provide a caring schooling environment

# ALTERNATIVE EDUCATIONAL PROGRAMMES

and working in solidarity with students to resist their continued marginalisation in schooling and beyond. For example, Faye, who attended Banksia College, commented:

> I got kicked out of home and I came in and saw the counsellor and straight away she got me straight onto housing. They do that little bit extra all the teachers here. It's more than just what a normal teacher does at a school. They look out for you in your entire life, not for just the 6 hours that I'm here for.

Additionally, many of the students we interviewed talked about how their prior schooling experiences contributed to the complexity of their lives, rather than providing a place of care and support. Drew, a student from Elkhorn Community College, provided us with an example:

> I was always 'your bad student'. I wasn't bad. Like, I was respectful in some ways but I couldn't concentrate on work and it was, like, hard, just coming from my old life ... drugs, drinking and wrong people and violence and – yeah.

Leanne, a student at Banksia College, contrasted her experiences with her former and current school. She said about the programme at Banksia:

> We get to come into school and you are not stressed. Like, when you have got family issues and that, you can sit down and, like, talk to Leigh and Stuart (teacher and deputy principal) and they will, like, help you through the day and that. And then you can go and make yourself a cup of tea. It's more relaxed and chilled. Like, you are not stressed about going into class and that. You are running a bit late on an assignments – they do help you out.

Irrespective of social class background, complex home environments can disrupt young people's engagement with schooling because they may be called upon, as we have observed, to exercise independence at an early age, to care of younger siblings and disabled parents, to manage relationships with neighbours and service providers and so on. While it is not the role of teachers to replace or substitute these primary relationships, even when complex, they can provide care and support that enhances young people's capacity to sustain their engagement in schooling. At Banksia College, for example, a teacher named Leigh came up constantly in our interviews with young people. We heard numerous stories of how she went beyond the role of 'teacher' in the ways she cared for her students. In one discussion with students Callum and Leanne, they joked: 'Leigh needs to clone herself!' and Leanne added 'Yeah – we need more Leighs!' Evidence of her high level of care was threaded through all the data from Banksia College. For example, in a discussion about the food available at the site, the conversation indicated that packs of noodles were once provided for students but this is no longer the case. Darren commented: 'Don't have them lately. If it was really bad, Leigh would probably just give you some money to go to the canteen or something'. And Robbie,

> I missed out on a lot of schoolwork because I was really sick, that was due last semester – not last semester, last term. And I have been allowed to catch up pretty much nearly all of it. In the last few days, I was supposed to get some other work done, but my mother is in hospital now. So Leigh is supporting me and making sure that I can get to places easily ... Pretty much anything that she can do, like, transport – I believe she's done it for other people.

It appeared that Leigh's approach was to develop modes of caring, which were appropriate for the needs of individual students as summed up here by Leanne:

> Yes, she works – she has a different relationship – she has a relationship with everyone but it's different, which is really good. She sits there and knows everyone but she will have to change her, like, talking and that. She's like, 'Alright, I am talking to this student now, so I have got to talk to her in this way', you know what I mean. Yeah, she's really good.

In the case of marginalised students, care and support are likely to involve solidarity expressed through curriculum and pedagogy that values, respects and builds upon the knowledge and cultural backgrounds of students, while also supporting their capacity to engage with the kinds of knowledge that contribute to success at school and beyond. This is a challenge faced by teachers in both alternative and mainstream settings. However, for the former, it requires finding ways to engage young people in learning that do not involve repeating or reinforcing students' prior experiences of failure (Hayes, 2012).

We contend that a concern with 'affective equality' is critical to the success of alternative schooling. This is achieved relationally and academically. We suggest that, as with the dimensions of justice outlined in Fraser's work, both types of affective equality are necessary, and neither is sufficient on its own for considering what makes up a socially just school. Kim and Taylor (2008), for example, examined one alternative school in the mid-west of the United States, attended by many young people who have not been served well by current educational practices, to explore the benefits or otherwise of this school for its students. Their view was that the school was, indeed, a caring place; however, they were also of the view that it did little to break 'the cycle of educational inequality' (Kim & Taylor, 2008, p. 208). In this school, many of the students indicated that they wanted to go to college; however, the school's focus on 'credit recovery', where students who have fallen behind on their grades or school work attempt to catch up with their peers in the mainstream school, did not facilitate this goal. However, as Kim and Taylor (2008) go on to say: 'Their dreams required a more rigorous college-bound curriculum and career counselling' (p. 213). Echoing De Jong and Griffiths (2006), Kim and Taylor (2008) claimed that:

> A school program is beneficial to students when it provides content, processes, rigor, and concepts that they need to develop and realize their future career goals. A school program that is beneficial to students engages them and leads them through varying processes to critical thinking and synthesis of the concepts and content. Conversely, a school program that is not beneficial to students is behavioristic, positivistic, and reductive. That is, the focus of the program is primarily on an either–or dichotomy: It addresses only lower order thinking and processing skills and does not move students toward their future career goals. (p. 208)

Others to critique the types of learning taking place in such settings include Thomson and Russell (2007) in the UK who suggested that there was a tendency to assume that all young people in alternative learning environments need and want is vocational options, which limits scope of provision (p. viii). Similarly, Dovemark and Beach (2014) in Sweden demonstrated some of the ways in which deficit understandings of students in a programme for non-academic, non-vocational students contributed to their already precarious existence. In such instances, it is imperative that teachers and workers in alternative schools become advocates for young people, enacting Lynch's notion of 'solidarity' in caring for the long-term prospects of their students. We have also witnessed the absence of engaging, intellectually challenging and meaningful classroom practice in the alternative schools that formed part of our study, as illustrated here by Anthony, a student at Boronia Flexi School, who commented about his English studies:

# ALTERNATIVE EDUCATIONAL PROGRAMMES

> The quality of work – for instance, if I was still going to [name of previous school] I'd be expected to do, in English say, a 3,000-word essay. You're not expected to do that in English here.

Both Anthony and another student, Colin, agreed that classes at the Flexi school were 'a lot easier'. When asked if they liked their current situation, Anthony replied:

> Yeah, it's good because it's a lot less workload, but bad because ... I honestly don't feel like I learn anything, like what I haven't already learned. It just feels like I'm just repeating.

The development of an appropriate and challenging curriculum for their students was clearly of great concern to the teachers in our case study schools. This kind of curriculum work is made even more complex in these settings because the students come from a variety of background learning experiences. Teachers are required to assess each student's learning needs and preferences, and map these to appropriate curriculum pathways. Maddy, a teacher at Elkhorn Community College, for example, explained how she got to know her student as learners:

> I have just recently started trying to do, 'what kind of learner am I?' That starts with a worksheet thing where they grade – put a scale, you know. They answer questions and then we have conversations, 'Why do you learn best in this way? What can we do in this setting to make it most beneficial for you, and the best way that I can support you in your learning?'

We acknowledge that many of the students who attend alternative schools have significant educational gaps that need to be addressed. Our concern is that rather than bridging the gaps and moving the learning forward, the 'gaps' will remain if learning is restricted to basic skills such as literacy and numeracy and 'job readiness'.

Branson from Elkhorn Community College spoke about a class that is offered at his college called employment, education and training:

> We have got a class that we can go to, if we want to do our job searches, résumés, certificates, get work experience. Yeah, I have got a couple so far. Heaps of stuff. It's pretty good here. TAFE is just down the road, so they take us down there in the bus, or they will come here; instead of finding your own way to TAFE.

In our experience, this state of affairs, as in lower streamed classes in mainstream schools, and lower expectations across whole schools located in low socioeconomic and marginalised communities, is justified often on the grounds of deficit understandings of students' abilities and dispositions. The absence of student work premised on high expectations and engaging activities, and the justifications for this absence would not be present in classrooms for 'gifted and talented' students or in schools proud of their academic reputations. Such attitudes may signify a lack of intellectual care and respect for the young people, their current abilities and their future potential. In recognising that there is a need to go beyond care, and indeed solidarity, as with Lynch, we have engaged with the work of Sayer and the notion of contributive justice. We argue here that this understanding of justice is crucial in ensuring that alternative schools consolidate their ethos of care as a basis for ensuring that their students have access to meaningful learning.

## ALTERNATIVE EDUCATIONAL PROGRAMMES

### Contributive justice and meaningful learning

Whilst affective justice has a focus upon care of and respect for the individual in terms of the material, relational and intellectual supports and opportunities provided, contributive justice (Gomberg, 2007; Sayer, 2009, 2011) is overtly concerned with what a person actually gets *to do*. Sayer (2011) stated that: 'contributive justice concerns what people are allowed, expected or required to do or contribute' (p. 9). As such, it contrasts with, but complements justices concerned with what a person gets (economic), who a person is (cultural), how a person is heard (political) and how a person is cared for (affective). He goes on to argue that:

> What people are allowed to contribute, particularly in terms of work, is at least as important as what they get in terms of resources, because the type of work that they do has far-reaching effects on the kinds of people they become, on how they view themselves and are viewed by others, and hence on the quality of their lives. (Sayer, 2011, p. 9)

This is an echo of his distinction between contributive justice and economic justice, when he argued that: 'what we *do* in life has at least as much influence on who we become and the quality of our lives, as does what we *get*' (Sayer, 2009, p. 2). For Sayer, there are two aspects to contributive justice. The first has a quantitative element to it and is concerned with doing a 'fair share' of the workload. Teachers, and indeed university academics, who set project work and group tasks are familiar with the complaints that others are not pulling their weight or are taking over – both relate to the notion of contributive justice. However, whilst important, we are more concerned here with the qualitative element of contributive justice. This relates to the type of work being done and the intrinsic and extrinsic rewards associated with this work. It also relates to the opportunities that people have to make a contribution to the conception and execution, and all stages in between, of a shared project. This form of injustice is also linked and works closely with those frames identified by Fraser. For example, there are times when boring, repetitive, low skilled tasks are necessary to complete a project. However, how those tasks are distributed and rewarded is a matter of social justice. The unfair distribution of work occurs in both the formal economy and in domestic life. In the formal economy, contributive injustice, according to Sayer, occurs both within and between occupations and workplaces.

Sayer provided a set of arguments from Murphy (1994) and Gomberg (2007), to indicate why this state of affairs is unjust. These all relate to a person's quality of life. The kind of work that a person does has an impact on who they become and on their emotional, physical and intellectual well-being. People experience enjoyment in doing complex tasks that enable them to employ and extend their capacities (see Griffiths, 2012, for a discussion of social justice and 'joy'). For example, Lilly from Banksia College who, after fleeing there from an abusive family relationship in another major city, had been homeless in the ACT, before finding her way to the College, excitedly told us about how she wanted to build her own computer and noted: 'At the moment I am working towards getting an IT apprenticeship – I would never been able to finish Year 12 without [this program]'.

Dignity is also enhanced when people have control over their labour in that they are trusted, understand their contribution to the larger project and have an opportunity to question their and others' roles throughout the process of conception and execution of a project. Understanding the various links in a project and reasons for embarking on a particular task also ensures that even mundane tasks when shared around are meaningful. There is great resonance here with schooling and classroom work. This was evident when

# ALTERNATIVE EDUCATIONAL PROGRAMMES

Stuart, the teacher in charge of the alternative programme at Banksia College, was describing the types of projects they undertook in their programme. A key aspect of their work involved students working on a range of tasks, including some menial ones, to develop a product that had real world impacts. Stuart told us:

> [For our next project] we are going to aim to make some swags[3] with an industrial sewing machine, roll them with toothpaste, toothbrushes, towel, whatever we find, soap, and then we will give them to one of our local homeless shelters for the winter because it's pretty harsh in [the city] – well, you know, it is not pleasant anyway. So wherever possible we take a leadership or a community service thing in addition.... We don't have too many students who wallow and they have – pretty much all have had difficult circumstances.

In this case, it was indicated that the students were proud of their achievements and developed a sense of contributing to their community.

Students who are deemed to be the most competent are often those most likely to be provided with opportunities to extend themselves and to receive diverse learning experiences (see for example, Charlton, Mills, Martino, & Beckett, 2007). Similar parallels can be found with a differentiated schooling system where certain schools specialise in academic learning and others have a more technical focus. The growing presence of flexible learning options points to a schooling system that is increasingly diversifying in ways that have the potential to exacerbate this situation (Hayes, 2013; Slee, 2011). The defence of such arrangements include arguments to the case that it is more efficient to have specialised or differentiated schools and classrooms that cater to differences in abilities, interests and behaviours. This, it is sometimes argued, helps to ensure that the schooling system is efficient, that it is stabilised in that disruptions and poor behaviours are minimised (at least to the extent that 'good students' do not have their work interfered with) and that this situation caters to different abilities, potential and dispositions. However, Bardsley (2007) has argued that:

> Where social stability and economic efficiency are valued above all else, the aim of education becomes the provision of basic skills to train citizens amongst the socioeconomically deprived classes to perform the menial tasks essential to keep society functioning, without disrupting established power structures (Laberee, 1997; Lynch & Lodge, 2002). Justice within education systems should be committed to the premise that all children must be adequately prepared for effective societal roles of their own choosing. (p.496)

Bardsley's (2007) work also suggests that a socially just education has to provide young people with the skills and knowledge to engage with 'emerging societal contexts'. This will entail school work engaging with technology, developing critical citizenship skills and understandings of contemporary society.

It is our contention that contributive justice is present in a classroom when students are presented with learning opportunities that enable them to develop a sense of pride in the outcomes of that learning – in much the same way as a craftsperson feels pride in the construction of a product (Sennett, 2009). This recount from Stuart, a deputy and head of the alternative programme at Banksia College, exemplifies this contention:

> We have Miriam who all of last year spent 6 months making polymers with one of our chemistry teachers and she explained it to me ... And she's a pretty eclectic little thinker. ... I missed the exhibition where her family came to the exhibition... And the family sees something that the kid is proud of and there is a moment where they do a little bit of readjustment. Yeah, they settle back – there is that moment when the kid goes, 'Oh, you

do actually see something good about me. I am making progress', and that's transformative for both sides. We have got parents that were reviewed as part of that review process. They are some of our biggest fans. As I said, they have enrolled second kids in it. I think that what they like about it is the concept that the kid has to do something fairly rigorous.

At Boronia Flexi School, the music teacher provided a similar example:

The staff and the students see people walking out of this room with such big chests, you know. The pride is just visibly obvious to see when they have just had some success. That I think is, I am not saying it is all about music, but some sort of high level professional product that is in the digital domain I think every school would benefit from.

What the data from our research indicate is that such learning occurs when it has a purpose (whether personal or instrumental) and that that purpose is evident to the student. Julian (a teacher at Boronia Flexi School) linked this to 'a sense of empowerment for the young people to be who they feel as though they want to be'. It also has some connection to the world beyond the classroom and stretches and challenges all young people, not just those deemed to be of 'high ability'.

## Conclusion

Our concern with what a socially just schooling system might look like and, in particular, how schools can meet the needs of the most marginalised students, led us to explore 'what works' in those schools catering to students who have been excluded from mainstream schools or have themselves rejected what the mainstream has to offer. In many instances, we have been impressed by these schools' efforts to address economic, cultural and political injustices. In this article, we have thus contended that a socially just education for students attends to Fraser's (1997, 2009) dimensions of social justice in respect of economic, cultural and political inequities. However, drawing upon the work of Lynch (2012) and Sayer (2009, 2011), we have also argued that these dimensions are enhanced by the inclusion of affective and contributive forms of justice, which pay attention to inequities in relational care and individual potential for meaningful participation.

The teacher participants in our study expressed a strong commitment to the social and emotional well-being of their students. Affective justice (in the forms of significant support structures and respectful, caring relationships) was of primary concern to them. Many of the students we interviewed indicated that its absence in their former school(s) had been a key factor in their departure from the mainstream sector. This concern with affective justice was thus critical to the success of such schools. However, we suggest that if it exists in isolation from other necessary elements, care is insufficient for ensuring the provision of socially just schooling. The quality of curriculum and pedagogy, which varied in some instances across the sites, is also of critical concern, and hence why we also argue that contributive justice needs to be incorporated into concerns about affective justice.

In this article, we have indicated examples of where we have come across flexible learning arrangements that facilitated students' engagement in meaningful learning, demonstrating a commitment to contributive justice; however, there were sometimes reservations expressed. In some instances, teachers indicated that in their alternative setting some students were not able to tackle challenging work and that this was why they were in the alternative school in the first place. Because of the patchy nature of the educational backgrounds of young people in alternative education, there was often a focus on literacy, numeracy and vocational options. Clearly, these skills are necessary for economic participation in society; however, if such competencies and training are considered sufficient education for these, usually marginalised and disadvantaged, young people it could be argued that this may also condemn them to a lifetime of political and social marginalisation despite their ability to obtain employment. We thus argue that the quality of curricular choices and pedagogical approaches made available to young people in alternative education sites is fundamental to the achievement of contributive justice, and hence social justice. We are also of the view that concerns with affective justice and contributive justice should have occurred long before students such as those interviewed for this project found themselves in alternative education provision.

## Acknowledgements

Martin would like to thank Kathleen Lynch for her comments at the Vere Foster Trust and the Institute of Educational Research in Ireland Lecture, 2013.

## Funding

This work was supported by the Australian Research Council under Grant DP120100620

## Notes

1. In this article, we have used the terms flexible learning centre and alternative school somewhat interchangeably. We note, as do Mills and McGregor (2014) that there is no agreed-upon definition and much contestation regarding what constitutes 'alternative education'. The schools involved here are those that cater to marginalised young people and are also often referred to as 'second chance' schools.
2. The Big Picture model of schooling has its origins in the USA. Its basic principles articulated on its Australian website state: 'highly personalised approach to education combines academic work with real world learning. It places the student, their passions and their interests, at the centre of the learning process' (See http://www.bigpicture.org.au/).
3. An Australian colloquial term for a bedroll containing all one's personal belongings.

# ALTERNATIVE EDUCATIONAL PROGRAMMES

## References

Abrams, F. (2010). *Learning to fail: How society lets young people down*. London: Routledge.

Bardsley, K. (2007). Education for all in a global era? The social justice of Australian secondary school education in a risk society. *Journal of Education Policy*, 22(5), 493–508. doi:10.1080/02680930701541691

Baroutsis, A., McGregor, G., & Mills, M. (2015). Pedagogic voice: Student voice in teaching and engagement pedagogies. *Pedagogy, Culture and Society*. Advance online publication. doi:10.1080/14681366.2015.1087044

Beane, J. A., & Apple, M. W. (1999). The case for democratic schools. In M. W. Apple & J. A. Beane (Eds.), *Democratic schools: Lessons from the chalk face*. Buckingham: Open University Press.

Beck, K., & Cassidy, W. (2009). Embedding the ethics of care in school policies and practices. In K. Te Riele (Ed.), *Making schools different: Alternative approaches to educating young people* (pp. 55–64). London: SAGE.

Bingham, C. (2004). *No education without relation*. (A. Sidorkin, Eds.). New York, NY: Peter Lang Publishing.

Black, R. (2011). Student participation and disadvantage: Limitations in policy and practice. *Journal of Youth Studies*, 14(4), 463–474. doi:10.1080/13676261.2010.533756

Blackmore, J. (1999). *Troubling women: Feminism, leadership and educational change*. Buckingham: Open University Press.

Blackmore, J. (2006). Social justice and the study and practice of leadership in education: A feminist history. *Journal of Educational Administration and History*, 38(2), 185–200. doi:10.1080/00220620600554876

Boler, M. (1999). *Feeling power: Emotions and education*. New York, NY: Routledge.

Charlton, E., Mills, M., Martino, W., & Beckett, L. (2007). Sacrificial girls: A case study of the impact of streaming and setting on gender reform. *British Educational Research Journal*, 33(4), 459–478. doi:10.1080/01411920701434011

Cribb, A., & Gewirtz, S. (2003). Towards a sociology of just practices. In C. Vincent (Ed.), *Social justice education and identity* (pp. 15–29). London: Routledge.

Darling-Hammond, L. (2010). *The flat world and education: How America's commitment to equity will determine our future*. New York, NY: Teachers College Press.

De Jong, T., & Griffiths, C. (2006). The role of alternative education programs in meeting the needs of adolescent students with challenging behaviour: Characteristics of best practice. *Australian Journal of Guidance & Counselling*, 16(1), 29–40. doi:10.1375/ajgc.16.1.29

Dewey, J. (1916). *Democracy and education: An introduction to the philosophy of education*. New York, NY: Macmillan.

Dovemark, M., & Beach, D. (2014). Academic work on a back-burner: Habituating students in the upper-secondary school towards marginality and a life in the precariat. *International Journal of Inclusive Education*. doi:10.1080/13603116.2014.961676

Evans, J., Meyer, D., Pinney, A., & Robinson, B. (2009). *Second chances: Re-engaging young people in education and training*. Essex: Barnardo's.

Falzon, M.-A. (2009). Introduction. In M.-A. Falzon (Ed.), *Multi-sited ethnography: Theory, praxis and locality in contemporary research* (pp. 1–23). Surrey: Ashgate.

Fielding, M., & Moss, P. (2011). *Radical education and the common school: A democratic alternative*. London: Routledge.

Fraser, N. (1997). *Justice interruptus: Critical reflections on the 'postsocialist' condition*. New York, NY: Routledge.

Fraser, N. (2009). *Scales of justice: Reimagining political space in a globalizing world*. New York, NY: Columbia University Press.

Gale, T., & Densmore, K. (2000). *Engaging teachers: Towards a radical democratic agenda for schooling*. Buckingham: Open University Press.

Gomberg, P. (2007). *How to make opportunity equal: Race and contributive justice*. Malden, MA: Blackwell Publishing.

Griffiths, M. (2012). Why joy in education is an issue for socially just policies. *Journal of Education Policy*, 27(5), 655–670. doi:10.1080/02680939.2012.710019

Hardy, I. (2013). A logic of appropriation: Enacting national testing (NAPLAN) in Australia. *Journal of Education Policy*, 29(1), 1–18. doi:10.1080/02680939.2013.782425

Hayes, D. (2012). Re-engaging marginalised young people in learning: The contribution of informal learning and community-based collaborations. *Journal of Education Policy*, *27*(5), 641–653. doi:10.1080/02680939.2012.710018

Hayes, D. (2013). Customization in schooling markets: The relationship between curriculum and pedagogy in a 'pop-up' learning project, and the epistemic opportunities afforded by students' interests and backgrounds. *International Journal of School Disaffection*, *10*(2), 3–22.

Hayes, D., Mills, M., Christie, P., & Lingard, B. (2006). *Teachers and schooling making a difference: Productive pedagogies, assessment and performance*. Crows Nest: Allen & Unwin.

Hochschild, A. (1983). *The managed heart*. Berkeley, CA: University of California Press.

Kane, J. (2011). *Social class, gender and exclusion from schools*. London: Routledge.

Keddie, A. (2012a). Schooling and social justice through the lenses of Nancy Fraser. *Critical Studies in Education*, *53*(3), 263–279. doi:10.1080/17508487.2012.709185

Keddie, A. (2012b). *Educating for diversity and social justice*. New York, NY: Routledge.

Kim, J.-H. (2011). Narrative inquiry into (re)imagining alternative schools: A case study of Kevin Gonzales. *International Journal of Qualitative Studies in Education*, *24*(1), 77–96. doi:10.1080/09518390903468321

Kim, J.-H., & Taylor, K. A. (2008). Rethinking alternative education to break the cycle of educational inequality and inequity. *The Journal of Educational Research*, *101*(4), 207–219. doi:10.3200/JOER.101.4.207-219

Kraftl, P. (2013). *Geographies of alternative education: Diverse learning spaces for children and young people*. Bristol: Policy Press.

Laberee, D. F. (1997). Public goods, private goods: The American struggle over educational goals. *American Educational Research Journal, 34*, 39–81.

Lingard, B., Martino, W., & Rezai-Rashti, G. (2013). Testing regimes, accountabilities and education policy: Commensurate global and national developments. *Journal of Education Policy*, *28*(5), 539–556. doi:10.1080/02680939.2013.820042

Lingard, B., & Sellar, S. (2013). 'Catalyst data': Perverse systemic effects of audit and accountability in Australian schooling. *Journal of Education Policy*, *28*(5), 634–656. doi:10.1080/02680939.2012.758815

Lipman, P. (2008). Mixed-income schools and housing: Advancing the neoliberal urban agenda. *Journal of Education Policy*, *23*(2), 119–134. doi:10.1080/02680930701853021

Lynch, K. (2012). Affective equality as a key issue of justice: A comment on Fraser's 3-dimensiponal framework. *Social Justice Series*, *12*(3), 45–64.

Lynch, K., & Lodge, A. (2002). *Equality and power in schools*: *Redistribution, recognition and representation*. London: RoutledgeFalmer.

Marcus, G. E. (1995). Ethnography in/of the world system: The emergence of multi-sited ethnography. *Annual Review of Anthropology, 24*, 95–117. doi:10.1146/annurev.an.24.100195.000523

McGregor, G., Mills, M., Te Riele, K., & Hayes, D. (2015). Excluded from school: Getting a second chance at a 'meaningful' education. *International Journal of Inclusive Education*, *19*(6), 608–625. doi:10.1080/13603116.2014.961684

Mills, C., & Gale, T. (2010). *Schooling in disadvantaged communities: Playing the game from the back of the field*. Dordrecht: Springer.

Mills, M., & McGregor, G. (2010). *Re-engaging students in education: Success factors in alternative schools*. Brisbane: Youth Affairs Network Queensland.

Mills, M., & McGregor, G. (2014). *Re-engaging young people in education: Learning from alternative schools*. London: Routledge.

Mills, M., McGregor, G., Hayes, D., & Te Riele, K. (2015). 'Schools are for us': The importance of distribution, recognition and representation to creating socially just schools. In K. Trimmer, A. Black, & S. Riddle (Eds.), *Researching mainstreams, margins and the spaces in-between* (pp. 150–167). London: Routledge.

Mills, M., McGregor, G., Martin, B., Tomaszewski, W., & Waters, R. (2014). *Engaging young people in education*. Brisbane: Department of Education, Training and Education.

Mills, M., McGregor, G., & Muspratt, S. (2013). *Flexible learning options/centres in the Australian Capital Territory (ACT)*. Canberra: ACT Education and Training Directorate.

Mills, M., Renshaw, P., & Zipin, L. (2013). Alternative education provision: A dumping ground for 'wasted lives' or a challenge to the mainstream? *Social Alternatives*, *32*(2), 13–18.

Mosen-Lowe, L. A. J., Vidovich, L., & Chapman, A. (2009). Students 'at-risk' policy: Competing social and economic discourses. *Journal of Education Policy*, *24*(4), 461–476. doi:10.1080/02680930902759712

Murphy, J. B. (1994). *The moral economy of labor*. New Haven, CT: Yale.

Noddings, N. (1988). An ethic of caring and its implications for instructional arrangements. *American Journal of Education*, *96*(2), 215–230. doi:10.1086/aje.1988.96.issue-2

OECD. (2012). *Equity and quality in education: Supporting disadvantaged students and schools*. Paris: OECD Publishing. doi:10.1787/9789264130852-en

Olsen, K. (Ed.). (2008). *Adding insult to injury: Nancy Fraser debates her critics*. London: Verso.

Pierides, D. (2010). Multi-sited ethnography and the field of educational research. *Critical Studies in Education*, *51*(2), 179–195. doi:10.1080/17508481003731059

Power, S., & Frandji, D. (2010). Education markets, the new politics of recognition and the increasing fatalism towards inequality. *Journal of Education Policy*, *25*(3), 385–396. doi:10.1080/02680930903576404

Sayer, A. (2009). Contributive justice and meaningful work. *Res Publica*, *15*, 1–16. doi:10.1007/s11158-008-9077-8

Sayer, A. (2011). Habitus, work and contributive justice. *Sociology*, *45*(1), 7–21. doi:10.1177/0038038510387188

Sennett, R. (2009). *The craftsman*. London: Penguin Books.

Slee, R. (2011). *The irregular school: Exclusion, schooling and inclusive education*. London: Routledge.

Smyth, J. (2006). Educational leadership that fosters 'student voice'. *International Journal of Leadership in Education: Theory and Practice*, *9*(4), 279–284. doi:10.1080/13603120600894216

Smyth, J., Angus, L., Down, B., & McInerney, P. (2008). *Critically engaged learning: Connecting to young lives*. New York, NY: Peter Lang Publishers.

Smyth, J., McInerney, P., & Fish, T. (2013). Re-engagement to where? Low SES students in alternative-education programmes on the path to low-status destinations? *Research in Post-Compulsory Education*, *18*(1–2), 194–207. doi:10.1080/13596748.2013.755862

Te Riele, K. (2006). Schooling practices for marginalized students – practice-with-hope. *International Journal of Inclusive Education*, *10*(1), 59–74. doi:10.1080/13603110500221750

Te Riele, K. (2007). Educational alternatives for marginalised youth. *The Australian Educational Researcher*, *34*(3), 53–68. doi:10.1007/BF03216865

Te Riele, K. (2011). Raising educational attainment: How young people's experiences speak back to the compact with young Australians. *Critical Studies in Education*, *52*(1), 93–107. doi:10.1080/17508487.2011.536515

Te Riele, K. (2012). Negotiating risk and hope: A case study of alternative education for marginalized youth in Australia. In W. Pink (Ed.), *Schools and marginalized youth: An international perspective* (pp. 31–79). Cresskill, NJ: Hampton Press.

Te Riele, K. (2014). *Putting the jigsaw together: Flexible learning programs in Australia. Final report*. Melbourne: The Victoria Institute for Education, Diversity and Lifelong Learning. Retrieved from: http://dusseldorp.org.au/priorities/alternative-learning/jigsaw/

Te Riele, K., Davies, M., & Baker, A. (2015). *Passport to a positive future. Evaluation of the Melbourne Academy*. Melbourne: The Victoria Institute for Education, Diversity and Lifelong Learning. Retrieved from http://www.vu.edu.au/sites/default/files/victoria-institute/pdfs/Passport-to-a-Positive-Future-%28web%29.pdf

Teese, R., & Polesel, J. (2003). *Undemocratic schooling: Equity and quality in mass secondary schooling in Australia*. Melbourne: Melbourne University Press.

Thomson, P., & Russell, L. (2007). *Mapping the alternatives to permanent exclusion*. New York, NY: Joseph Rowntree Foundation.

# The force of habit: channelling young bodies at alternative education spaces

Peter Kraftl

This article develops a novel conceptual framework for examining the (re)formulation of habits in education spaces. It is based on the premise that education spaces are key sites for channelling and intervening in children's habits, to various ends. The article focuses on the ways educators at alternative education spaces in the United Kingdom seek to (re)formulate children's habits. In some cases, they do so to combat social exclusion, dealing with some of the most vulnerable children in the UK's educational system. Drawing on the habit-theories of Ravaisson and Dewey, and commensurate post-human, more-than-social approaches to childhood, the article proposes a two-fold conceptualisation of habit: as '(re)calibration' and as 'contagion'. The article draws on empirical examples taken from 10 years' research across 59 alternative education spaces in the United Kingdom. Developing recent educational scholarship on bodies, emotions and affects, it develops an expanded, post-human notion of 'collective' habits that might offer a conceptual language for challenging and imagining alternatives to the perceived problems of the neoliberal educational mainstream. However, the article closes by posing some critical questions for further scholarship about why educators might specifically choose to intervene into children's habits – not least in terms of inclusion and social justice.

## 14 June 2011: A scout hut in London[1]

*I am sitting on a wall, in the sun, facing the scout hut, and chatting to a group of mothers who homeschool their children. They come here every Monday afternoon, for their children to play, socialise and take part in organised activities. As we talk, the sound of screaming interrupts us; we look over to the hut where a man appears from an office doorway, looking harassed. Just out of his sight, four children – boys and girls, various ages between four and fourteen – scamper around the nearest corner, squealing with delight; I catch a glimpse of a red plastic bucket, water splashing onto the concrete. The man stares pointedly in our direction before disappearing into the darkened hallway. I am not sure what has happened, but Annette, one of the mothers, tells me this is a weekly occurrence: an ongoing, low-level spat between the children and the caretaker. Annette's explanation sparks a discussion about how homeschooled children are, collectively, 'different' from schooled children. She explains:*

# ALTERNATIVE EDUCATIONAL PROGRAMMES

*'When a school kid comes to our group, they act in a certain way. And it's almost like our children de-school them, and mould them, without really saying anything at all [...].*

Rowena, another mother, suggests that the 'bucket' incident is symptomatic:

*'When you go to educational places, the staff expect them to behave as school children. Like learning to queue up [...] and ours are lounging around [...].Or, homeschooled children don't know how to sit on chairs. Some will sit on them, others will turn them upside down, others will sit on them backwards.'*

## Introduction

Prompted by examples such as the one above, this article is premised upon the observation that education spaces are key sites for the channelling of habits. Such habits may be expressed as generic descriptors of bodily comportment – like 'grace' – or as more context-specific skills: as Rowena observed, sitting on a chair. Habits are characterised as routine, repetitive acts, performed instinctively in a given situation. The main contribution of this article is to offer a novel conceptual language for articulating how adults attempt to (re)formulate habits in children in education spaces. In doing so, the article opens out several critical questions about inclusion – focussing on both why and, especially, how alternative educators seek to intervene differently into children's habits from a perceived mainstream. It debates the relative merits of a potentially radical conceptualisation of habits that sees them as *mutable* and *collective*, rather than as stable properties of apparently individuated human subjects.

The article progresses through empirical vignettes from research at 59 alternative education spaces in the United Kingdom. The term 'alternative' glosses multiple complexities (Kraftl, 2013a; Woods & Woods, 2009), but denotes education spaces that deliberately differentiate themselves from 'mainstream' schools, which are usually State-funded and follow the UK National Curriculum. In this study, these included Homeschooling, Steiner, Montessori, Democratic, Small-Scale and Forest Schools and Care Farms[2]. Although diverse, all pursue knowingly alternative pedagogies, and provide a replacement for all or part of a child's education in a context where it is assumed that children aged 4–16 attend school. Alternative education spaces offer a significant starting place for discussion about inclusion, because they are rooted in pedagogies that seek to evade the apparent problems of mainstream education (rote learning, didactic teaching, standardised testing/progression), whilst privileging the development of human relationships, bodily movements, the arts and dialogic learning. Alternative educators also wrestle directly with inclusiveness in two senses: first, in that their democratic, dialogic approaches are often viewed as pedagogically and socially inclusive; second, in that alternative education spaces frequently take children with a range of emotional, social and bodily differences, who have often struggled at mainstream schools. Some alternative education spaces do not *expressly* cater for such children, but have developed a reputation for working with them – in the case of Steiner Schools, for working with children on the autistic spectrum. Others, like Care Farms, explicitly offer therapeutic learning experiences for children at risk of exclusion from mainstream schools, sometimes as part of attempts to reintegrate a child for life in a mainstream school, training or paid work. The article's central premise is that the (re)learning of habits is foundational to the work of alternative educators, but that processes of habit (re)formation require much greater analysis and conceptualisation – not least in order to critically assess their possible implications for 'mainstream' settings.

117

The article begins by briefly situating my project within educational research on embodiment and emotion. Thereafter, and building on that work, it specifies two theorisations of habit, which are deployed in the article's empirical analyses. These are based around the contrasting but in some senses complementary work of two habit theorists: Félix Ravaisson and John Dewey. The second section summarises the research project upon which this article was based, and introduces the key education spaces appearing in the article. The third and fourth sections offer two steps towards a conceptual language for articulating habit (re)formation in educational spaces: habit as '(re)calibration'; habit as 'contagion'.

## The force of habit in education

With its focus on habit, this article extends a recent groundswell of research within education studies on bodies/emotions. Evans, Davies, and Rich (2009) summarise how bodies/emotions have been conceptualised threefold (also Cook & Hemming, 2011). First, children's bodies have been understood as socially constructed, produced and regulated via ideological messages, policies and laws. This viewpoint undergirded well-established 'new social studies of childhood', prompting analyses of how children's bodies/emotions were often framed as either vulnerable or dangerous (Valentine, 1996). Notably, a key early assumption – since questioned – was that a focus upon emotions in both research and classroom teaching was de facto progressive (Evans, Rich, Davies, & Allwood, 2005). Second, education scholars have examined how teachers' and children's bodies feel, especially in terms of the affects produced through their interactions (Probyn, 2005; Zembylas, 2009). Rather than categorisable emotions felt individually, affects denote shared feelings, atmospheres or ineffable energies that connect (and divide) bodies in the classroom. As Youdell (2010) demonstrates, the classroom is marked not only by entrenched flows of bodies, practices, affects and subjectivities, but also cut across by potential new becomings – new constellations, performances or knowledges that move beyond scripted performativities in schools. Third, bodies/emotions may be made flesh, in education spaces (Evans et al., 2009). Significantly, this observation chimes with a 'new wave' of childhood studies (Kraftl, 2013b; Prout, 2005; Ryan, 2011), in which erstwhile attention to the *socially* constituted child's body is tempered by attentiveness to the fleshy processes of bodies constituted through shifting combinations of matter, human and non-human. As Prout (2005, p. 3-4) argues, this is a 'requirement that childhood studies move beyond the opposition of nature and culture [to] a hybrid form [wherein] children's capacities are extended and supplemented by all kinds of material artefacts and technologies, which are also hybrids of nature and culture'. Prout therefore examines the ways in which childhoods are produced and experienced through complex, dynamic constellations into which children (and adults) enter with information technologies, genetics and psychopharmaceuticals. More recently, scholars have examined how new neuroscientific knowledges have been deployed in schools for citizenship education (Pykett, 2012), and have critiqued how anti-obesity policies not only mark but also intervene in fleshy processes of eating and exercising (Evans, 2010; Pike & Kelly, 2014).

These ways of understanding bodies/emotions in education offer a starting point for some of this article's analyses. However – and in extending the latter two approaches – it is necessary to develop a theoretical language more attuned to how *habit*-formation takes place at alternative education spaces. Everyday usage of the term sees habit as a conservative force that stultifies individual human creativity and reflexivity; a force acting upon the body, 'below the level of consciousness and language' (Carlisle, 2013; Crossley, 2001). Recently, however, scholars have explicated the malleability of habit.

# ALTERNATIVE EDUCATIONAL PROGRAMMES

Drawing on Ravaisson (2008), there has been growing acceptance that habits may be cultivated, albeit with disagreement on the level of conscious reflection required (Carlisle, 2010). Thus, as a habit takes hold over time, an individual may, simultaneously, be increasingly *bound* by their habits whilst also *free* to undertake other tasks whilst performing them (e.g. an accomplished car driver able to hold a conversation whilst driving). This is what Ravaisson (2008, p. 37) – a key inspiration for contemporary habit theories – termed 'the double law of habit'. Thus, for Carlisle (2013), habit is an 'ambivalent' component of human embodiment, sitting between freedom and necessity, routine and creativity.

Radically, such scholarship also enables attunement to *collective* facets of habituation. Looking across a range of habit scholarship, there is insistence that habit is, variously, central to social reproduction, skilling and power (Bissell, 2015), a 'switchpoint' between isolated individual actions and collective laws (Crook, 2013), and entrained in 'affective habit ecologies' dispersed across individual bodies (Dewsbury, 2012).[1] The most radical element of this work – with its roots in Ravaisson's (2008) observation of a continuity between human will and 'nature' – is that the 'collective' referred to here is not merely a *social* one, but material, or more-than-social (Kraftl, 2013b). Resonating with more recent post-human scholarship and the 'new wave' of childhood studies discussed above, in Ravaissonian conceptions of habit the primacy of the sovereign human agent is radically overhauled (Bennett, 2010). As air, water, food and chemicals flow into, through and out of a 'human body', it becomes apparent that this body is constituted not only socially, but also via molecular, pre-conscious, for-the-moment flows of life itself. If, as post-humanists have now clearly established (Bennett, 2010), we follow those *processes* rather than start a priori with the bodies they constitute, then such a manoeuvre breaks down assumed boundaries between self and other, human and non-human, and, indeed, the idea of the sovereign human agent.

The above scholarship provides important signposts for developing a conceptual language of habit in education spaces. It provides a set of resources for explicating how alternative educators embrace both emergent, contingent events and how they seek to stabilise shifting constellations of affect and (non)human bodies in the concretisation of new habits (Kraftl, 2013a). Moreover, as I demonstrate below, this scholarship – contra the focus on individual children's bodies/emotions in much childhood studies research and, indeed, in neoliberal educational agendas – enables much sharper attunement to the ways in which *collective*, contagious habits exceed and (re)combine apparently individual agents (e.g. Tarde, 1903). Thus, this article extends (via a language of habit) other recent work on how bodies/affects are 'made flesh' in the classroom (Youdell, 2010) and nascent 'more-than-social' or hybrid approaches to a new wave of childhood studies (Kraftl, 2013b). As I argue in conclusion, such an expanded, collective conception of habit may contain radical political potential for both critiquing and imagining alternatives to what many commentators view as the exclusionary and unjust machinations of neoliberal educational models.

Nevertheless, Ravaissonian theories of habit do not (quite) provide the conceptual tools for analysing moral judgements about inclusion; nor do they deal explicitly with education. Here, broadly conceived pragmatist conceptions of habit could come into play. Given his influence in educational circles – and upon many alternative educators themselves – I emphasise Dewey's work here. There exist some important similarities and productive tensions between Ravaisson's and Dewey's approaches to habit. Like Ravaisson, Dewey saw habit as malleable, developed in interaction with the environment, and a force that enabled agency rather than constrained it (Dewey, 1921). Moreover, like

119

Ravaisson, Dewey ascribed a moral dimension to habit acquisition – tethered into judgements about what is 'good' or 'bad' (Dewey, 1921, p. 120).

However, Dewey placed greater emphasis upon the active cultivation of 'good' habits (whose nature will remain undefined here). Dewey recognised – in parallel with post-humanist conceptions of agency – that the stimulus for such cultivation may not be individual, reflective thought. He devotes considerable attention to 'impulses' – 'pivot points', surprises, immediate responses, whose event-al properties provoke the recalibration of old habits (Cuffari, 2011). From here, though, Ravaisson and Dewey diverged. In the service of bettering habits, Ravaisson favoured non-cognitive tasks, like meditation and yoga (Ravaisson, 2008; also Lea, 2009). Dewey preferred more directed, less passive process of working with habit: through moral reflection upon and programmes to achieve tangible goals (Dewey, 1921).

Critically, Dewey ascribed great importance to education as a force for habit formation. Rooted in his 'theory of experience' (Dewey, 1997), Dewey directed the goals of education in terms of their relevance for society's future needs, 'ground[ed] in the human life process' (Harris, 2012, p. 24). Yet these 'needs' were not necessarily teleological: recursively, such goals should be both imagined and realised through educational processes that would foster habits of questioning and imagination (hence their importance to alternative education: see Kraftl, 2013a). Education, then, is a proliferative, embodied, contingent, but *also reflexive* exercise that capitalises upon impulsive 'pivot points'. This is what Sullivan (2001, p. 104) calls 'rebodying': a form of embodied experimentation, but one which is not totally fluid, formless or un-planned:'[w]hat education should do, paradoxical though it might sound, is to enable people to develop firm habits that support flexible modes of being'. Following Dewey, Sullivan also argues that the cultivation of habit may not simply occur through a uni-directional process of transmission from teacher to learner. Rather, when different habit-regimes (for instance, those of adults and children) come into contact, those habits may conflict; different habits may 'challenge and influence one another', potentially, 'opening up possibilities for reconfigurations of habit and thus of culture as well (Sullivan, 2001, p. 105)'. The next section of the article examines how these processes may occur.

Whilst not philosophically entirely commensurate, Ravaisson's and Dewey's habit-theories offer a basis for articulating how habits might be (re)formed in education spaces. They indicate that whilst habits may coalesce within individuated, reflective human subjects, recursively, habits emerge from pre-cognitive, contingent relationships between bodies-in-worlds, and can therefore be *collective*, in a more-than-social, expanded sense of the term. Yet, as Dewey argues, habits may also be subject to active planning and experimentation, such that they could be a proper realm for intervention by educators. The rest of this article examines how alternative educators articulate these possibilities.

**Researching geographies of alternative education**

This article is based upon a large-scale research project, which examined 59 alternative education spaces across the United Kingdom, over 10 years. I sampled a diverse range of educational approaches (stratified by both type and location in the United Kingdom), visiting each site, and using relatively traditional qualitative methods of data collection. I spent a minimum of one day (usually two or three) at most sites, observing, taking part in activities, and talking with children,[2] parents, teachers, educators/practitioners and volunteers. I engaged in several informal conversations at each site, alongside a total of 114 formal, semi-structured interviews. Interviewees were selected through a mixture of

# ALTERNATIVE EDUCATIONAL PROGRAMMES

convenience (i.e. those present when I visited) and more targeted processes (pre-arranging interviews with headteachers/directors/leaders and some young people). The formal interviews followed standard, strict ethical procedures in terms of confidentiality, anonymity, freedom to withdraw and informed consent. The only (minimal) ethical challenge was presented during more informal, ad-hoc discussions with adults (which were not tape-recorded): in those cases, my research was still overt, verbal consent was obtained, and, as with all interviews, interviewees were given my contact details as a failsafe should they have wished to withdraw from the study later. The whole project received institutional ethical approval from the two separate universities at which I was based during periods of data collection. I kept detailed field notebooks (again overtly, and always with consent from a gatekeeper) during periods of observation, and made sketches of key places and 'moments' during the research. Importantly, 49 of the interviews were with children: as a childhood scholar, a fundamental aim was to understand their experiences of alternative education. There is not space to provide more than brief excerpts from my research with children in this article, since my aim is to explore how *adult* alternative educators sought to (re)formulate children's habits. Some of the empirical material provides some sense of children's responses, but their occasional appearance in this article is not an attempt to downplay their 'agency' (although given the conceptualisation of habit deployed here, that term is itself problematic: see Kraftl, 2013b for a detailed critique of the notion of children's agency).

All data were subject to manual thematic analysis. This approach was made systematic through the use of open, axial and selective coding strategies (Strauss & Corbin, 1990). I undertook repeated reading, coding and re-coding of transcripts alongside the contents of my field notebooks – a process that began in the second year of my research, and was developed and interrogated at regular intervals. Therefore, analysis was integral to the research process, progressively focussed and empirically tested, through iterative data production and analysis.

The vast majority of educators/practitioners were familiar with the notion of habit as something that somehow resonated with their chosen pedagogies. This was unsurprising: most definitions of alternative education – which draw on the 'radical' pedagogies of Dewey, Holt, Freire, Illich and others – recognise that alternative educational practices are 'holistic'. Whilst day-to-day practicalities may vary, holistic forms of learning frequently involve closer attention to children's bodies/emotions, the creation of appropriate learning atmospheres that may enable mutual respect (Kraftl, 2006), often with some common root in Dewey's notion of 'experience'. Nevertheless, whilst many educators/practitioners recognised the importance of children gaining particular habits, they were wary of the ethical implications of claims to instil 'good' habits.

The article's analysis draws on indicative examples from three forms of alternative education. First, from *Homeschooling*: the practice, usually undertaken by parents, of educating one's children at home instead of at school. Around 150,000 children are homeschooled in the United Kingdom, through diverse learning styles (Lees, 2013). My research focused upon families who use child-centred techniques, which follow the interests and perceived needs of individual children. I draw largely on vignettes and quotations from self-organised homeschooling groups, attended by homeschooling families to provide opportunities for play, co-learning and socialisation. Second, *Care Farms* are either existing farms that have diversified from agriculture to provide learning experiences, or purpose-built farms that offer activities such as horticulture, gardening and animal care. With their bases in Dutch models of 'Green Care' (Hine, Peacock, & Pretty, 2008), Care Farms are not purely educational spaces, as they cater for a range of 'clients', including: disabled children and adults, for whom contact with animals and plants might be 'therapeutic'; children with emotional-behavioural differences, for whom human–animal relationships may (re)establish 'improved' relationships with human others (Berget & Braastad, 2008); mainstream school groups, who make occasional day visits. In 2012, there were approximately 180 Care Farms in the United Kingdom (Kraftl, 2013a). Third, *Forest Schools* are intended to allow children to (re)connect with 'nature', where it is argued that many have lost meaningful contact with the natural world (O'Brien, 2009). Forest Schools operate in patches of woodland where children engage in various tasks they might ordinarily not: firelighting, den-building, using knives, story-telling and 'free' play (Knight, 2009). In terms of habit, a key feature of learning at both Care Farms and Forest Schools is repetition. Children are considered to benefit if they visit regularly, for a defined period of time, in a carefully boundaried space, building upon similar skills during each visit. Cognisant of the differences between the case studies, I nevertheless attune my analyses to constructing a conceptual focuses upon two broad, non-exhaustive, overlapping types of habit-formation: '(re)calibration' and 'contagion'.

## (Re)calibrating habits, 'channelling the same energy'

### A Care Farm, on a squally April day in Scotland

*I amble along a muddy grass path, sided by wire fences and small paddocks that separate sheep and horses. Clive, a practitioner, leads the way. Further ahead, fourteen-year-old Ben has disappeared through a small stand of pine trees. When we catch up, on the other side of the trees, Ben is hand-feeding some hens, having let himself into their enclosure, talking to the birds in a voice so quiet we cannot hear. Immediately he hears us arrive, he starts, looks up, and around, but not directly at us; he seems unsure what to do; after a couple of long seconds, he strides purposefully inside the wooden chicken coup, emerging with an egg in each hand. He passes the warm eggs to us, one each, without a word to me. He cocks his head slightly, face expressionless, looking briefly at Clive, as if to say – 'see?'. Then he heads off after one of the farm dogs, and away, into a larger field, from where we occasionally hear him calling the dog's name.*

The moment at which Ben passed over the eggs was a Deweyian 'pivot point' in several ways. It demonstrated, perhaps more than any other encounter in my research, the potential fragility of habit-formation. Ben's response was, I learned afterwards, somewhat unprecedented. Perhaps not a habit at all, perhaps a proto-habit, Ben had been attending the Farm for five weeks and had only recently gained the confidence to enter the chicken coup on his own. Before coming to the Farm, he had, according to his teachers, lost virtually all capacity to interact with other people, and had been temporarily excluded from school. That he had given an egg to me – a complete stranger – was indicative of a change, but surprised even Clive. The Farm had, over time, acted as some kind of pivotal space and time such that Ben's apparently instinctual reaction to our startling him was to collect an egg for us. There was something a little raw – stilted even – about this performance, sharpened by the ironic nod that followed. It afforded a sense that what we were seeing was a motivation, at least, for the 'reorganizing or redirecting of old habits' (Cuffari, 2011, p. 539), their intentional modification through the carefully designed, repetitive activities through which Clive had engaged Ben. As Bissell (2015) notes, via Ravaisson, repetition is not only central to habit-formation itself, but to the exercise of authority through the inculcation of apparently 'good' habits (also Kraftl,

# ALTERNATIVE EDUCATIONAL PROGRAMMES

2015). After Ben had given us the eggs, Clive explained how the recalibration of 'good' habits was central to the *inclusive* mission of his Care Farm.

> *Over time, lads like Ben, they will become more confident to make decisions – how much food for the hens. Say, I'll show them for the first couple of weeks, but then, taking a step back, I won't. They're doing it without thinking, without me. Gradually, it will be distanced from me. [...].With young people, it's mostly about changing behaviour. Seeing the world's not all bad out there. [...] They need something to make them feel good about themselves. [...] Not too much pressure, and reorienting, so that when they see a half-broken pipe, they don't just instinctively kick it, they ask straight away, how can I fix that? It's channelling the same energy [...] using a power tool, you get the same kind of buzz, release, but look at the end result.*

Strikingly, this vignette speaks of the (re)calibration of habit as *motive*, in a triple sense. Firstly, as a move away from thought, towards the pre-reflective accomplishment of a physical task – when 'they're doing it without thinking', as Clive put it. Or, as Dewey (1921, p. 180) posited: '[i]n this period of redistribution, impulse determines the direction of movement. It furnishes the focus about which reorganization [of habit] swirls'. Second, habit emerges as a form of movement (which may include being emotionally moved) away from particular habit-bundles towards others. Third, the recalibration of habits presents a kind of motivation to change that fulfils some kind of personal or social 'good' that is potentially inclusive – whether 'feeling good' or 'seeing that the world's not all bad', in Clive's words. For Ravaisson (2008), the repetition of habits constituted a movement towards the fulfilment of particular desire drives; in Ben's case, through whatever sensuous pleasure is derived from using a power tool. As previously discussed, Dewey also highlighted the motivating power of habit, although rather more pragmatically towards a 'deliberate yet undetermined project of transformation' (Cuffari, 2011, p. 549). This sentiment was echoed at several Care Farms I visited. Clearly, there is a desire to change what are deemed 'problematic' or 'anti-social' behaviours – and perhaps this desire diverges little from the exercise of power through neoliberal education and youth policies in the United Kingdom (compare Pykett, 2012). Yet the ultimate goals of doing so are rather less defined. They may be inclusive in an instrumental sense – to enable Ben to return to school, for instance. Yet even in such cases, it is the *process* of motivation – expressed by Clive as a 'channelling' of the same energy – that represents the kernel of such interventions, and, importantly, a *good-in-itself*.

### London: a conversation with James, aged fifteen

*Until he was fifteen, James had been home-schooled and had never been to school. Recently, his parents had sent him to a fee-paying independent school, in London. We spent time reflecting on this transition. James told me that although he has no desire to break any rules, some aspects of his behaviour that he had never even thought about before had been deemed problematic by teachers and other pupils.*

> *'I was told to calm down, because I hug too many people. I was like, yeah. That's not calming down. I'm the calmest person there. [...] It's kind of weird, it makes me cringe, the difference between the seriousness. It's seriousness of two kinds. I am serious when I am into something. But this is something else. They're even serious about having fun. Like so competitive.'*

'Seriousness' was, for James, something habituated: something pre-reflective, but something that in whichever brand – being 'into something' or being 'competitive' – seemed to permeate aspects of his own and his classmates' being. In acknowledging two kinds of seriousness, James' experience resonates with Clive's conceptualisation of 'energy', where the energy in this case is 'seriousness'. Seriousness was, for James, a character trait that we could all hold, yet something expressed, habitually, in different ways.

James' experience prompts the first of three reflections about a movement from habit as something contained within an *individual* subject to a Ravaissonian and post-human sense of habit as inter-subjective, more-than-human and, hence, *collective*. These reflections are also salient to the scout hut vignette with which this article began. First, habits are thrown into sharp relief when different habit-worlds collide (Sullivan, 2001), and especially when the same 'energy' is expressed in two divergent (but similarly named) habits: seriousness. This collision is a harbinger of power relations of inclusivity/exclusivity: James is an 'outsider' at his new school and is subject to scrutiny from teachers and peers because of his particular brand of 'seriousness'. Nevertheless, James' rather unusual educational history *enables reflection upon habit*: upon entering the school, James noted that his habituated actions were different from his peers' *shared* habituated dispositions. The latter performed such habits collectively: in their treatment of James, and in how James was able to observe their shared 'competitiveness'.

Indeed, James' experience offered a unique opportunity to shed some light upon the bodily capacities, affects and habits that are performed in neoliberal educational contexts. Perhaps these kinds of habits are heightened, even, in the context of a fee-paying school in which pupil achievement and league-table positioning dominate pupils' educational experiences. On one hand, as Pykett (2012) argues, James' transition to this school marks out how neoliberal education (and schooling) operate via a range of somatic, affective and bodily registers – from neuroscientific knowledge about brain functioning to 'acceptable' forms of collective behavioural traits that will lead to educational 'success'. On the other hand, they add flesh – literally – to the well-worn observation that neoliberal educational agendas have sought to 'skill' school children in ways that prepare them – as future adults – for work in contemporary economies (Zembylas, 2009). The kinds of 'seriousness' James recounts are, in other words, produced through discursive, affective and performative logics that are highly redolent of the 'soft' forms of capitalism identified by Thrift (1997), which in turn predicated on new styles of management that – like some forms of neoliberal education – privilege attention to emotions and bodily skills in the formation of more 'productive' subjects (see also Pykett & Enright, 2015).

Second, I argue that the (re)calibration of apparently individual habits is nonetheless a collective process, which involves a degree of *harmonisation*. A practitioner at a Forest School, where young people are taught woodworking skills, stated:

> [w]hen I teach a young person how to saw wood, I make the sound of how it should sound. I go shoo, shoo, I put my hand on the saw with them, to feel the rhythm of it. Sometimes, you need to see, to hear, to feel, together (Andy, Forest School practitioner)

Harmonisation is, however, not about delicately choreographing the same literal performance, whether weighing out seed or sawing wood. It is also a matter of knowing when to withdraw, so that, as Clive indicated, 'they just start doing it'. The pivot-point of this harmonisation process is the transition from mimickery (performing the same skill together) to withdrawal. In that moment, habits 'are the means of knowledge and thought' (Dewey, 1921, p. 176); when combined with impulses, and when responsive enough to a given situation, they allow what conventionally passes for individuated, reflective human agency. Thus, as a reminder of the possible commensurability of Ravaisson's and Dewey's conceptions of habit, habits may also move from apparently collective to ostensibly individual properties. Reliance upon a habit-companion – necessary to learn a new habit – may be rescinded in a movement towards the (partial) freedom of an individual human being (compare Carlisle, 2013).

Third, after a shared, 'good' habit takes hold in an individual, there remains the possibility for the re-collectivisation of that habit, towards a sense of 'inclusion', however tenuous. After our discussion about Ben, Clive depicted a scenario in which some young people were gently introduced to others at the Farm: 'if things work out for an individual young person, we try to match them up with another young person, or a small group, gradually building up their confidence – but only if they are broadly similar in their behaviour'. Significantly, not all young people are simply inculcated with the same 'good' habits. Rather, energies are channelled such that the habits of one young person *may* resonate with one, but not another. Thus, the orchestration of resonant habits affords what one might rather glibly term the '(re)socialisation' process that forms an important part of many Care Farms' work: a step towards some kind of social inclusion.

Thus far, I have argued that the habit-theories of Ravaisson and Dewey can be brought together to *specify* how habits could be formulated through (re)calibration. Such a conceptualisation of habit – specified further via tropes of the motive and the collective – offers a starting point for a novel theoretical language for articulating how educators seek (of course not always successfully) to intervene into young people's habits. Most significantly, given James' experience of entering a more mainstream school environment, this theoretical language might enable the formulation of similar, critical questions about how neoliberal educational systems make their own demands on children's bodily habits, both individually and *collectively*. I develop this discussion through the rest of the article.

## Habit as contagion: Group dynamics and co-learning habits

### *A Care Farm in the outer suburb of a medium-sized city in Eastern England*

*Maura, a Care Farm practitioner, is showing me around the Farm. The main building serves many functions for the disadvantaged, suburban estate that surrounds it: a nursery, a Sure Start[3] Centre, a youth club. The small outside space is similarly multi-purpose. Maura shows me a stand of several pine trees, with some blackened ground scarred by fire, used for Forest School. A small pen contains a pig, some chickens and ducks, which is used for Care Farming. The rest of the site is given over to an enormous, colourful adventure playground, built twenty years ago. We head to a portakabin, where Maura tells me about the role the Farm plays for local teenagers:*

> *'This is a space to experience challenging behaviour, deal with it, and talk about it. A space to just be, kind of between the school and the street. [...] It's more supervised [than the street] but not so regimented [as school]. The difference is that we take a step back, as professional adults. Their attitudes and dispositions do change. They learn alongside playing with other children: [...] how to take themselves away, sometimes, if they're feeling angry. They learn to deal with situations, without anybody else stepping in. It's not just the theory, that they might learn in citizenship ed at school. It's the immediate thing, the immediate, impulse response, almost emotional.'*

I argued above that collective habits might somehow resonate, unspoken, between two individuals or a group. Yet, as Dewey argued, this does not efface more deliberative or reflective forms of communication. These are *education* spaces, which rarely work without some measure of reflection and dialogue. In developing an argument around habits as more-than-individual properties (as per Ravaisson), I want to theorise this process of both spoken and unspoken transmission as *contagion*. My analysis evokes theories that view contagion not only as biological infection (i.e. disease) but in how bodily/emotional states (such as excitement) can be transmitted between people (Tarde, 1903). Critically, there is little agreement about *how*, exactly, social contagion proceeds, although the term is usually used to describe affects and habits that permeate large-scale crowd events or denote the mood of a populace (for instance, following a national election) (Kraftl, 2010). Therefore, explanations of social contagion usually refer to processes affecting a large-scale collective, and refer to emotional/affective states (Levy & Nail, 1993). By distinction, I use the term contagion – perhaps provocatively – to characterise smaller-scale, but nonetheless inter-subjective processes of habit-formation that are emotional, embodied *and* materialised. Bearing in mind Maura's words, I use the term contagion to foreground three further considerations about habit.

The first relates to the framing of group interaction as 'impulsive' and 'emotional', in Maura's words. Her words could be interpreted as a generic descriptor for the kinds of unspoken, pre-cognitive, affective energies that drive wordly interaction (Anderson, 2006). Yet they obtain particular significance for habit-formation when cross-referenced with what Maura terms changing 'dispositions' and 'attitudes'. Whilst habits may be communicated through oral instructions, Maura describes how habits may also be transmitted and choreographed through gestures. Something similar was evident in earlier examples: from the Scout Hut, to Andy's depiction of learning to saw, to Clive's gradual, quiet withdrawal. The critical point is that habits are *somehow* transmitted, once a *body* becomes receptive-enough (or, being provocative, vulnerable-enough). Habits are contracted through repeated exposure: they are contagious.

The second consideration is inspired by James' experience of attending school and Maura's explanation of how young people 'learn to deal with situations'. It pertains to the role of adults in transmitting habits. In these two examples, young people appear to exhibit considerable agency through self-policing challenging habits ('problem behaviours'), without adult intervention. Something similar happened at the scout hut, where exposure to the contagious collective habits of Homeschooled children might 'de-school' newcomers. However, if one adopts a Foucauldian conception of power and habit (Cuffari, 2011), adults' presence seeps through children's apparently autonomous habit-regulation. The acts of withdrawal recounted by Clive and Maura are premised upon sets of carefully honed ground rules, material environments and spatio-temporal boundaries that are instilled at Care Farms and Forest Schools (Knight, 2009). Those rules, materialities and boundaries themselves have been learned: perhaps deliberately instilled through Homeschoolers' cogitation of the pedagogic 'greats'; perhaps through consideration about what constitute 'bad' habits, and which consideration itself is founded in broader, societal understandings (or habituation) about what constitutes 'anti-social' behaviour, in the United Kingdom, in 2011. However the teenagers at Maura's Care Farm work out their differences in-the-moment, their provisional solutions will likely (but not always) match predominant moral schema – not least because if they diverge too greatly, Maura and her colleagues *will* intervene. Thus, collective habit-formation is contagious in a second sense: adults transmit habits to some children, who – in exhibiting some measure of 'agency' – in turn ensure that other children's bodies contract resonant habits. The identity of the original 'host' is (perhaps deliberately) obscured – sometimes through planned 'withdrawal' – so that future contagion takes place.

Thirdly, I have termed the transmissive properties of habit 'contagion' to provoke debate. The term contagion can be read pejoratively, indicative of how there may be disagreement as to the moral fortitude of particular habits, with little in the way of guidance as to what are 'good' habits. Certainly, alternative pedagogies affirm certain principles, which are contrasted with apparently deficient principles in mainstream education. These principles deliberately offer an antidote to what might be read (from the previous point) as an almost inescapably, structuralist, fatalist reading of societal contagion – they are attempts to practice 'alter-childhoods' (Kraftl, 2015). Yet that does not mean that such values are *a priori* any more morally worthy, despite the many critiques of neoliberal educational policies that exist. They are, simply, alternative, and it may be that these habits themselves are viewed as deficient or threatening by other critics (see for instance, Ecclestone & Hayes, 2008 critique of therapeutic education). The difficulty in making such judgements is compounded by the fact that in fomenting (re)channelled habits, practitioners such as Care Farmers may not only value change (for 'therapy', for instance), but may pursue instrumental goals, such as a young person returning to school. These are goals to combat certain forms of social exclusion with which some in the mainstream may agree, even if they do not agree with the particular habits being acquired.

## Conclusions

This article's main contribution has been to formulate a novel conceptual language through which educational scholars can articulate how habits might be (re)formulated in education spaces. Via Ravaisson, Dewey and related post-human/more-than-social theories, the article proposed a non-exhaustive conceptualisation of the channelling of habits at alternative education spaces in the United Kingdom. That conceptualisation was characterised by two key, inter-linked properties: (re)calibration and contagion. In terms (re)calibration, habits act as a switchpoint, oscillating between individual and group behaviours. They operate through harmonisation and motivation, as the practices of individual bodies are (re)orchestrated such that they may – however temporarily – resonate with one another, towards forms of inclusion that may be localised and momentary, and/or more enduring. The term (re)channelling also pointed towards similar energies (like 'seriousness') that are articulated in divergent ways, becoming most apparent when an 'outsider' is exposed to the habits of a pre-existing group. The idea of contagion further sharpens the properties of habit-formation in three ways. First, through both the transmission (unspoken *and* spoken) of habits between educators and learners, and between learners and learners. Second, through the ongoing effects of contagion by 'adult'-designated habits that, even in the (deliberate) absence of their originators, continue to be contracted by other bodies. Third, given that the contagiousness of habits entails a multiply scaled, materialised and – timed series of power relations, the term 'contagion' is meant provocatively: to prompt further reflection as to the relative moral worth of intentional habit formation.

These final observations – both moral and political – require far greater discussion than possible here. Indeed, the article's main contribution has been to open out processes and practices of habit-formation, via a novel conceptual language surrounding habit, to prompt future scholarship by education and childhood studies scholars. Yet I would argue here that questions of power and moral judgement could be addressed through the conceptual languages I have formulated in this article. In particular, scholars might critically analyse the role of *collective* (and contagious) habits in diverse educational settings, and especially in 'mainstream' schools. In closing, I argue that this is because to theorise habit as *collective* – rather than individual – is both a potentially radical political move and one open to further debate.

Ravaisson and, especially, Dewey are so helpful for conceptualising alternative education because many alternative pedagogues seek to efface teleology in education (preferring creativity and contingency) and emphasise the educational collective over individual gain. Specifically, the post-human, more-than-social conceptions of habit in this article challenge the ontological primacy of the sovereign human subject in education, albeit to varying degrees in the examples cited. Thus, to perform what especially in neoliberal contexts is a counter-intuitive manoeuvre – to posit habits as *collective* – is radically inclusive in both conceptual and political senses. This is because – like related work on affect (Youdell, 2010; Zembylas, 2009) – doing so runs against the grain (or, rather, the granularity) of contemporary neoliberal educational praxes. One might ask, then: what possibilities might be imagined (or already exist) in mainstream educational settings for the formulation of collective habits amongst young people? By extension, educational scholars and practitioners might ask whether and how such collective habits – whether or not inspired by the praxes of alternative educators – might offer models of schooling that are in any way more progressive, inclusive or socially just than those of predominant neoliberal models.

However, and in part answering the above question, the ultimate *aims* towards which particular kinds of habit are put sometimes still remain unclear at many alternative education spaces. In some cases, notions of inclusion or democracy that are deployed by alternative educators are quite vague, ranging from simple inclusion in education of any kind to more pragmatic attempts to return a child to mainstream schooling. Therefore, notwithstanding the radical conceptual and political potential of a language of collective habits, that potential might be hollowed out if attention to the for-the-moment, embodied-emotional registers of habit is divorced from their implication in *better-specified*, more durable and broader-scaled power relations. As I argued in the final section of the article, these effects and power relations striate apparently momentary events of habit-acquisition, produced through contextual understandings of 'anti-social behaviour' and citizenship in the twenty-first century United Kingdom, and adults' preferences for 'good habits' that may structure children's behaviour, but be deliberately hidden from them. The process of instilling and (re)formulating habits – let alone the process of identifying 'good habits' – is a fraught one. Even if posited as a form radically inclusive, collective education that might remedy the perceived injustices of neoliberal education, the very *idea* of educating habits requires further sustained and critical scrutiny. This article has offered the beginnings of a conceptual language for doing so.

### Acknowledgements

I would like to thank the educators, young people, volunteers, parents and others who supported my research at the 59 alternative education spaces included in the study reported in this article. I would also like to thank the guest editors for inviting me to submit an article to this special issue, and for their constructive and insightful comments on an earlier draft. Finally, I would like to thank two anonymous referees for their generous, positive and constructive critiques.

### Notes

1. The italicised sections in this article recount notes from the field diary I kept during my alternative education research.

## ALTERNATIVE EDUCATIONAL PROGRAMMES

2. An explanation of the learning sites included in this article is provided in the next section. For a full introduction to these sites, see Kraftl (2013a).
3. Introduced by the UK New Labour Government, Sure Start Centres (and, latterly, Children's Centres) were located in socio-economically disadvantaged communities to provide support for parents and early years education (Jupp, 2012).

## References

Anderson, B. (2006). Becoming and being hopeful: Towards a theory of affect. *Environment and Planning D: Society and Space, 24,* 733–752. doi:10.1068/d393t

Bennett, J. (2010). *Vibrant matter.* Durham: Duke UP.

Berget, B., & Braastad, B. (2008). Animal-assisted therapy with farm animals for persons with psychiatric disorders. *Annals Ist Super Sanita, 47,* 384–390. doi:10.1186/1745-0179-4-9

Bissell, D. (2015). Virtual infrastructures of habit: The changing intensities of habit through gracefulness, restlessness and clumsiness. *Cultural Geographies, 22,* 127–146. doi:10.1177/1474474013482812

Carlisle, C. (2010). Between freedom and necessity: Félix Ravaisson on habit and the moral life. *Inquiry: A Journal of Medical Care Organization, Provision and Financing, 53,* 123–145. doi:10.1080/00201741003612146

Carlisle, C. (2013). The question of habit in Theology and philosophy: From hexis to plasticity. *Body & Society, 19,* 30–57. doi:10.1177/1357034X12474475

Cook, V., & Hemming, P. (2011). Education spaces: Embodied dimensions and dynamics. *Social & Cultural Geography, 12,* 1–8. doi:10.1080/14649365.2011.542483

Crook, T. (2013). Habit as switchpoint. *Body & Society, 19,* 275–281. doi:10.1177/1357034X13484372

Crossley, N. (2001). The phenomenological habitus and its construction. *Theory and Society, 30,* 81–120. doi:10.1023/A:1011070710987

Cuffari, E. (2011). Habits of transformation. *Hypatia, 26,* 535–553. doi:10.1111/j.1527-2001.2011.01186.x

Dewey, J. (1921). *Human nature and conduct.* London: Allen and Unwin.

Dewey, J. (1997). *Experience and education.* New York: Touchstone.

Dewsbury, J.-D. (2012). Affective habit Ecologies: Material dispositions and immanent inhabitations. *Performance Research, 17,* 74–82. doi:10.1080/13528165.2012.712263

Ecclestone, K., & Hayes, D. (2008). *The dangerous rise in therapeutic education.* London: Routledge.

Evans, B. (2010). Anticipating fatness: Childhood, affect and the pre-emptive 'war on obesity'. *Transactions of the Institute of British Geographers, 35,* 21–38. doi:10.1111/j.1475-5661.2009.00363.x

Evans, J., Davies, B., & Rich, E. (2009). The body made flesh: Embodied learning and the corporeal device. *British Journal of Sociology of Education, 30,* 391–406. doi:10.1080/01425690902954588

Evans, J., Rich, E., Davies, B., & Allwood, R. (2005). The embodiment of learning: What the sociology of education doesn't say about 'risk' in going to school. *International Studies in Sociology of Education, 15,* 129–148. doi:10.1080/09620210500200136

Harris, F. (2012). The grammar of the human life process. *Educational Philosophy and Theory, 44,* 18–30. doi:10.1111/j.1469-5812.2011.00744.x

Hine, R., Peacock, J., & Pretty, J. (2008). Care farming in the UK. *Therapeutic Communities, 29,* 245–260. Retrieved from http://www.carefarminguk.org/sites/carefarminguk.org/files/UK%20Care%20Farming%20Research%20Summary.pdf.pdf

Jupp, E. (2012). Enacting parenting policy? The hybrid spaces of sure start children's centres. *Children's Geographies, 11,* 173–187. doi:10.1080/14733285.2013.779449

Knight, S. (2009). *Forest schools and outdoor learning in the early years.* London: SAGE.

Kraftl, P. (2006). Building an idea: The material construction of an ideal childhood. *Transactions of the Institute of British Geographers*, *31*, 488–504. doi:10.1111/j.1475-5661.2006.00225.x

Kraftl, P. (2010). Events of hope and events of crisis: Young people and hope in the UK. In J. Leaman & M. Woerthing (Eds.), *Youth in Contemporary Europe* (pp. 103–119). London: Routledge.

Kraftl, P. (2013a). *Geographies of alternative education: Diverse learning spaces for children and young people*. Bristol: Policy Press.

Kraftl, P. (2013b). Beyond 'voice', beyond 'agency', beyond 'politics'? Hybrid childhoods and some critical reflections on children's emotional geographies. *Emotion, Space and Society*, *9*, 13–23. doi:10.1016/j.emospa.2013.01.004

Kraftl, P. (2015). Alter-childhoods: Biopolitics and childhoods in alternative education spaces. *Annals of the Association of American Geographers*, *105*, 219–237. doi:10.1080/00045608.2014.962969

Lea, J. (2009). Liberation or limitation? Understanding Iyengar Yoga as a practice of the self. *Body and Society*, *15*, 71–92. doi:10.1177/1357034X09339100

Lees, H. (2013). *Education without schools*. Bristol: Policy.

Levy, D., & Nail, P. (1993). Contagion: A theoretical and empirical review and reconceptualization. *Genetic, Social and General Psychology Monographs*, *119*, 235–283. Retrieved from http://connection.ebscohost.com/c/articles/9607211195/contagion-theoretical-empirical-review-reconceptualization

O'Brien, E. (2009). Learning outdoors: The forest school approach. *Education, 3-13*, *37*, 45–60. doi:10.1080/03004270802291798

Pike, J., & Kelly, P. (2014). *The moral geographies of children, young people and food: Beyond Jamie's school dinners*. Basingstoke: Palgrave Macmillan.

Probyn, E. (2005). Teaching bodies: Affects in the classroom. *Body & Society*, *10*, 21–43. doi:10.1177/1357034X04047854

Prout, A. (2005). *The future of childhood*. London: Routledge. doi:10.1177/1357034X04047854

Pykett, J. (2012). Making "youth publics" and "neuro-citizens": Critical geographies of contemporary education practice in the UK. In P. Kraftl, J. Horton, & F. Tucker (Eds.), *Critical geographies of childhood and youth* (pp. 27–42). Bristol: Policy Press.

Pykett, J., & Enright, B. (2015, online early). Geographies of brain culture: Optimism and optimisation in workplace training programmes. *Cultural Geographies*, doi:10.1177/1474474015591122.

Ravaisson, F. (2008). *Of habit*. London: Continuum.

Ryan, K. (2011). The new wave of childhood studies: Breaking the grip of bio-social dualism? *Childhood*, *19*, 439–452. doi:10.1177/0907568211427612

Strauss, A., & Corbin, J. (1990). *Basics of qualitative research*. London: SAGE.

Sullivan, S. (2001). *Living across and through skins*. Carbondale: University of Indiana Press.

Tarde, G. (1903) (1963). *The laws of imitation*. Massachusetts: Peter Smith.

Thrift, N. (1997). The rise of soft capitalism. *Cultural Values*, *1*, 29–57. doi:10.1080/14797589709367133

Valentine, G. (1996). Angels and devils: Moral landscapes of childhood. *Environment and Planning D: Society and Space*, *14*, 581–599. doi:10.1068/d140581

Woods, P., & Woods, G. (2009). *Alternative education for the 21st century*. London: Routledge.

Youdell, D. (2010). Pedagogies of becoming in an end-of-the-line 'special' school. *Critical Studies in Education*, *51*, 313–324. doi:10.1080/17508487.2010.508810

Zembylas, M. (2009). Global economies of fear: Affect, politics and pedagogical implications. *Critical Studies in Education*, *50*, 187–199. doi:10.1080/17508480902859458

# Teachers' work and innovation in alternative schools

Nina Bascia and Rhiannon Maton

> Toronto boasts a large and diverse system of public alternative schools: schools where democratic practices, student access and a commitment to public education are fundamental. There are academic schools; schools with thematically focused curricula; schools driven by social movement principles such as antiracism and global education; schools for students who do not thrive in mainstream schools; and schools with alternative scheduling and delivery practices for students who must work. The schools are small, supporting personalized relationships among teachers and students, with teacher-driven curricular programs that are responsive to student interests. Curricular innovation is made possible because alternative schools are only loosely coupled with the rest of the public education system, but they still must comply with school system regulations. This paper describes how teachers' work and the structural elements of alternative schools support school-based innovation.

Alternative schools allow publicly funded school systems to meet the social, emotional and physical challenges of children and youth that are not addressed by mainstream schools (Bascia & Fine, 2012). Many alternative schools experiment with different modes of organization that encourage curricular innovation (Raywid, 1994). In such alternative schools, teachers and students may take an active role in designing innovative courses and programs. Democratic practices involving students and teachers, and small school and class sizes that allow for personalized relationships among staff and students (McLaughlin, Talbert, Kahne, & Powell, 1990; Raywid, 1994; Te Riele, 2007), appear to be the major features that distinguish alternative schools from mainstream schools.

This paper focuses on *publicly funded and managed* alternative schools. Charter or academy schools are predicated on the loosening of ties with the regulatory structures of public school system and may host curricular programs developed by teachers, parents, religious institutions or private firms. The distinction between such schools and the alternative schools described in this paper is that the latter are proudly public: student accessibility to diverse programming is a priority, as is a commitment to supporting students who 'fall through the cracks' of more mainstream schools. They are accountable to school systems and adhere to governmental regulations.

That public alternative schools are able to develop and maintain innovative programs is remarkable given the bureaucratic, top-down nature of the school systems in which they operate (Darling-Hammond, 1997) – the same systems that promote the standardized programs at mainstream schools that alienate some students (Wehlage, 1989). How is this possible? What structural factors buffer alternative schools from the currently prevalent educational practices that constrain teachers' work (Ball, 2003)? How does teachers' work in alternative schools mediate the effects of bureaucratic educational systems in order to maintain innovative programming that is responsive to students' interests? This paper attempts to answer these questions.

This paper explores the conditions of teaching in secondary alternative schools in the Toronto District School Board, the largest school district (local educational authority) in Canada, which arguably boasts the largest number of public alternative schools in North America. The paper reviews the literature on diverse forms of public alternative schooling in Canada and the United States. It uses the concept of organizational 'loose coupling' to describe how alternative school teachers (and students) may actively choose and craft courses and programs within the context of school district (local educational authority) and provincial policy constraints.[1] The concept of loose coupling helps explain alternative school teachers' abilities to innovate, as well as the limits of alternative school teachers' influence beyond their own schools and thus inhibit curricular cross-fertilization. Research on teachers' careers helps us discern the continuities between teachers' lives and their work.

The data informing this paper are derived from an exploratory study (Bascia, Carr-Harris, Fine-Meyer, & Zurzolo, 2014) that focused on the work of five Toronto teachers, each in a different secondary alternative school. This study took as its point of departure the literature on teachers' lives, work and careers in mainstream public secondary schools (see, for example, Goodson, 1992; Little & McLaughlin, 1993; Siskin & Little, 1995). The schools the teachers worked in reflect the diversity of secondary public alternative schools in Toronto. They include academically oriented schools, schools that focus on social movement goals (such as feminism, global education, and recognition of Aboriginal sovereignty), schools geared to the education of working class students, schools emphasizing student accessibility, and 'transitional' schools for students who have left school and now wish to come back. Two hour-long interviews with each teacher resulted in analyses of how teachers came to work in the school, how they determined what and how to teach, their working relationships with students and colleagues, school administration and governance, and challenges and opportunities posed by their work (Table 1).

## Public alternative schools

In North America, publicly funded and managed alternative schools have existed, in one form or another, for about one hundred years – nearly as long as there have been systems of mass public education (Semel & Sadovnik, 2008). A review of the literature suggests that, rather than arising within a particular era, alternative schooling options continue to proliferate. For example, in the past decade, new schools – and new kinds of schools – have opened in all of the school districts in the Greater Toronto Area, and in Toronto, where there have been public alternative schools since the 1960s, four new schools opened in the 2012–2013 school year alone (Bascia & Fine, 2012; Hammer, 2012).

Some alternative schools are schools of choice for students, parents and teachers (Darling-Hammond, Ancess, & Ort, 2002; DeVore & Gentilcore, 1999; Duke & Griesdorn, 1999; Rutherford & Quinn, 1999; Tobin & Sprague, 2000). In Raywid's (1994) widely referenced typology of alternative schools, these are Type I schools: schools that reflect organizational and administrative 'departures from the traditional, as well as programmatic innovations ... likely to reflect programmatic themes or emphases pertaining to content or instructional strategy, or both' (p. 27). This end of the spectrum

# ALTERNATIVE EDUCATIONAL PROGRAMMES

Table 1. School descriptions.

| School pseudonym | School characteristics |
|---|---|
| Downtown Academy | Highly academic program designed for 'intellectually curious' learners who are responsible and capable of handling decreased structure. |
| Open Access Alternative School | 'Personalized learning experiences, flexible, one-on-one or small group learning sessions replace classroom structures. Individual attention and open concept workspaces create an inclusive learning community.' |
| Democratic Alternative School | 'For students whose needs are not met in mainstream secondary schools. We provide a warm, supportive atmosphere for you to complete your secondary school credits.' |
| Oracle | 'This program is ideal for creative, self-motivated students who value community and collaborative learning. The inviting atmosphere, diverse student population, innovative curriculum, inspired teaching, and small size make Oracle an appealing alternative to mainstream high schools.' |
| Art Shop | Art Shop is a transitional school, helping youth re-engage in a small educational setting. Students have a variety of goals: credit accumulation; becoming ready to take the next step into the world of work and active citizenship; earning a high school diploma; or transitioning to post-secondary education. |
| Engage! | Engage! is a full-time academic alternative secondary school serving youth who have left high school and now want to return or students who are attending another secondary school but feel they could benefit from a program that emphasizes social justice and community. |

includes alternative schools based on child-centered, Deweyan or Waldorfian models as well as any of a number of more recent educational priorities such as antiracism, culturally responsive pedagogy, and programs emphasizing the arts or sports. At the other end of the spectrum, many school systems establish alternative schools to manage 'students "unwanted" by personnel in regular school settings ... as repositories for disruptive students and ineffective teachers' (McLaughlin, Atkupawu & Williamson, 2008, p. 9; see also Kelly, 1993). These schools correspond to Raywid's Type II – 'programs to which students are sentenced – usually as one last chance prior to expulsion' (p. 27). Raywid's Type III schools are 'for students who are presumed to need remediation or rehabilitation ... They often focus on remedial work and on stimulating social and emotional growth – often through emphasizing the school as a community' (p. 27). Some of these alternative schools allow students to earn academic credits without the distractions and obligations of comprehensive academic programs (Gagne & Robertson, 1995).

Toronto has many kinds of alternative schools, but roughly half of the over 20 secondary alternative schools serve marginalized student populations.[2] Despite their commitments to students who do not thrive in mainstream schools, Toronto's alternatives have characteristics that correspond to Raywid's (1994) Type I schools, but they contain elements of each of the school types, sometimes in the same schools. For example, as one teacher in the study reported, '[Even though this is a highly academic school] we also deal with kids in crisis, or students who have had difficulties adapting to a larger collegiate environment.' (Downtown Academy)

A hallmark of many Toronto alternative schools is the extent to which staff (and students) experiment with different modes of organization and, in particular, encourage curricular innovation (Bascia, Carr-Harris, Fine-Meyer, & Zurzolo, 2014). Several courses and practices that are now part of Toronto's and Ontario's official curriculum were developed and delivered early in alternative schools; examples include gender and women's studies, holocaust and genocide education, and peace-making and conflict resolution. While new courses and programs also may be developed in mainstream school settings, Toronto's alternative schools are a rich source of such teacher-driven innovation. But because alternative schools tend to operate in a sphere separate from mainstream schools, these curricular 'gifts' only rarely enjoy broader dissemination.

## Educational organizations in tightly and loosely coupled systems

Organizational theorist Weick (1976) developed the concepts of tight and loose coupling to describe organizational structure in educational institutions in the USA. According to Weick, a tightly coupled organization has a set of mutually understood rules enforced by an inspection and feedback system. In tightly coupled organizations, supervisors know exactly what employees are doing and can coordinate all the activities of different departments according to a central strategy.

In loosely coupled organizations or systems, some of the characteristics of tight coupling are not in effect. Understanding an organization as a loose coupling of actors, rewards, and technology may explain how it can adapt to its environment and survive amidst uncertainties. Weick observed that in loosely coupled systems, several means might produce the same ends, with minimal coordination or regulation. While this loose control may seem problematic from a managerial perspective, it actually may allow an organization to persist through rapid environmental fluctuations; improve the organization's sensitivity to the environment, allowing local adaptations and creative solutions to develop; permit sub-system breakdown or change without damaging the entire organization; and allow more self-determination by actors.

In loosely coupled organizations, employees have more autonomy, and different departments may operate without much coordination between them. Organizational sub-units (such as schools within a larger educational system) may exhibit varying degrees of tight and loose coupling. Organizations can be tightly coupled in some dimensions and loosely coupled in others. Both structures have advantages and disadvantages (faculty. babson.edu/krollaf/org_site/org_theory/Scott_articles/weick_lcs.html).

School systems are assumed to be tightly coupled by both US and Canadian societies as a whole (Meyer & Rowan, 1977). Certain educational practices are assumed to be uniform across public school systems and schools: for example, sorting students by age and presumed academic ability, dividing the curriculum into subjects and grades, and the nature of student–teacher and teacher–teacher relationships – and fidelity with officially prescribed curriculum policy (Miles & Darling-Hammond, 1998; Siskin, 1994). These regularities produce what Metz (1989; also Hemmings & Metz, 1992) has termed 'real school,' and what Tyack and Tobin (1994) call the 'grammar of schooling.'

Metz writes that expectations for 'real school' are easily fulfilled when students 'accept the staff's agenda as worthwhile' (p. 87), but when students are disengaged from school, these expectations are more difficult to meet. Educators may respond to such challenges by developing distinct programs within schools (e.g., special education, English Language Learners, vocational programs) that act as add-ons, pull-outs, and augmentations to the 'regular' academic program without seriously challenging its primacy (Miles & Darling-Hammond, 1998). In this way, schools may resort to loose coupling to cope with students who do not conform to system expectations.

# ALTERNATIVE EDUCATIONAL PROGRAMMES

School systems require public schools and educators to comply with system rules and expectations for 'real school' with at least the appearance of tight coupling (Meyer & Rowan, 1977). But bureaucratic school systems also may use alternative schools to help manage of the dissonance that arises when they are confronted by diverse populations of students. In a sense, the existence of alternative schools reduces the pressure on regular schools to change in response to diverse students' needs. This point has raised the concern of researchers as having system-wide consequences (e.g., Darling-Hammond et al., 2002; Duke & Griesdorn, 1999).

In order to maintain their unique programs while ensuring their continued existence within public school systems, alternative schools may challenge some – but not all – of the expectations for 'real school'. In this study, alternative school teachers acknowledge the district and province's expectations for 'real school' but they also understand their special roles as requiring something more and different from 'real teaching'.

## Loose coupling and alternative schools

In the Toronto District School Board, there is tension 'between the diversity required for innovation and the standardization assumed by the normal operating procedures of the Board of Education' (Darling-Hammond et al., 2002, pp. 665–6). A special mid-level administrator for alternative schools operates at the district level: in this way, even though alternative schools maintain unique educational programs, from the school district's perspective, coordination and communication are managed efficiently (Bascia & Fine, 2012). Alternative schools nominally are headed by principals, but often these principals have responsibility for multiple schools. A lead teacher ('curriculum leader') may handle daily decision making, and teachers may experience greater autonomy than in traditional school settings. This enables small alternative schools to maintain a system-required student–administrator ratio while also serving to loosen organizational coupling by reducing administrative oversight. To accommodate provincial student–teacher ratios, Toronto's alternative schools have small teaching staffs, with each teacher typically responsible for multiple grades or subjects.

Secondary alternative schools' small size means that most subject areas have only a single teacher and there are no academic departments managing and standardizing teachers' work. A teacher in the study reported that 'I am the philosophy teacher, I don't have to work with a colleague and we don't have to write the same tests, so every semester I customize my class reading lists' (Democratic School). At a second school, a teacher notes the absence of overt external control over teaching: 'There are no curriculum police here' (Open Access School). Loose coupling characterizes the nature of the relationship between what teachers do in their classrooms and what occurs at the school or district level.

The philosophy teacher said:

> We're really able to handle a lot of curriculum innovation because it is directed from the ground up. There's a lot of staff collaboration here. One of our recent courses that we created here is called the Art of Math, and it involves two of our teachers who have collaborated – our art teacher and our mathematics teacher – to create a course that deals with mathematics and aesthetics. It's a few years old now and it's been met with a lot of success. So that's the first arm that drives curriculum innovation, the small size and freedom and autonomy that comes with the alternative format. It's really hard, I would imagine, to innovate in a [regular-system] collegiate setting, simply because of the vagaries of all the bureaucracy that occur there. If you have fifteen sections of English, and you want to innovate in a broad way, you

want to create a new course, it's difficult to – I would imagine – have that mesh with the outcomes and understandings and purchase of curriculum materials that all the other sections require. (Downtown Academy)

This quotation demonstrates how some alternative school teachers were able to create curricular platforms with which allowed them to teach to the strengths and interests developed in their personal and professional lives.

In the schools where the teachers we interviewed worked, democratic practices involving students as well as teachers appeared to play a significant role in shaping course content, activities, assignments and assessments:

Certainly the choices of subjects we have here are greatly based on student input. We have a survey every semester, with all the courses that we are able to offer, given our qualifications, and then they choose and can make suggestions. Actually both women's studies and gay and lesbian studies were student suggestions.

Students like the fact that they have a voice on what courses we offer. We do offer the basic compulsory ones just so they can make sure they get all their credits for their diploma. But they do have a voice on what we offer, and within each course, we begin with a look of what issues they'd like to be looking at. I would say all the teachers do that. We really try to incorporate what the students would like in the courses. We follow the [provincial curriculum] guidelines, but there's a lot of room. Sometimes we're looking at specific issues more than others … or bringing in international perspectives. With me, for example, sometimes they'll say we want to look more at what's happening with LGBT communities around the world. By bringing in new courses all the time too, there is a fair amount of curriculum development here. I've been teaching my courses for a number of years but they are different, the units stay the same, but the content of the units change. Obviously there's no text so I'm bringing in a lot of articles, and every year there are some that I repeat but there are so many new ones that come in every year. (Democratic School)

A teacher at another school describes how he and other teachers provided a unique physical education course requested by students:

Students over the last couple of years have said that they really would like physical education, a curricular strand that isn't too typical in most alternative schools. And what we did was, in order to allow for at least some teaching of phys ed, we team-taught. Three different teachers taught the phys ed course this year. One brought an experience and an understanding of yoga and alternative health practices to the course. Another was much more traditional and dealt with group athleticism. And another was more academic and addressed health issues in terms of body image and gender awareness and things like that. So the students actually got this very interesting sort of tripartite physical education and health course that probably won't be replicated, but that's absolutely fine … … You don't have three different teachers from three different departments from a three story school.… .We had three out of the six teachers in a four-room school here [teaching the physical education course]. (Downtown Academy)

One mode of innovation is thematic teaching that connects various subject areas. In some schools, at some times, several teachers, or the whole staff, had agreed to focus on a common theme across courses. Because of the intense nature of their workloads, teachers sometimes also chose to have all of their own courses theme-based:

… in terms of that sort of workload, you know, when you teach so many courses in our job, you're juggling, and in some ways it's survivor mode and in some ways it's thematic, right? So, if I had to teach 8 courses, the theme of that semester might be, I don't know, I'm just going to throw out an idea, carbon footprints. So if I'm teaching World Issues, Grade 11, maybe the focus would be water as a human right. And maybe in Philosophy it would be about the ethics about, you know, the earth's resources. So I do not really have to overextend myself in terms of my own knowledge base or the sort of good questions that I can come up with. But they're still getting different lenses, or different access points to enter new ideas, right? (Open Access School)

Minimal administrative oversight, small size, demanding teaching schedules and involving students in decision making together create a situation where authority is pushed down to the school and classroom level, and where curricular innovation is the norm. But teachers must walk a fine line between the priority to deliver curriculum that students find engaging and ensuring that students earn the credits required to graduate from secondary school and be admitted to college or university. For this reason, innovative curriculum is offered under the aegis of regularly approved courses. For example, gender and women's studies courses offered at Democratic School and Public Access School were listed on students' academic transcripts as fulfilling requirements for High School Philosophy. At Art Shop, an entrepreneurship course fulfilled provincial Business Studies course requirements.

## Continuities and ruptures

A line of inquiry on teachers' personal and professional lives in the late 1980s and 1990s explored the ways teachers' biographies shaped their activities inside and beyond their classrooms, in their daily work and longer term career paths. The life history approach emphasized the motivations and career paths of teachers of divergent backgrounds and social identities including racialized teachers, immigrant teachers, teachers with political and social commitments, working class teachers, and women teachers (Casey, 1993; Goodson, 1997). It emphasized continuities between teachers' biographies, their current work, and their life trajectories. Life/career history research became less popular as educational reforms of the 1990s and 2000s constrained and regimented teachers' work by scripting their formal responsibilities, curtailing their time and opportunities to be involved in activities beyond their classrooms (Ball, 2003; Thiessen, Bascia, & Goodson, 1996; Verger, Kosar Altinyelkin & Dekonig, 2013).

There were obvious threads in the interviews we conducted that joined the work and lives of alternative school teachers with their activities at school. Here, for example, a teacher describes how his life choices led to the kind of work he had created for himself in alternative schools:

In September I'll have been teaching in the school board for 15 years, most of that time in the alternative schools. I never wanted to be a teacher. I went to university to study theatre and visual art, which was very unusual for my social circle growing up. I started being a catalyst teacher at [an alternative school]. The catalysts are basically people who teach from the community. I was teaching an arts and social change kind of project that engaged a whole bunch of community youth, and we did some crazy projects. It had mostly to do with art in public space. . . . I taught street art classes. And I've always believed that you shouldn't do fake school projects, you should do real projects. So then the kids were successful doing these art shows and all this stuff. So I pitched the idea – the school is like, 'have our whole focus be through the arts.' (Art Shop)

Three of the five teachers we interviewed had spent their entire teaching careers in alternative schools, sometimes only in their current school. Two teachers had started teaching in mainstream high schools; one said he had no intention of going back. The other took on a position in a school district unit, from which she participated in bringing to fruition the formal creation of a 'locally developed course' that had its roots in the time she spent at Engage!.

Alternative schools in Toronto exist in a kind of bubble: that is, curricular inventions that occur in alternative schools do not often find their way into general circulation in mainstream schools. Teachers' comments suggest that this may be partly due to constraints on their opportunities to interact with teachers beyond their own schools. Given the time and energy they put into working with students, several teachers in the study said they rarely attended teacher union or subject area organizations.

One study teacher said that she believed alternative school teachers had less influence in the district and province than teachers from more traditional schools.

> It seems as these [district-level and provincial teams of teachers] that write curriculum, if you're not in the 'in group,' you don't get invited. So I'll give an example, I knew a teacher and she says oh yeah, as part of my summer I'm getting paid to write curriculum for the [provincial] Grade 10 History course. I would say well cool, how do you get in that gig, you know, it's like how do you get invited to that party? (Laughter) Yeah, and again, you know when you work in a small environment, maybe you're not as visible – I don't know, if I were in a larger school [I would be visible to more educators]. Maybe it's just an access issue ... Well, I always find it interesting that we never get invited to host or sponsor [professional development sessions]. You know, if you are at a big school you're more on the radar. If you're at a small, I've just found that nobody is looking at the alternative schools and their programs and asking them to be consultants or advisors, or specialists. (Public Access School)

There are obvious continuities between teachers' past interests and present professional activities. Alternative school contexts allow teachers to develop curriculum around their own (and students') interests. Alternative schools appear to be buffered from the constraints of neoliberal educational reforms that researchers claim limit and regiment teachers' work in many jurisdictions worldwide. Loose coupling between alternative and mainstream schools may serve to inhibit the spread of innovation.

## Conclusion: implications for the spread of innovation

Drawing on interviews with teachers in the Toronto District School Board's alternative schools, this paper has explored the structural factors and work by teachers that enable curricular innovation, as well as those that inhibit the expansion of innovation beyond them. Using the notion of loose coupling, it described the contradictory relationship that exists between district and provincial policy expectations and the actual curricular practices in alternative schools. On the one hand, teachers and students create or modify courses by using district or provincially approved course expectations as scaffolding to ensure students can earn the credits they need for academic advancement and graduation from high school. On the other hand, student and teacher interests are major drivers in developing course content, activities and assignment practices.

This paper identified several features of alternative schools (the small size of staff and student cohorts, minimal administrative oversight, and teachers' heavy workloads) that support curricular invention. Yet these same factors may serve to limit the spread of innovation to mainstream schools by limiting the access – and therefore the influence – of alternative school teachers to educators beyond their own school walls.

The teachers' comments suggest that structural features of mainstream secondary school programs also make it unlikely that alternative schools' innovative curricular

## ALTERNATIVE EDUCATIONAL PROGRAMMES

practices could be adopted there. Most secondary schools' large size and organizational division into academic departments, with teachers' work more tightly coordinated within, and weaker bounds between, subjects (Siskin, 1994; Siskin & Little, 1995); greater anonymity among teachers and students due to large cohort size and lack of spatial proximity (Hargreaves, 1994); greater administrative scrutiny given hierarchical relations between teachers, department heads and school administrators, and between school and district administrators; and tighter bonds between at least some teachers and officially sanctioned curriculum given the greater likelihood of mainstream school teachers' participation in professional development and curriculum writing activities.

Mainstream and alternative schools exist at different points along a continuum between innovation and prescription, with limited opportunity for curricular cross-fertilization. While it seems unfortunate that alternative school innovations are rarely, if ever, taken up by other schools (Te Riele, 2007), transforming structural aspects of schooling takes more than good intentions. In the meantime and conversely, loose coupling serves to enable innovation within alternative school bounds.

### Notes

1. In Canada, provinces have constitutional authority to set and ensure overall educational policy, including curriculum. Different provinces devolve particular aspects of educational decision making to school districts (local educational authorities). In Ontario, for example, academic program and course expectations are established at the provincial level (Anderson & Ben Jaafar, 2007; Bascia, Carr-Harris, Fine, & Zurzolo, 2014).
2. Toronto's public alternative schools provide educational programs for students of all ages. There are primary alternative schools for children between grades Kindergarten to 6, or grades 4–6 or grades 4–8; secondary alternative schools for students between grades 9 and 12, or 10 and 12 (http://www.tdsb.on.ca/). Toronto alternative schools provide students with the same grade-level qualifications offered by mainstream schools: secondary alternative schools confer the same high school diploma on students who successfully complete Grade 12 as any other secondary school. In most cases, students and/or their parents choose to attend an alternative school voluntarily, although a minority may be 'steered' to alternative schooling by mainstream teachers and educational staff.

### Disclosure Statement

No potential conflict of interest was reported by the authors.

### References

Anderson, S., & Ben Jaafar, S. (2007). *Policy trends in Ontario education*. International Centre for Educational Change (ICEC) Working Paper #1. Toronto: Ontario Institute for Studies in Education.

Ball, S. J. (2003). The teacher's soul and the terrors of performativity. *Journal of Education Policy*, *18*(2), 215–228. doi:10.1080/0268093022000043065

Bascia, N., Carr-Harris, S., Fine-Meyer, R., & Zurzolo, C. (2014). Teachers, curriculum innovation and policy formation. *Curriculum Inquiry, 44*(2), 228–248.

Bascia, N., & Fine, E. (2012). *Alternative schools: Models and challenges*. Report Prepared for Toronto Catholic District School Board. Toronto: Ontario Institute for Studies in Education.

Casey, K. (1993). *I answer with my life*. New York, NY: Routledge.

Darling-Hammond, L. (1997). The limits of education bureaucracy. *The Right to Learn: A Blueprint for Creating Schools That Work*. San Francisco, CA: Jossey-Bass, 37–68.

Darling-Hammond, L., Ancess, J., & Ort, S. W. (2002). Reinventing high school: Outcomes of the coalition campus schools project. *American Educational Research Journal, 39*(3), 639–673. doi:10.3102/00028312039003639

DeVore, D., & Gentilcore, K. (1999). Balanced and restorative justice and educational programming for youth at-risk. *The Clearing House, 73*(2), 96–100. doi:10.1080/00098659909600157

Duke, D. L., & Griesdorn, J. (1999). Considerations in the design of alternative schools. *The Clearing House, 73*(2), 89–92. doi:10.1080/00098659909600155

Gagne, A., & Robertson, M. B. (1995). *Contact school: Landscapes of possibilities in the inner city: An alternative high school in the toronto board of education*. Toronto: Canadian Education Association.

Goodson, I. (1992). *Studying teachers' lives*. London: Routledge.

Goodson, I. (1997). The life and work of teachers. In B. Biddle, T. Good, & I. Goodson (Eds.), *International handbook of teachers and teaching* (pp. 437–458). Dordrecht: Kluwer Academic.

Hammer, K. (2012). More alternative schools opening than ever in Toronto. *Globe and Mail*, August 23, 2012.

Hargreaves, A. (1994). *Changing teachers, changing times: Teachers' work and culture in the postmodern age*. New York, NY: Teachers College Press.

Hemmings, A., & Metz, M. (1992). Real teaching: How high school teachers negotiate societal, local community, and student pressures when they define their work. In L. Valli & R. Page (Eds.), *Curriculum differentiation: Interpretive studies in U.S. secondary schools* (pp. 91–111). Albany: SUNY Press.

Kelly, D. M. (1993). *Last chance high: How girls and boys drop in and out of alternative schools*. New Haven: Yale University Press.

Little, J., & McLaughlin, M. (1993). *Teachers' work*. New York, NY: Teachers College Press.

McLaughlin, M., Atukpawu, G., & Williamson, D. (2008). Alternative education options in California: A view from counties and districts. Retrieved July 12, 2009.

McLaughlin, M. W., Talbert, J., Kahne, J., & Powell, J. (1990). Constructing a personalized school environment. *Phi Delta Kappan*, p. 230–235.

Metz, M. H. (1989). Real school: A universal drama amid disparate experience. *Politics of Education Association Yearbook, 4*(5), 75–91.

Meyer, J. W., & Rowan, B. (1977). Institutionalized organizations: Formal structure as myth and ceremony. *American Journal of Sociology, 83*, 340–363. doi:10.1086/ajs.1977.83.issue-2

Miles, K. H., & Darling-Hammond, L. (1998). Rethinking the allocation of teaching resources: Some lessons from high-performing schools. *Educational Evaluation and Policy Analysis, 20*(1), 9–29. doi:10.3102/01623737020001009

Raywid, M. A. (1994). Alternative schools: The state of the art. *Educational Leadership, 52*(1), 26–31.

Rutherford, R. B., Jr., & Quinn, M. M. (1999). Special education in alternative education programs. *The Clearing House, 73*(2), 79–81. doi:10.1080/00098659909600152

Semel, S. F., & Sadovnik, A. R. (2008). The contemporary small-school movement: Lessons from the history of progressive education. *The Teachers College Record, 110*(9), 1744–1771.

Siskin, L., & Little, J. (1995). *The subjects in question*. New York, NY: Teachers College Press.

Siskin, L. S. (1994). *Realms of knowledge: Academic departments in secondary schools*. London: Routledge.

Te Riele, K. (2007). Educational alternatives for marginalised youth. *The Australian Educational Researcher, 34*(3), 53–68. doi:10.1007/BF03216865

Thiessen, D., Bascia, N., & Goodson, I. (Eds.). (1996). *Making a difference about difference*. Calgary: Detselig.

Tobin, T., & Sprague, J. (2000). Alternative education strategies: Reducing violence in school and the community. *Journal of Emotional and Behavioral Disorders, 8*(3), 177–186. doi:10.1177/106342660000800305

Tyack, D., & Tobin, W. (1994). The 'grammar' of schooling: Why has it been so hard to change? *American Educational Research Journal, 31*(3), 453–479. doi:10.3102/00028312031003453

Verger, A., Kosar Altinyelken, H., & de Koning, M. (2013). *Global managerial education reforms and teachers –emerging policies, controversies and issues in developing contexts*. Brussels: Education International.

Wehlage, G. G. (1989). *Reducing the risk: Schools as communities of support*. Philadelphia, PA: The Falmer Press.

Weick, K. E. (1976). Educational organizations as loosely coupled systems. *Administrative Science Quarterly, 21*, 1–19. doi:10.2307/2391875

# Index

*Note*: **Boldface** page numbers refer to tables and italic page numbers refer to figures

Aboriginal communities 8, 11, 12
academic achievement: black males 22; young women 65
academic advancement 138
academic provision 56, 72
Adult Literacy and Numeracy (ALaN) 58
AE *see* alternative education
affect, as epistemological tool 9, 18
affective equality, in school 105, 107
affective habit ecologies 119
affective justice 3, 103, 104; educational inequality 107; and learning environments 104–8; relational care work 105
affective storytelling 9–11
African-Caribbean heritage 22, 26
ALaN *see* Adult Literacy and Numeracy
alternative education (AE) 84–5; alternative educators 117, 119–21, 128; disciplinary regime in 87–8; literatures on 86, 88; Major Tom's 88–92; programmes 95; Thursday's Child Farm 92–5
alternative learning spaces 16
alternative schools, in Toronto District School Board 1, 4; continuities between teachers 137–8; educational organizations 134–5; loose coupling and 135–7; Raywid's type 133
anti-social behaviour 126, 128
aspirational capital 25–6

Bailey, Simon 86
Banksia College 104
Baroutsis, Aspa 3
Bascia, Nina 4
Becker, Sophie 2
Bergen, Penny Van 2
Bernstein, Basil 4
Bjarnadóttir, Valgerður S. 3
black masculinity 21
bodies/emotions, in education 118, 119

boot-camp-style training 91
Boronia Flexi School 104
Bottrell, Dorothy 7
bureaucratic educational systems 132, 135

care farms 121–3, 125–7
citizenship education 118
Coleman, J. 56
collective facets of habituation 119
collectivism 4
communities of color 25
community-based alternative learning program 7
community cultural wealth 25
Compact for Young Australians 6
complementary alternative education 84–5, 96; disciplinary regime in AE provision 87–8; Major Tom's team-builders 88–92; orientation to care 85–6; research 87; Thursday's Child Farm 92–5
contagion habit 3, 125–7
continuities between teachers 137–8
contributive justice 3, 101, 103; and meaningful learning 109–11
Cowley, Sue 86
critical race theory (CRT) 24, 25
cultural capital 25
cultural injustice 102
cultural justice 101
curricular innovation 131, 133, 137, 138

Daszkiewicz, T. 63
Davies, H. 63
Dawson, N. 56
Dennison, C. 56
Devine, John 86
Dewey, John 118–20
'difference,' concept of 57
*Discipline and Punish* (Foucault) 85
disruptive behaviour 37–40
dropout rates, Icelandic upper secondary schools 71–2

143

# INDEX

economic injustice 101, 102
economic justice 101, 109
Education Act (1990) 37
educational achievement 22
educational exclusion 4
educational organizations: expectations for 'real school' 134–5; teacher–teacher relationships 134; in tightly and loosely coupled systems 134–5
educational progression 24
elite private schools 11
Elkhorn Community College 104
'embodied intersectionality' 24
emotionally and behaviourally disturbed (ED/BD) schools 36
entry-to-employment (E2E) programmes 57, 58
exclusion from school 25–6

familial capital 25
Federation of Icelandic Industries 81
flexible learning 110; and social justice 101–3
force of habit, in education 118–20; bodies/emotions 118, 119; citizenship education 118; 'the double law of habit' 119; post-human scholarship 119; Ravaissonian theories 119; scholarship 119
forest schools 122
Foucault, M. 85, 86
Fraser, Nancy 100–1
Friedel, Tracy 7
Fuller, C. 64

Gareth case 9–10
General Certificate of Secondary Education (GCSE) 57, 59, 63, 64
geographies, of alternative education 120–2; care farms 121; forest schools 122; homeschooling 121
globalised modernity 29
Graham, Linda 2
Gutherson, P. 63

habit scholarship 119
hands-on-learning program 73
Hayes, Debra 2, 3
heightened flow of affect 12
high school suspension rates 23
homeschooling 3, 117, 121
Hosie, A. 56
Hunter, Ian 85

Iceland, upper secondary education in 70; analysis of data 74–5; dropout rates 71–2; education system 71; ethical issues and value of research 75; interviews 74; participants 74; pedagogy of 72–3; reasons for leaving previous school 75–6; re-enter academic 71; research setting 73–4; return-to-school options 72 *see also* Long Hill

index of community socio-educational advantage (ICSEA) 39, **39**
Indigenous students 6, 13; alternative learning program 7; relational epistemologies 7–9
individuation 15–17
innovative curriculum 137
intersectionality 24–5

Jóhannesson, Ingólfur Ásgeir 3

Kelly, D. 56
kidbrain 15
Kraftl, Peter 3

language of habit, in education 119
learning environments, affective justice and 104–8
linguistic capital 25
Long Hill: assessment policy 77, 79; journey to 75–6; mature returning-to-school student 78–9; online learning platform 75, 80; pedagogy of 75–6; re-entering students, teaching 80–1; school location 80; student–teacher relationships 76–7, 79; teachers 77–8
loosely coupled systems 4; and alternative schools 135–7; educational organizations in 134–5; grammar of schooling 134; organizational subunits 134
Luttrell, W. 56, 63, 66
Lynch, Kathleen 101, 105, 107, 108

Macfadyen, T. 64
Major Tom's 95, 96; as disciplinary regime 91–2; programme 88–90
'managed moves' programmes 85
Martin, Karen 7, 14; relational epistemologies 7–9; 'Ways of Knowing, Being and Doing' framework 8
Maton, Rhiannon 4
Maylork, Uvanney 2
McGregor, Glenda 3
'meaningful' education 73
meaningful learning, contributive justice and 109–11
medicalised discourse practices 86
Mills, Martin 3
Mirraboop, Booran 14
multi-sited ethnography, of alternative schools 103–4

National Foundation for Educational Research (NFER) 85
National Vocational Qualification (NVQ) 58
navigational capital 25, 28–9
neo-liberal education 2
net black advantage, black students 24

# INDEX

New South Wales behaviour schools 36–7; alternative placement options 50; behavioural explanations **45**; dislike school *41*, 41–3; disruptive behaviour 37–40; Education Act (1990) 37; emotionally and behaviourally disturbed 36; feeling happy in 45–7; learning choice 36; like school 41; policy and school practice 49–51; schoolwork 42–3, 46, 49; Special Education Plan 36; students experiences 37–9; support classes 35; teacher–student relationship 46, 49; violent 37

NFER *see* National Foundation for Educational Research

Nolan, Kathleen 86

NVQ *see* National Vocational Qualification

Obama, Barack 23

OCN *see* Open College Network

OECD *see* Organization for Economic Co-operation and Development

Office for National Statistics (ONS) 22

online learning 3

online learning platform 75, 77, 80

Open College Network (OCN) 58

opportunity classes 36

Organization for Economic Co-operation and Development (OECD) 72, 79

Pennacchia, Jodie 3

'permanence of structural racism' 22

Pillow, W. 56, 63, 66

political injustice 101

post-compulsory schooling 2

post-exclusionary schooling 2

post-human scholarship 119

pregnant teenager 55–6; positive identity as 61

Prince's Trust 87

PRU *see* pupil referral unit

public alternative schools 132–4; school descriptions **133**

'pupil premium' funding 85

pupil referral unit (PRU) 57–8

racial inequality: in education 24, 27; in employment 30

Ravaisson, Félix 118, 119

'real school,' expectations for 134–5

(re)calibrating habits 3, 122–5; care farm 122–3; harmonisation 124; seriousness 124

re-engagement programs 17

(re)formulate habits 117, 121

regular schools 1, 84

relational epistemologies 7–9

(re)learning of habits 117

resistant capital 25–6

Riele, Kitty Te 3

Rogers, Bill 86

Rudoe, N. 56

Russell, L. 64

Sayer, Andrew 101, 108, 109

school disciplinary regimes 86

school exclusion 1

schoolgirl mothers 56, 57

schooling structures: amplification systems 14–15; individuation and relatedness 15–17; stories of 11–14, 17

'schools for specific purposes' 35

school systems 134–5

schoolwork 42–3, 46, 49

secondary alternative schools 135

second chance education 70

securing equality 105

self-awareness 49

self-enhancement 49

Skattebol, Jennifer 2

Skinnerian regimes 88

Slee, Roger 84, 85

social capital 25, 28–9

social justice 1, 3, 4, 100; affective equality 105, 107; affective justice and learning environments 104–8; and alternative education 105; care relations 105; contributive justice and meaningful learning 109–11; flexible learning and 101–3; multi-sited ethnography 103–4; parity of participation 102; securing equality 105; solidarity relations 105

'sociological imagination' 6, 7

special education 50

Stepping Stones 58, 59, 61, 64

storytelling, affective 9–11

students: attitudes 38; educational gaps 108; in flexible learning 101; knowledge and cultural backgrounds 107; low socioeconomic background 102; memories 38; poor outcomes 103; reintegration 38

student–teacher relationships 76–7, 79, 134

subsidies, issue of 11–12

support classes 35

Sweller, Naomi 2

teachers: attitudes 42; behaviour 42, 49; Long Hill 77–8; student conflict 43

teacher–student relationship 46, 49

teacher–teacher relationships 134

teenage mothers' experiences 55–7; in America 56; education 55–6; entry-to-employment programmes 57, 58; positive identity as pregnant 61; pregnancy 55–6; pupil referral unit 57–8; students' perceptions of 57

teenage pregnancy strategy evaluation 55

Thomson, Pat 3, 64

Thursday's Child Farm 96; as disciplinary regime 94–5; farm tasks 93; residential programme 92–4

## INDEX

tightly coupled systems 4; educational organizations in 134–5; grammar of schooling 134
Torres Strait Islander communities 9
traditional programs 72
'turnaround narrative' 27, 28

unemployment: black male 22; youth 29
United Kingdom: alternative education 120; anti-social behaviour 126, 128; care farms in 122, 125–7; citizenship 128; education and youth policies 123; homeschooling 121
Upper Secondary School Act 72
US National Center for Educational Statistics 24

Vincent, Kerry 2
violent behaviour 37
vocational education 65, 72, 85

'Ways of Knowing, Being and Doing' framework 8
Wright, Cecile 2

YMTB *see* Young Mums To Be
young black males: academic achievement 22; aspirational and resistant capital 26–7; black masculinity 21; cultural action 28–9; different forms of capital 26; educational achievement 23; educational and employment outcomes 23; educational progression of 24; exclusion from school 25–6; family and parenting role 27–8; intersectionality 24–5; net black advantage 24; unemployment 22
Young Mums To Be (YMTB) 57, 58, 59
young women's experiences: benefits 58; detrimental impact on 66; flexible approach 62; limitations of 62–5; non-authoritarian approach 61; recognition and non-recognition of difference 65–6; Shae's educational 63; specialist provision 62; teaching and learning strategies 58